The
CAT CARE
Question and Answer Book

The CAT CARE
Question and Answer Book

Barry Bush BVSc PhD FRCVS

Bloomsbury Books
London

To Mave

First published in Great Britain by
Orbis Publishing Limited, London 1981
© Barry Rush 1981

This edition 1986 published by
Bloomsbury Books an imprint of
Godfrey Cave Associates Limited
42 Bloomsbury Street, London WC1B 3QT
by arrangement with Orbis Publishing Limited.

Printed and bound in
Yugoslavia by
Mladinska Knjiga
Ljubljana
ISBN: 0 906223 44 X

Contents

Introduction

When I first began to practise as a veterinary surgeon twenty years ago, I soon realized that many cat and dog owners wanted not only help with specific problems but also general advice about the care of their animals. Since that time the demand for reliable information about pets, and in particular the cat, has grown enormously. Faced with conflicting statements about the value, or otherwise, of various commercially-prepared foods, and no longer content to accept, let alone believe, the advice passed on by friends, many owners are obviously anxious to discover the facts for themselves.

Over the same period veterinary scientists have also shown a much greater interest in cats than formerly, with the result that there have been major advances in our knowledge of feline behaviour, nutrition and diseases. In the past twenty years important 'new' diseases have been described, and the causes of others, such as feline leukaemia, have been established.

Unfortunately, because so much information has become available recently, the type of wide-ranging discussion that most cat owners would like to arrange with their vets would be prohibitively time-consuming. With a busy practice to run it is shortage of time that makes vets keep their consultations short.

It was this problem in communication that prompted me to present in book form a type of 'extended consultation' that would make it possible to answer fully those questions about cats which are asked most frequently, and to discuss other topics of general interest. Like many of my colleagues whose main concern is the teaching of veterinary undergraduates, I believe that the best and quickest way to raise the standard of care of pet animals is to disseminate accurate information as widely as possible. And I feel sure that the one thing we would all agree about is the need to look after our pet animals to the best of our ability.

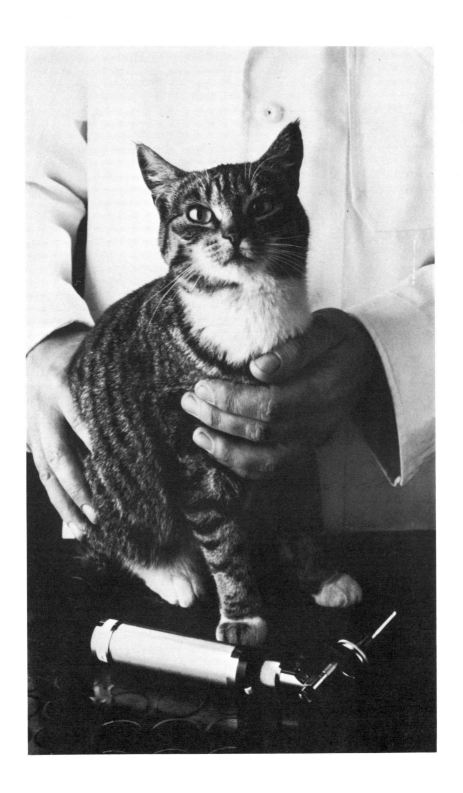

Helping Your Vet

Q *Is it worthwhile taking an apparently healthy cat for a regular check-up?*

A Certainly it is advisable for all cats to be vaccinated against certain diseases and, in order for them to maintain a high level of immunity, re-vaccination should be carried out every one or two years. The interval should depend on the type of vaccine used. At the time of each vaccination, the cat *will* be routinely examined by a vet to ensure that it is clinically healthy. If there is any evidence that the cat is currently combating an infection (e.g. an abnormally high temperature), the vaccination is best delayed. Otherwise, the body's immune responses may be engaged in fighting the infection to the extent that they cannot respond fully to the stimulus of the vaccine.

It is doubtful whether any other check-up is required, provided the cat remains apparently healthy, unless it is in response to a particular problem. For example, it may be desirable to check a cat for evidence of FeLV infection if it has been in contact with another cat known to be infected, or to check whether it is a carrier of ringworm if a human in the household develops this disease. However, such examinations are very specific and would not normally form part of a routine check-up.

It has been suggested that there might be merit in a routine examination of blood samples from cats, say every one to two years, to determine the numbers of the different cell types and the levels of certain blood constituents. Such testing might reveal evidence of some developing, and as yet unsuspected, disorder, but it has also been argued that it would provide a record of the normal values for that individual animal. If the cat subsequently developed signs of disease and the blood was re-examined, knowledge of the previous 'normal' values would permit any relatively small change to be detected, thereby assisting diagnosis of the condition. Unfortunately, tests have shown that the concentration of some cells and substances in the blood can fluctuate considerably from day to day in an individual, thus making it difficult to use information in this way. It is also debatable whether, at least in some cats, the benefits of such routine blood sampling would outweigh the difficulties of collection.

Q *Do vets specialize in treating any one type of animal, and how can I be sure that a vet is knowledgeable about cats?*

A All veterinary surgeons receive the same basic training so that they are competent to deal with all domesticated species. These are chiefly the meat-producing animals (cattle, sheep and pigs) and the companion animals (horses, dogs and cats). Cats and dogs, together with other smaller pet animals such as rabbits, guinea pigs and hamsters, are referred to professionally as 'small animals', whilst the other species are known as 'large animals'. Poultry, exotic animals (i.e. zoo animals) and fish are also dealt with in veterinary training, but less extensively.

After qualification, some vets feel that they would prefer to treat all these species of animals in order to utilize all that they have learned, and consequently they take employment in a 'mixed practice', i.e. one treating both large and small animals. Others prefer to deal solely with either small or large animals and therefore may establish, or find employment in, a practice which concentrates on that particular group. Alternatively, they may work with other veterinarians in a mixed practice but take responsibility for just the small or large animal patients.

Increasingly there is a tendency for vets to concentrate on just one species; this is particularly so in the large animal field and there are, for example, a number of specialist equine practices. In general, small animal practices will treat both cats and dogs, although in North America there is a trend towards purely feline specialists. At the present time in Great Britain the governing body of the veterinary profession, the Royal College of Veterinary Surgeons, is still formulating its ideas about specialization and currently no British vet is able to describe himself as a specialist in any particular field, even though this may be so.

However, a telephone call to your local veterinary practice will usually establish whether one or more of the veterinarians has a special interest in small animals, and in particular in cats. In North America interested veterinary surgeons are often members of the American Association of Feline Practitioners, and in Britain veterinary surgeons, as well as members of the public, may belong to the Feline Advisory Bureau. However, it is not easy to establish that a vet is a member of either society, nor in fact does it indicate anything more than an interest in cats.

Veterinary practices in urban areas are invariably solely or predominantly concerned with treating small animals, and in both North America and Great Britain many such practices are described as 'hospitals', most of which deal solely or mainly with small animals. The term hospital implies the provision of certain facilities over and above those of a routine practice.

Finally, the recommendation of other cat owners is valuable in choosing a veterinary surgeon to treat your pet, for example, friends, neighbours or fellow members of a club devoted to cat owning or breeding. Certainly, once you have found a veterinary surgeon that you find helpful and sympathetic and in whom you have confidence, you should take his advice.

Q *My cat has been behaving oddly and he must be ill. How can I best help my vet to find out what is wrong?*

A Most human patients will be able to answer questions about their illness but clearly cats are unable to do this. So it is important that whoever consults the veterinary surgeon should be able to express exactly what it is that they are worried about; in other words the nature of the problem. The person who is present when the cat is examined should be prepared to supply information about both recent and past events; this is known as the 'history' of the case. Usually questions will be asked about the animal's diet, appetite and thirst, its temperament and willingness to play or exercise, the passage of urine and motions, past illnesses and injuries, how long it has been owned, whether it has been neutered and, in the case of entire (i.e. unspayed) females, the date of birth of any litters and whether the animal has been 'calling' recently. You will also be asked for details of any abnormal signs that have been observed. Where abnormalities have been noted, it is important to be able to say, at least approximately, how long they have been present (for months, weeks, or days) and whether they have been present continuously or intermittently (i.e. have come and gone). If it is possible to give exact dates, so much the better.

Some owners keep a diary, or at least make notes about the sequence of events in an illness, and certainly, whenever the succession of events becomes complex and therefore difficult to remember, it is useful to have a written record of the salient points. Most vets are very busy and therefore won't relish the idea of ploughing through page after page of unimportant details, but all of them will welcome an accurate and concise step-by-step account of what has occurred. Whenever you have additional documentation (e.g. the cat's pedigree or vaccination certificates), these should be made available, especially when you are consulting a particular veterinary surgeon for the first time.

From what has already been stated, most owners will appreciate the problems that are created for the vet, and therefore for the patient, if the person present with the animal knows little or nothing of the background to the illness. This is frequently so when children or helpful neighbours bring a sick cat to the consulting room. Wherever possible therefore, the owner, or whoever normally looks after the cat, should be available. When this isn't possible, the best substitute is a written record of the facts together with a telephone number at which the owner can be contacted – in case further details are required, or it is necessary to obtain their consent for anaesthesia or other procedures to be performed.

Q *Are there any other ways in which I could help my vet?*

A Well, if you know that your cat is difficult to handle, the nurses and vets would appreciate learning this fact beforehand so that they can take any necessary precautions in dealing with him.

In situations where the cat's thirst is greatly increased, it is also very helpful if you are able to measure the total amount drunk in twenty-four hours. If you know that the cat normally drinks two to three bowlsful a day, measure how much the bowl holds; the capacities of cat bowls are, like the lengths of pieces of string, very variable. Or even better, measure the total amount provided during twenty-four hours and subtract the amount remaining undrunk at the end of that period.

Q *The vet has told me he would like to do some 'diagnostic tests' on my cat. What does this mean?*

A Often the history of events combined with a clinical examination of the cat are sufficient for your vet to diagnose what is wrong and to recommend a course of treatment. However, this information may be inadequate for a precise diagnosis to be made so the vet may advise that one or more diagnostic tests should be performed. This may involve collecting samples of blood, urine or motions for laboratory examination. In fact, you might be asked to collect some urine or motion samples yourself and to deliver them to the vet's premises. Sometimes other types of sample may be collected for laboratory tests, such as bacterial swabs or fluid from the abdomen. Radiographic examination may be recommended and occasionally the performance of an electrocardiograph (E.C.G.) or electro-encephalograph (E.E.G.) which record the electrical signals coming from the heart and brain respectively. At times, investigatory surgery may be advised, and usually this takes the form of an exploratory laparotomy (opening the abdomen and examining the organs within) or a biopsy (taking a small piece of tissue for microscopic examination).

Some of these procedures must always be performed under a general anaesthetic to avoid pain (e.g. surgery) or prevent the risk of damage arising from sudden movement (e.g. collection of cerebrospinal fluid); at other times anaesthesia is useful to keep the animal still (e.g. during radiography) or simply because the animal's temperament makes it difficult to handle otherwise. If there is a *possibility* that anaesthesia might be required, it is important for the cat not to have been fed for at least eight hours beforehand. This can also help with blood tests which are best performed on 'fasted' animals.

It is important for the owner's family to have discussed the situation and to have decided whether to consent to anaesthesia and/or surgery. Whoever presents the animal should have the authority to make a decision about what is to happen next: whether the animal should be investigated further (if necessary under general anaesthesia), whether it should be hospitalized for tests and/or observation, or whether surgery can be undertaken immediately to treat the condition. Most veterinary surgeons will be pleased to explain precisely what the problems are, what possible conditions the tests may help to confirm or eliminate, and the purpose of any treatment. It is helpful if this is matched by a clear decision on the owner's part as to what should happen to his pet.

Q *Should I continue giving my cat his course of tablets now that he looks so much better?*

A When treatment of an illness is in progress, the vet's instructions should be *always* carefully followed. Most owners will do this to the best of their ability but there are some who vary the treatment as they see fit and may discontinue a course of tablets if they feel the animal has improved sufficiently, not realizing that by so doing they risk the animal relapsing. On the other hand, if the animal has entirely recovered from a condition and the vet has advised stopping treatment, it could be harmful to prolong drug therapy. Some owners even obtain drugs from other sources and give them indiscriminately, thereby damaging the health of their pet.

Q *On what occasions would my cat have to stay in hospital?*

A In the treatment of many feline conditions it is usually not necessary to hospitalize the animal. But there are circumstances in which hospitalization of a cat is desirable to ensure efficient diagnosis and therapy, and in some situations it is essential to increase the animal's chances of survival.

A critically ill animal, suffering from such conditions as massive blood loss, severe shock, difficulty in breathing or maintaining normal heart action, unconsciousness, extensive injuries or acute pain, is obviously best hospitalized because of its need for continuing expert treatment and nursing. This may involve blood transfusions or intravenous fluid therapy, the administration of oxygen, the use of special heating devices and heart monitors, and of course the injection of drugs including pain killers. This type of intensive care simply could not be provided at home.

It is also imperative for animals receiving general anaesthesia to be hospitalized until they are sufficiently recovered to be allowed home. Animals requiring general anaesthesia prior to radiography or the performance of some comparatively straight forward procedure can often be discharged later the same day, or on the following day. Those that have undergone major surgical operations should stay in hospital until they are sufficiently improved and this period can vary from a few days upwards, depending upon the animal's response.

Hospitalization may also be required for the performance of specialized diagnostic tests. Where the owner has difficulty in collecting routine urine or motion samples, again it may be preferable to hospitalize the cat to obtain them. Certain types of treatment are difficult for owners to deal with, such as the stabilization of a diabetic cat, the administration of an enema or at times even the combing out of a cat that is difficult to handle.

Finally, hospitalization may be advisable so that the veterinary surgeon can observe the animal for a period, particularly where neurological disturbances or behavioural problems are suspected.

In all instances where admission to hospital is advised, owners will naturally be upset at being separated from their pet. In fact, in most cases the owners are probably more upset than the cats, most of whom adapt very quickly to their new surroundings. Owners can rest assured that a veterinary surgeon will not want to prolong the period of hospitalization unnecessarily but on the other hand there is no sense in discharging the cat before diagnosis or treatment is completed or, following an emergency admission, before recovery is assured.

Q *If my cat is hospitalized should I visit it?*

A It is better not to visit your cat if the period of hospitalization is going to be comparatively short. An animal is usually very pleased to see its owner again and naturally believes that they will be permanently reunited. Consequently, when the owner leaves again after only a few minutes, the cat feels rejected.

Fortunately, the feelings of most pet animals seem to be more objective than subjective and whilst the owner is absent they usually do not pine or fret as the owners anticipate, particularly if there is a certain amount of activity in the hospital to occupy their attention.

On the other hand, if hospitalization is unduly prolonged for whatever reason, then the question of the advisability of visiting should be discussed with the vet in charge of the case.

Q *Why is veterinary treatment sometimes thought to be expensive?*

A The establishment and running of a private small animal practice or hospital is a private business venture just like any other. The veterinary surgeon(s) involved will have to raise sufficient capital initially to build, buy or lease the premises, and to pay for highly specialized equipment and instruments without any preferential loan or subsidy from the government or any other organization. Subsequently the business must generate sufficient money to pay all the expenses – charges for water, electricity, telephones, insurance, rates, and probably the interest on mortgage or bank loans, the cost of drugs and replacement equipment, in addition to providing the salaries of the veterinary surgeon(s) and the other staff required to run the practice efficiently.

Obviously, if the return on the money put into the enterprise is not at least comparable to that which could be provided by other forms of investment, there will be no incentive to undertake all the hard work required, a lot of it during 'unsocial' hours. However, when the cost of veterinary attention is compared with that of other services such as routine car maintenance, taxi journeys or simply getting a repair man to call and examine the washing machine, it is usually found to be low, bearing in mind the level of skill which is demanded.

In North America pet owners are well aware of the high cost of private medical attention for themselves and their families. In Great Britain the way in which the National Health Service is financed disguises the true cost of medical care and many people are unaware that modern drugs and vaccines are extremely expensive. Consequently, owners are sometimes very surprised when they discover the real cost of drugs and may perhaps resent paying so much for their animal's treatment.

There are of course pet insurance policies available which provide some degree of protection against having to pay really hefty bills for operations and treatment, although it's important to read the exclusion clauses carefully before deciding whether what is offered is either adequate or fair.

If you are genuinely unable to afford the fees of a veterinarian, assistance can usually be obtained from one of the animal welfare societies, although it should be borne in mind that these charitable organizations have limited resources and should not be asked to help unless you genuinely cannot afford normal veterinary fees.

Q *Is it advisable to telephone my veterinary surgeon for advice?*

A Whenever there is a real emergency it is always preferable to make a telephone call before taking your cat to the vet's premises, particularly when it occurs outside normal surgery hours. This is because the practice/ hospital can make arrangements to receive and treat the cat as soon as possible (maybe even at home), as well as offering advice on how to proceed in the meantime.

Of course, a telephone call will also enable you to enquire about consultation times or to arrange an appointment, as well as checking on the arrangements for, and costs of, such routine procedures as vaccinations and spay operations.

However, most vets are unwilling to spend a long time on the telephone whilst you relate what has happened to a cat which they may never have attended, and then to be asked questions about what should be done. Even if the animal *has* been seen before, the veterinarian will not usually have the cat's notes to hand to refer to. And, of course, it will not be possible to examine the animal to establish a diagnosis, nor to hand out drugs or a prescription for treatment. Since it is also unlikely that the vet will be able to recall the details of the conversation later, it is usually better to make an appointment for a proper consultation at the outset. Telephone calls like this can block the line for a long time preventing other more urgent calls from being received. And perhaps you should not be surprised if your vet appears reluctant to give out advice for nothing; after all, he also has a living to make.

It is of course a different matter if, whilst the animal is on a course of treatment, it develops signs which you find worrying; often a telephone call will then establish whether there is in fact anything to be concerned about. Indeed, often you may be asked to telephone and report the cat's progress. Also, if your cat is hospitalized, it is reasonable that you should telephone and enquire about his condition. However, if you have been asked to telephone at a particular time, it is always much appreciated if you can keep to that arrangement. It may be that the vet dealing with your cat knows that he will only be available at that time and wishes to speak to you personally about what is happening. Co-operation is always appreciated and helps to cement good relationships to ensure the best possible treatment for your animal.

Q *I don't want to offend my vet but is it possible to obtain a second opinion on my cat's illness?*

A Yes of course it is, though usually this is only necessary if your animal is thought to be suffering from a serious disorder which might involve complex and expensive diagnostic methods or treatment, or if previous therapy has not resulted in satisfactory improvement.

It may be that your vet will suggest a second opinion – if not, you can raise the matter yourself. Most veterinarians will be happy to have the benefit of another professional opinion and in many cases will be able to suggest the best person for you to consult. They can even make arrangements for the consultation. Then all the information on the case, the details of clinical signs and treatment, the results of any laboratory tests and any radiographs or E.C.G. traces, can be supplied to the consultant for analysis. Usually, the second clinician will refer you back to your original vet with recommendations for future treatment, but this can depend upon a variety of factors.

Certainly, this procedure is much better than simply moving on to one (or more) of the other vets in your area should you be disenchanted with what has already been achieved. If another vet has to start from scratch, without knowing any of the previous history, it will inevitably result in unnecessary expense and in a delay which could prove critical to the cat's health. If you are really dissatisfied with your existing vet, tell him; knowing the difficulties which have arisen in your case may allow your vet to take steps to prevent this type of situation recurring. And if you still decide to transfer to another practice, telling your vet might at least ensure that your cat's records get transferred.

2
Choosing and Living with a Cat

Q *If I'm out all day is it fair to keep a cat?*

A Although there are some people who believe the answer should always be no, it really depends on your individual circumstances. It would be reasonable to keep a cat if you are absent only during the normal working day and are home in the evenings and at weekends, and provided that the cat is able to enter and leave the premises (through a cat door) when you are not around. However, if you are away from home more frequently than that, it is doubtful whether the arrangement is fair to the cat. Of course, you might arrange for a neighbour to feed the cat when you are away, but usually there is no permanency about such arrangements. If you really care about the cat and put its interests first, which you should, it is clearly a very poor home that you are offering.

If you live in an apartment, it may prove impossible to let the cat have access to outdoors. With a ground floor or basement apartment the situation is obviously different. If you live in an apartment above that level, it may even be possible for a cat to reach the ground via roofs or a cat ladder, which will not support the weight of any heavier animal, including potential housebreakers. But always ensure that the cat has free access back into the premises and to its bed. Make sure too that fresh water is always available when no-one is at home.

Since a kitten would require feeding three or four times a day and house training, it would be better for single working people to take in an older cat, even though it will almost certainly take longer for it to adapt to its new home. Bear in mind that you could encounter problems when you want to go on holiday, or if either you or the cat is taken ill – especially if you have to go into hospital.

If you really can't arrange all this, then you shouldn't have a cat. Some less demanding creature such as a budgerigar, a golden hamster or a gold-fish might be suitable, but even these will require regular cleaning even though they do allow more flexibility, in feeding for example. Any cat that cannot be let free outdoors must be provided with a litter tray and with regular exercise, perhaps by providing an outdoor run.

Q *As cat owners, are there likely to be problems if we have a baby?*

A The problems which may arise fall into two categories. One is the behaviour of the cat towards the baby, and the other is the health risk.

The established cat may resent the arrival of the baby, feeling that it has been replaced in the owner's affections. Consequently, it may show all the signs of jealousy and resentment, i.e. the deliberate breakdown of toilet training with urine spraying, and refusal to eat or groom. In very extreme cases, the baby might even be attacked.

It is therefore important to give increased affection and attention to the cat when the infant arrives to reassure it about its position in the household. And to minimize the transmission of disease from cat to child, they should be segregated, care taken to prevent each from consuming the other's food or using the same utensils, and for the child not to approach the cat's toilet area.

Q *Will a cat damage my furniture?*

A Unfortunately, this is always possible, unless the cat is excluded from the house, though for many people this would rather defeat the object of keeping one.

Apparently destructive behaviour arises primarily from the need of the cat to sharpen its nails by removing the damaged and blunted outer cuticles, and also to mark its territory. Methods of preventing this behaviour are dealt with on page 91.

Q *Is one breed of cat more trouble than another?*

A Well, firstly it should be pointed out that long-haired cats, whether pedigree or mongrel, will require more grooming than those with short hair, and often more bathing as well. Remember too that the hairs of black and dark-coloured cats are usually less obvious on furniture or carpets, though this, of course, depends on the colour of the carpet and upholstery.

Certainly, different pedigree breeds of cat have different characteristics: what you regard as 'trouble' depends on your own temperament and individual circumstances – your accommodation, whether you have a family, and so on. It is as well to be aware of these characteristics so as to obtain a pet that will suit your requirements. Even so, there will inevitably be differences between the temperament of individuals even of the *same* breed.

First, the short-haired cats. The most popular pedigree cats are Siamese, which differ from most cats in being very outgoing with strangers and generally more sociable. A pair of cats reared together usually get on very well. Nevertheless, they are very strongly attached to their owners and very demanding of attention and affection. Because they enjoy being held and stroked, Siamese often fit in well with older children, provided they are handled carefully. On the 'problem' side, they have loud raucous voices which they tend to use excessively. This can be a problem with neighbours, especially in small apartments. The noise is particularly loud when a female on heat is 'calling' and the breed does tend to have prolonged seasons. In general, they are intelligent, highly-strung cats, at times tending towards the neurotic. Because they have been so popular, some strains have become excessively inbred, resulting in severe squints (strabismus or 'crossed eyes'), skeletal disease (osteogenesis imperfecta), kinked tails (due to misalignment of the vertebrae), or abnormal temperaments, some individuals being very aggressive, others very timid. Some Siamese have wool-sucking tendencies and some are absolute spitfires when handled. Like other oriental breeds, they are often easily trained and will frequently walk on a lead or leash.

Burmese cats are closely related to Siamese, though less vocal and more withdrawn with strangers. In general, they are easy-going cats, good as family pets and tolerant of children.

The Abyssinian is a shy cat, apprehensive with strangers, and not at all happy about sitting on your lap. It is rather too nervous for children, though it is an increasingly popular breed, especially with men. This may well be because the Abyssinian, more than any other breed, resembles a wild cat in appearance.

The Russian Blue is an attractive-looking cat but very shy and not at all sociable. When other cats are around, it will probably spend most of its time in hiding.

The curly-coated Rex cats ('poodle cats') are often considered suitable pets for people who are allergic to other breeds of cat. This is attributed to the absence of any long body hairs (guard hairs). In fact, only in the Cornish Rex (otherwise called the German Rex) are these truly absent; in other Rex cats the guard hairs are still present, though modified into soft curly hairs. Consequently, it would be advisable to test the alleged 'freedom from allergy' if this is important to you. Probably the most popular of the Rex breeds is the Devon Rex; its pixie looks are attractive to some people, but disturbing to others. The breed is renowned for its quicksilver temperament – apprehensive, highly-strung, easily upset, and tending to go into sulky moods. However, it has a quiet voice and can be trained to walk on a lead. Regrettably, Devon Rex cats have a high incidence of patella luxation, i.e. a tendency for the knee-cap to slip out of place.

Now, the long-haired breeds. In Great Britain these breeds are not so fertile as the short-hairs, so there are fewer kittens born (two or three is the average litter size of Persians) and the prices asked for them are correspondingly higher.

The Persian is a rather reserved cat, not particularly demanding in affection (not terribly keen to sit on your lap for instance) and quite happy as the only cat in the household. Indeed, some people find the breed almost lethargic, which may be associated with its poorly developed predatory instincts, towards birds for example. Blue-eyed white Persians may be deaf (see page 36).

The Himalayan is a breed which is growing in popularity, especially in North America, and it makes a good pet. Its temperament is between the reserved Persian and the more outgoing Siamese.

Finally, we should mention the Turkish (Turkish Angora) breed which is rather a nervous cat but notable because it has a reputation for liking water and enjoying swimming.

In the domestication of cats, it seems probable that the animals selected were the ones with the most kittenish qualities, i.e. those with a less independent nature and more likely to form a cat-owner relationship similar to the natural kitten-mother bond. Unfortunately, in the breeding of pedigree cats, animals seem to have been selected largely on the basis of appearance, without regard for their desirable behavioural characteristics as pets.

Q *Are cats suitable pets to have in the home with children?*

A Certainly for older children, i.e. above the toddler stage, there can be considerable educational benefit in looking after a cat, as with any pet. The child learns consideration for living creatures and through having responsibility, for example for feeding and grooming, gains confidence in himself. In owning a female cat, there is also an opportunity for learning about sex and birth and the care of the young. Burmese, Himalayan and Siamese cats are pedigree animals which are particularly suited to children, if you are considering a pedigree cat.

If you intend to buy a cat for your children, don't do so unless *you* really like cats, because in a family one of the parents *must* take responsibility for looking after the cat. This isn't something that can be delegated to a child; at worst they may tire of the novelty of having a cat very quickly and at best they may at times become so engrossed in another activity that they forget to feed or groom the cat. Perhaps this change of interest is of no great importance to them, but it certainly is vital to the cat's well-being. And never buy a cat as a present for someone else's children without consulting and obtaining the consent of the parents. There may well be important factors to consider which you know nothing about.

It is important to avoid the cat being ill-treated; usually this results from not knowing the correct way to handle the animal (squeezing and pulling) and from carelessness and a misplaced sense of fun. The children should be asked to consider how they would like to be treated, and shown the correct way to handle a cat. Deliberate maltreatment of animals is most common in children who are themselves ill-treated.

Children between three and six years old should be sat down before being given a cat or kitten to hold as they can easily drop it, especially when the animal wriggles or, as a kitten will, digs its claws in.

For children below toddler age, there can be problems with cats. Babies and toddlers certainly like to stroke cats and many cats like it. But there should always be an adult around. If the child pulls at the cat's tail or hair, or steps on it, the cat may attack (pain-induced aggression). Very young children (under two years old) have a natural tendency to suddenly grab at objects, which kittens find alarming. Cats can also snuggle into a pram or cot with a baby for warmth, and may suffocate it. Cat nets will, if properly fastened, prevent this occurring.

In addition, two important zoonoses (diseases spread by animals to man) can be transmitted by the cat, and children are particularly at risk because of their habit of putting fingers and objects in their mouths. These diseases are visceral larva migrans and toxoplasmosis, and they are discussed in more detail on page 163.

Cats and children should be prevented from eating each other's food, and the cat should be stopped from licking the child's face. After stroking the cat, the child's hands should be washed; until then it should not be allowed to put its fingers into its mouth. Babies and toddlers should be kept away from the cat's toilet tray, and the child's sandpit should be covered when not in use to prevent cats using it as a toilet box. Cat faeces should be cleaned from children's play areas as soon as possible.

Q *Is a female cat a better companion than a male cat?*

A Of course, both males and females can be neutered and there is then little to choose between them. On balance, however, a spayed female cat seems marginally less aggressive and less likely to spray urine indoors (see page 87) than is a castrated male cat. (It does, however, cost slightly more to neuter a female than a male.)

If the cat is not neutered, then a female cat is definitely preferable because it will fit in better with normal human family life. Even so, when she is 'in season' ('on heat') she will be difficult to confine indoors and will make the typical loud calling noises. And she may easily become pregnant and produce a litter of kittens, a process which might be repeated several times. You could of course have her spayed later, which would eliminate these problems.

An uncastrated (entire) male, i.e. a tom cat, usually does not make an acceptable pet because of his habit of leaving home for long periods, sometimes several days, being more aggressive and getting into fights. He will also tend to spray his pungent urine in the house, which impregnates everything, including clothes, with a smell that most people find objectionable. Most boarding catteries are unwilling to board a tom cat. Incidentally, a tom cat's skin is exceptionally tough and giving an injection can prove a problem because the needle may bend rather than penetrate, particularly around the neck region.

Q *Should I get a kitten, or will an older cat eventually fit into our family?*

A This choice depends on individual circumstances. A kitten usually fits in better than an older cat, which sometimes takes a long time to adapt to different people and a different regimen. However, a kitten requires feeding three or four times a day and needs house training, which really means that someone has to be at home with it all day. For these reasons, an older cat is preferable for people who are out all day, as well as for elderly people who can find it difficult to cope with a lively and demanding young kitten.

An older cat will usually integrate more readily with a single person than with a complete household, i.e. a family with existing pets. But if you do opt for an older cat, be careful both about animals that people want to give you, or a stray cat that wants to adopt you. Have the cat checked first by your vet to make sure that you are not taking on a chronic invalid or a diseased animal which may infect existing pets.

Q *What points should I look for when buying a kitten?*

A First of all, the kitten must have been properly weaned (see page 187). Since most cats are weaned at six to eight weeks old under domestic conditions, this means that the kitten should be a minimum of eight weeks old before it leaves its mother.

If it has already been handled frequently as a kitten (though of course not ill-treated) it will usually accept humans readily and prove an affectionate pet. A kitten over twelve weeks old, reared in a cattery with little human contact, is best not purchased because it will tend always to be fearful of humans and rather distant.

By this age of seven or eight weeks old the kitten will have all, or virtually all, of its needle-sharp milk teeth (deciduous teeth); fourteen in the upper jaw and twelve in the lower, twenty-six in all. Also, at that age most kittens will weigh about 25 to 29 oz (700 to 800 g).

The kitten should be adequately nourished, neither thin with its backbone and ribs sticking out, nor pot-bellied. If the mother of the litter appears poorly cared for, it's likely that the kittens have had the same treatment. Kittens should appear clean and well-groomed, strong, active and alert, taking an interest in what is going on around them, including your behaviour. There should be no evidence of fleas or ear mites (see later) or anything else wrong with the coat, e.g. yellow staining of diarrhoea beneath the tail.

There should be no abnormality of the limbs or any defect in walking, and no discharge around the eyes and nose. With a white kitten with one or both eyes blue, it is as well to test for possible deafness (see page 36). If you choose from a litter, choose a friendly, bright animal, but not the most aggressive (i.e. the one who fights all his litter-mates) or at the other extreme, a timid shrinking kitten. And don't choose the 'runt' of the litter, i.e. the smallest and most put-upon, even though you probably feel very sorry for him. These kittens are more likely to develop physical and emotional problems. They begin life less well-nourished and with less immunity to disease and, because of the treatment they have received from their litter-mates, they are more likely to grow up either excessively timid or very aggressive. If you want to test a kitten's emotional state, place it in a room where there are no other cats to distract it and see whether it will chase a paper ball or piece of string. Then clap your hands loudly and speak to it for five to ten seconds. If it scurries away and hides and doesn't cease this behaviour quickly when you come to coax it, the chances are that it won't fit in well with a house full of noisy children.

Lastly, find out what, if any, vaccinations the kitten has received and take it to your own vet for a check-up.

Q *Is it always kinder to get two kittens as company for each other?*

A Although keeping two cats is often advocated so that they can keep each other company, especially if you are out most of the day, it would appear that because domestic cats do not form social groups they do not actually *need* the company of other cats. Essentially, cats are loners and adapted to a solitary existence; this is true of all members of the cat family with the exception of the lion and the cheetah. The only lasting relationship that occurs naturally between cats is that which is formed between a mother and her kittens, but even this doesn't last beyond the time at which the kittens reach puberty, whereupon the group splits up and each individual goes its own way.

Consequently unless you *want* to have two cats it is not imperative for the cat's sake to provide a companion. (Remember that where a new cat is introduced into a household the resident cat may feel initially that its established territory is being usurped and could respond with anger and frustration.) However, if two kittens are *raised* together they usually accept each other's right to be present and these problems are unlikely to occur.

One advantage of having two cats can be that if they ever have to be left in a boarding cattery they will have a familiar companion with them. In Britain only about a quarter of all cat owners keep two or more cats.

Where a number of cats are *obliged* to live together because they are all confined in the same breeding colony or household, they usually learn to tolerate each other and get along without too much trouble. In these groups there is often one cat (usually a male) who is dominant and demands to feed first and sit or sleep wherever it chooses. Sometimes, a 'second-in-command' can also be identified, and at times there may be one or two cats who are clearly social outcasts and have to feed after all the rest and occupy the least desirable sleeping places. But otherwise there is not the same rigid hierarchical structure for cats as seen in the social species, such as dogs, where the 'rank' of each individual is well established.

If they can, cats generally prefer to avoid each other and therefore avoid trouble. To this end, the scent marking of territory may serve to warn other cats that they might encounter the 'occupying' cat and therefore to be cautious. Because of the absence of a hierarchy of dominance, chance encounters between cats, especially males, often end in fights because neither recognizes his own position as being inferior.

Notwithstanding this, it is known that at nightfall both the male and female cats of a neighbourhood will often meet on neutral ground, that is to say, away from their own territories. The purpose of such meetings is uncertain but they are not related to mating or to asserting dominance. The cats just sit around, usually about six feet (2 m) or more apart, though sometimes they will sit close together and groom each other. Such gatherings may go on all night, particularly just before the start of the breeding season, though in general they will break up by midnight or soon after.

Q *I have had a cat for eight years. If we get a new kitten, will they get along together?*

A There is unlikely to be any problem about the kitten accepting its new companion if they are introduced before the kitten reaches three months of age, ideally close to the age of eight weeks. As the kitten gets older it will take progressively longer to adapt to new surroundings and to other animals.

The main problem, however, is likely to lie in the older cat accepting the newcomer. The established cat in the household usually feels threatened on two counts: firstly, its territory is being invaded by another cat, and secondly, it feels jealous because there is competition for the owner's attention and affection. The feeling of insecurity which is created may, in extreme cases, result in the newcomer being savagely attacked. If this occurs, then the animals must be kept separated and only re-introduced in a series of meetings when you are present.

However, a certain amount of 'bossy behaviour' on the part of the older cat is normal and is intended to teach the newcomer its place. Often the older cat will initially ignore the kitten totally and it can take a long time for the kitten to be accepted.

At times the jealousy and resentment felt by the older cat will result in abnormal behaviour, even psychosomatic illness. There may be a break-down of toilet training (i.e. urine spraying in the home or the deposition of urine and faeces in inappropriate areas), sulking, and a failure to eat and/or to groom. In some cases, though, furious grooming is seen and in extreme instances diarrhoea, vomiting and hair loss can occur. Siamese in particular may be very resentful and leap on to the owner's shoulder for affection.

How can this process of acceptance be made smoother? Well, firstly, don't provoke a confrontation by bringing the two animals face to face to 'meet' each other. If they do come into contact, it should be in a fairly large room, and not a confined space, with you present. Secondly, make a particular fuss of the established cat, *not* the newcomer. The older cat must be made to realize that it has not been displaced in your affections. So don't lavish attention on the kitten, no matter how attractive it appears, when the resident cat is around to see this.

Finally, feed both cats at the *same* time from separate dishes of their own, either in different rooms or at opposite ends of the same room, if necessary with some furniture between to separate them. After a week these rules can be relaxed somewhat and hopefully within six to eight weeks the two cats will get along amicably.

Q *Will my cat get along happily with other types of pets?*

A Because of its natural predatory instincts, it is unreasonable and unrealistic to expect a cat not to attack the smaller pet mammals (such as hamsters, guinea pigs, or even rabbits), fish and cage birds. Where a kitten and the young of one of these species have been raised together, they may accept each other as equals and co-exist in harmony, but in practice this situation is rare. Therefore these pets should be segregated in their own cages, runs etc., and the cat allowed no opportunity to interfere with them.

The household pet with which they are most likely to get along happily is the dog, especially if kitten and puppy were introduced into the household at the same time.

If a kitten is brought into a house where there is already a dog, there is a danger of the dog becoming jealous and attacking the kitten. Therefore much the same procedure should be adopted as when introducing a kitten and an older cat (see above), i.e. giving increased attention to the dog and feeding the animals separately, particularly as they will have different food requirements and the dog will usually finish its meal first. Generally there will be gradual acceptance. Introduction of an older cat may present greater difficulty, but again it should be attempted along the same lines.

Q *Should I have my cat neutered? I want to do what is best.*

A The term 'neutering' means, in the female, spaying (i.e. the removal of the uterus and the ovaries) and, in the male, castration (i.e. the removal of the testicles). These operations have two main effects.

Firstly neutering prevents cats producing litters of unwanted kittens that will either have to be destroyed or become strays. There are already large numbers of unwanted stray animals around. Any more will have to compete with existing stray animals for food and will often die prematurely from disease or injury. It is also worth noting that female cats who regularly produce kittens are subjected to greater stress and do not live as long, e.g. a maximum of twelve years old compared with fourteen or fifteen years for a spayed female.

Secondly, neutering prevents the formation of sex hormones by the gonads (testosterone by the testicles and oestrogen by the ovaries) and thereby alters the behaviour of the cat.

Entire female cats show signs of heat two or three times in the year, and at those times they will want to wander off to find a mate. Attempting to keep the cat indoors to prevent her mating is an almost impossible task; sooner or later the cat will manage to slip out. She will show typical mating behaviour, crouching and rolling about making a raucous howling noise ('calling'), which owners often interpret as evidence of severe pain. In Siamese in particular, the heat cycles can be prolonged *or* constant (often referred to as nymphomania). And, of course, the presence of a female on heat will attract the local tom cats, who will congregate round the house in the hopes of mating, will yowl, spray urine and fight each other.

Entire male cats will roam the neighbourhood seeking mates, often for days on end, and they will spray their characteristically strong smelling urine in the home. They can also develop the condition of stud tail. Tom cats are certainly more aggressive; they frequently fight other male cats and as a result often get bitten and develop abscesses. Not surprisingly, these additional stresses shorten their lifespan compared with a neutered male. And, because of their frequent wanderings, they are also more likely to be injured in a road traffic accident.

Q *At what age should my cat be neutered? Will it cause a personality change?*

A Usually veterinary surgeons prefer to perform these neutering operations when the animal is old enough to withstand the operation and for the anatomical structures to be easily seen, but *before* puberty when breeding is possible and the cat develops the sexual behaviour described above. This usually means a minimum age of five to six months for the female and a little older for the male (it's necessary for the testicles to have descended into the scrotum).

Removing the gonads makes the cat develop into a much more acceptable pet, especially in the case of males. Male cats 'doctored' before puberty will not usually develop the urine spraying habit or any undue aggressiveness. Rarely, this behaviour does develop in castrated males where they are subjected to abnormal stress, for example, another cat invading their territory.

Q *Is a cat ever too old to be neutered?*

A There is no maximum age at which these neutering operations can be performed, i.e. no cat is too old, but in general there is no point in delaying the operation unless:

1 You wish to breed from a female. If you feel you *might* want to breed in the future, a drug (progestagen/progestin) can be given in the meanwhile to prevent her from coming into heat and displaying the behaviour mentioned earlier, or

2 You wish a male to develop the characteristic tom cat features of a wide head, puffy cheeks and larger body. You could then have him castrated at two to three years' old. Castrating an older tom cat may not stop him spraying urine, though it is 90% effective, but as least it stops the objectionable smell. He may also still want to roam, fight or even mate; this behaviour occasionally persists, particularly in very sexually experienced males. But certainly his appearance will improve from a smelly, rough-looking cat into a well-groomed individual. In general most males and females show a gradual decline in sexual behaviour after neutering.

Currently, the 'chemical castration' of male cats is being actively investigated; one or two injections of the drug cyprodione acetate permanently inhibits the effects of male sex hormone on the body.

Q *Is the neutering operation cruel?*

A The neutering operation is not cruel; in both sexes it is done under general anaesthetic. In the male it involves removing the testicles through an incision into the scrotum; the small surgical wound is usually not sutured and heals quickly. In the female the operation is a little more serious, involving opening into the abdomen. The incision is made either on the side, i.e. the flank, of the cat (favoured in Europe and Australia) or in the middle of the underside (favoured more in the United States). A mid-line incision is often preferred if there is a possibility of the hair removed from the cat growing back a different colour afterwards – as often happens with Siamese. There is very little risk of a cat dying during this routine operation and the day afterwards most cats are almost as active as normal. However, after the operation *they should not be handled roughly and therefore are best kept separated from young children.* Two or three sutures are inserted to keep the wound edges together and these are removed seven to ten days later when healing is complete. Before then, it is important to prevent the cat and other pets in the household from licking the wound unduly or from interfering with the stitches. Occasionally a cat will bite through the stitches leading to a wound breakdown. If the animal won't leave the site alone, it may need to be covered with a crêpe bandage around the abdomen, or the cat fitted with an Elizabethan collar (page 201).

Q *Do neutered cats become fat?*

A Neutered cats, both male and female, are more likely than entire cats to become overweight as they grow older, but this is easily corrected by simply reducing their food consumption.

Q *Shouldn't I let my female cat have one litter before she is spayed?*

A Unless you particularly want the litter of kittens and can find homes for all of them, it is best not to let her have kittens at all. Having a litter confers no benefit; indeed, if anything it slightly increases the possibility of problems occurring. There could be difficulties during the pregnancy and at the time of the birth, and because the uterus (womb) and its blood supply are now better developed, marginally more risk is associated with the spay operation.

Sometimes it happens that an owner intends to have a cat spayed but delays doing anything about it until after puberty and then discovers that the cat is pregnant. In this situation, it would be possible to remove the uterus containing the developing kittens and the ovaries, but many owners prefer to let the cat have the kittens and then for the cat to be spayed. If this is decided upon, the operation should be delayed until the kittens are weaned (a *minimum* of six weeks after birth). However, it is very important to try to avoid the animal mating again during this period; it is perfectly possible for a female cat to come into heat again during the period when the kittens are suckling.

Of course, none of these difficulties will arise if the cat is spayed at around five to six months of age, that is to say, *before* puberty.

3
Understanding Your Cat's Body

Q *How does my cat purr?*

A The sounds which constitute the 'voice' of an animal (including man) are produced by vibration of the vocal cords within the larynx as air passes over them. The larynx, or voice box, in the throat is part of the respiratory tract along which air passes to and from the lungs. The shorter the vocal cords, because the greater the tension in them, the higher the pitch of the sound. The normal cat's miaow is produced in this way.

However, the purring noise of many members of the cat family, including our domestic cats, actually consists of rapidly recurring bursts of sound, though again originating in the larynx. Each separate sound is due to a sudden release of air pressure following separation of the right and left vocal cords. The laryngeal muscles are briefly stimulated by nerve impulses between twenty and thirty times per second. Each time this happens, the vocal cords come together so that the glottis (the opening between the cords) is closed, and as a result air pressure begins to build up. When the muscle stimulation ceases the vocal cords suddenly part and the air pressure is released producing a sound.

This sequence of events occurs during both breathing in (inspiration) and breathing out (expiration), though there is a brief pause, detectable by a listener, between each phase. In addition, during inspiration, to prevent the air pressure being dissipated, the diaphragm does not contract continuously (which is usual) but in a succession of short bursts which alternate with the contractions of the laryngeal muscles.

The intensity of the purring sound depends upon the degree to which the cat is being stimulated, for example by stroking or being spoken to. Often purring occurs at a low level in the presence of humans and is barely audible, though a finger placed over the throat can detect vibrations in the larynx.

An alternative theory for the mechanism of purring has been put forward, but appears unlikely. This suggests that purring is due to an increase in the velocity and turbulence of blood flow in the posterior vena cava, which is the major vein returning blood from the hind part of the

The site of purring

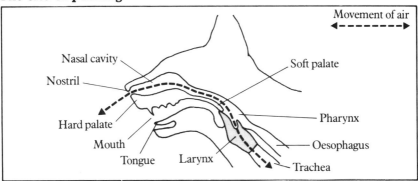

The larynx (voice box) lies in front of the trachea (or windpipe) and air passes through it on the way to and from the lungs. It is constructed of five pieces of cartilage, held together by ligaments and muscles, and is lined by membrane.

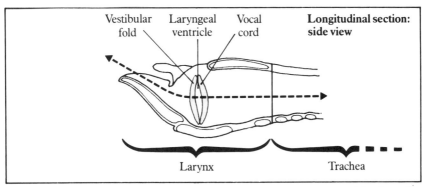

Close up, the membrane is seen to be arranged in two folds on either side. One of these is the true vocal cord and in front of it is the vestibular fold (or false vocal cord). Between them is a minute pocket, the laryngeal ventricle.

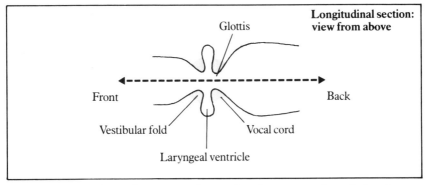

When the laryngeal muscles contract the vocal cords come together, closing the glottis; when the muscles relax it opens again. Each time it opens air pressure is released, making a sound. If this recurs rapidly the resultant noise is purring.

body. The turbulence creates a vibration in the wall of this blood vessel as it passes through the chest, and this vibration is then transmitted through the air passages to the head. However, whereas there is scientific evidence for the explanation given earlier, this one appears to be purely hypothetical.

Q *Now can you tell me why my cat purrs?*

A It is believed that the original purpose of purring was to serve as a signal from the suckling kitten to its mother that it was contented, and kittens from about one week of age are able to purr. Its special value is that because this sound can be produced with the mouth closed the kitten does not have to let go of the teat.

As the cat gets older, purring is used in other situations, again usually to signify a sense of well-being. For example, mother cats purr both when approaching their kittens and during suckling to re-assure the young that all is well.

And of course cats use purring as a greeting and sign of affection for their owner. Purring as a greeting between cats is sometimes shown by a young cat wanting to play with an older cat or by a dominant but friendly cat which wishes to reassure an inferior or younger cat that it means no harm. By purring whilst rubbing against the owner's legs, or when being stroked on the owner's lap, the cat is behaving rather as a kitten does towards its mother. Indeed, some cats even show a 'kneading' action when being held (a gentle up and down movement of the forelegs) which resembles the way in which kittens 'knead' the mammary gland of the mother cat during suckling. A few cats even show this obviously pleasurable reaction on a fur rug or pile of washing – kneading and purring with great satisfaction.

Paradoxically, an injured, ill or timid cat may sometimes purr when it feels threatened in some way, for example by a more dominant animal. In this context, a deep purring appears to act not as a sign of well-being but rather as a plea for mercy.

Cats appear to purr less frequently as they get older, although with age they can use two or three notes in purring compared with the single note of kittens.

Q *Can cats see in the dark?*

A Animals see because light enters the eye and stimulates the nerve endings of the light-sensitive layer, the retina. These sensations are then transmitted along the nerve fibres of the optic nerve to the brain and there interpreted as a 'picture'. If there is absolutely *no* light present, then the cat will be quite unable to see anything, simply because there will be no light entering the eye to stimulate the retinal nerve endings. So in *total* darkness the cat has no advantage over any other animal.

But in dim light, indeed sometimes so dim that to human eyes it may *appear* as complete darkness, the cat is much better able than ourselves to perceive objects, especially if they move. There are three main reasons for this.

1 In the retina there are two types of nerve endings which are named, according to their shape, as rods and cones. The cones are most strongly stimulated by bright light and these nerve endings are responsible for colour vision in man and for the perception of fine details. The rods, on the other hand, are stimulated by light of lower intensity but are not capable of producing such sharp images.

Night vision, or more correctly, twilight vision, in all animals is due to the functioning of the rods. The eye of the cat contains a much higher proportion of rods to cones (approximately 25:1) than the human eye (approximately 4:1).

2 The cat, in common with many other domesticated animals but unlike man, has a reflecting layer (tapetum lucidum) situated just behind the retina. The effect of this is that light rays which have entered the eye and penetrated the retina, thereby stimulating the nerve endings, are immediately reflected back onto exactly the same nerve endings. Consequently each ray of light produces double stimulation of a particular nerve ending giving a type of image intensification.

The presence of the tapetum also accounts for the typical 'cat's eyes' effect when a beam of light, e.g. from car headlights, is shone into the eyes in the dark. The light is reflected back from the greenish-yellow tapetum so that the eyes appear to glow yellow or green in the dark.

3 In all animals the pupil of the eye dilates in dim light and constricts in bright light in an attempt to keep the amount of light entering the eye constant at a level at which the eye works best. The pupil of the cat is able to dilate to a very considerable extent. When constricted in bright light, the cat's pupil appears as a mere vertical slit, but, when fully dilated in dim light, it is circular and can be almost half an inch in diameter. The eyes of the cat are large in relation to its body size anyway and this ability of the pupil to open so wide in dim light obviously permits much more light to enter the eye and to stimulate the rods.

The combined effect of these three factors is such that in poor lighting conditions the cat receives much more visual information compared with a human. In fact it is able to detect objects and other animals with less than 20% of the minimum amount of light needed by the human eye.

Q *Do cats see as we do? Can they see in colour?*

A As mentioned previously, cats are able to see their surroundings more clearly than ourselves when the lighting conditions are poor. But in stronger light, the eye of the cat is not able to distinguish details as well as a human eye can. The eyes of the cat are reasonably close together, like those of man, so that the image seen by each eye is practically the same. This makes it possible for the brain to superimpose these two images to produce a stereoscopic effect, i.e. to give a three-dimensional impression of the surrounding area; this is called binocular vision. Objects are in sharpest focus when they are between six and twenty feet (2 to 6 m) away. Undoubtedly, this is very important to the cat in enabling it to judge distances accurately in such activities as hunting and jumping. Animals in which the eyes are placed on the side of the head (e.g. the horse) see two separate pictures with little overlap and therefore do not experience stereoscopic vision.

Some Siamese cats have difficulty in superimposing the two images because of faulty transmission of the nerve impulses from the eyes to the brain. These animals experience 'double vision' and squint in an attempt to correct this defect.

At one time it was thought that cats, like most domesticated animals, were colour-blind and saw things merely in black, white and shades of grey – like the picture on a black and white television set. But following a series of investigations, it has been demonstrated that, although limited in number, the cone-shaped nerve endings in the retina of the cat's eyes are able to provide some degree of colour vision. Cones sensitive to the primary colours green and blue, though not to red, have been shown to be present. However, the cat's ability to discriminate different shades of colour is clearly inferior to that of man.

Q *If my cat injures his eye in a fight, could he manage with one?*

A An eye may sometimes have to be removed following severe injury. Then, the eyelids would be sewn together so as not to leave a gaping wound. Such one-eyed cats manage perfectly well in most circumstances although obviously they are at some disadvantage in hunting or fighting. There will be some loss of vision on the affected side, and a loss of stereoscopic vision (the superimposition of images from both eyes which gives a feeling of depth). Nevertheless, the animal quickly compensates for these deficiencies and essentially behaves as any other cat.

Q *How old are kittens when their eyes open?*

A At birth the edges of the upper and lower eyelids of a kitten are firmly united. Separation of the eyelids usually occurs five to ten days after birth. In Siamese cats they may open as early as two or three days after birth, but sometimes not until twelve days in domestic cats. If the lids continue to remain together after that time it is considered abnormal. So if the eyes of a kitten are not open after a fortnight, a veterinary surgeon should be consulted.

Closure of one or both eyes in an older cat shouldn't be ignored because this often happens in cases of eye infection. The eyelids become stuck together with discharge, and pus, containing multiplying bacteria, accumulates at the back of the eyelids. If neglected, the eyeball may be permanently damaged. An attempt should be made to gently bathe the eyelids apart, but if any difficulty is encountered the cat should receive veterinary attention without delay.

Q *Is it true that cats only have sweat glands on their pads?*

A No, there are sweat glands over the entire skin surface with the exception of the skin of the nose which is completely free of glands.

The misunderstanding probably arises because the sweat glands are of two types, eccrine sweat glands found only in the pads of the feet, and apocrine sweat glands found everywhere else, especially in the skin of the scrotum (the pouch covering the testicles of tom cats).

The apocrine glands produce a secretion which is broken down by the bacteria normally present on the skin to substances that are responsible for the cat's characteristic body odour. The mammary glands are also apocrine glands but specially modified to produce milk.

In man, the eccrine glands are important as the source of sweat, which in a hot environment cools the body as it evaporates. In this way the glands assist in regulating the body temperature, i.e. maintaining a constant temperature. But in the cat, where these glands are confined to the pads, they are of little importance in temperature regulation. Nevertheless, on a hot day it is noticeable that the cat leaves wet footprints behind it. These glands are also activated by emotional stimuli, just like the glands on the palms of the hand in man which cause 'sweaty palms' at times of anxiety. Consequently, a frightened cat, e.g. one being examined by the vet, can also be seen to leave damp footprints, which are particularly obvious on a dark surface.

Q *Is it an old wives' tale that cats always land on their feet?*

A Well, cats *normally* land on their feet after a fall, provided what is called the head-on-body righting reflex functions correctly.

In the inner ear on both sides of the head are three fluid-filled semi-circular tubes (called the semi-circular canals), each of which is arranged at right angles to the others, i.e. each is in one of the three planes of space. In their walls are nerve endings (vestibular receptors) which detect movement of the fluid and send information about their relative spatial positions to the brain. This means that even when the cat is unable to see it is aware of the position of its head in relation to the ground.

If the cat should happen to fall from a height, it first twists its head so that the top of the head is directed upwards (head-righting reflex). Then it twists its neck and the rest of its body so that they 'line-up' in the normal way with the head – the feet will thus be downwards towards the ground. Simultaneous rotation of the body in one direction and rotation of the tail in the other (one moving clockwise and the other counter-clockwise) allows this stage to occur rapidly, even though the cat has nothing to grip on to whilst falling.

The entire series of reflex (automatic) movements takes only milliseconds to happen so that the cat is 'righted' very quickly and can land on its feet, thereby avoiding or minimizing any injury. In daylight, when the cat can see, visual orientation will inevitably also play a part, but these righting reflexes are not dependent on vision and will also occur in total darkness.

Of course, at times these reflexes may not function correctly, or the animal may sustain an injury during its fall, such as hitting a projecting object, with the result that it does not land on its feet. Even if it is correctly righted, the force of the impact with a hard surface, such as concrete, after a lengthy fall can produce serious injuries, especially fractures of the lower jaw and limb bones and damage to internal organs.

Q *How do cats keep their balance?*

A The cat has a very well-developed sense of balance. He can move surefootedly and without any qualms along narrow shelves and ledges, and even on the tops of walls several feet above the ground. Cats will also climb trees rapidly and without difficulty; although a kitten's nerve may fail at the prospect of the descent, necessitating a 'rescue' by the owner or firemen.

Following the amputation of a limb, fore or hind, a cat experiences little difficulty in balancing or moving and it is able to compensate almost completely.

As mentioned previously, it is the movement of fluid in the semi-circular canals of the inner ear which produces information about the position of the head relative to the ground. This information is conveyed in the form of electrical impulses along the eighth cranial nerve to the brain. The part of the brain known as the cerebellum interprets these signals, together with sensations of touch and pressure from the paw pads and other parts of the body, and then sends nerve impulses to move the appropriate body muscles that will enable the animal to maintain its equilibrium.

The tail acts as a useful counterweight when the cat is moving along very narrow edges, rather like the balancing pole of a tightrope walker. It swings from side to side to compensate for changes in the distribution of bodyweight as each step is taken. It is also held straight out behind at the end of a jump to help arrest the cat's forward movement.

It is interesting to note that the well-known tail-less Manx cat has hind legs longer than its forelegs and that these hind legs have well-developed heavy muscles, which must inevitably shift some weight to the animal's rear end and probably help compensate for the lack of a tail.

34

Q *What do cats use their whiskers for?*

A The whiskers of a cat are large, long hairs which grow out at right-angles to the skin. They are unlike other hairs, which grow at an oblique angle, and the follicles from which they develop are rich in sensory nerve endings. This makes the whiskers very sensitive to touch and their alternative name is tactile hairs or vibrissae. (Incidentally, the skin between them is also extra sensitive.)

The whiskers are useful to the cat on its journeys through its home range and territory. At night they can be used to detect objects which are in its path. When on familiar routes they permit navigation, i.e. the recognition of familiar features which permit the cat to know what point he has reached on his journey. It is believed that if the whiskers of a cat can pass through a narrow opening when fully spread then the rest of the cat can too, i.e. there is no risk of the cat's body becoming jammed. The way that the wind moves the whiskers means that in jumping the cat can make an appropriate correction for windspeed and direction, and also that the cat can more readily locate the source of an attractive or repellant wind-borne odour.

When it is holding a prey animal in its mouth after biting the animal's neck, the cat protrudes its whiskers forward so as to touch the prey. In this way it can detect any movements of the prey, helping to establish when the animal is dead and therefore safe to put down.

The whiskers are also used to 'feel' a strange cat during the mutual inspection and sniffing which occurs when cats encounter each other. Furthermore, whiskers can be used to indicate emotion – they can, for example be rubbed against objects or people they like while at the same time marking these objects with scent from the cheek gland, or they can be fully extended in threat displays to other cats.

There are variations in forms of whiskers just as in other types of hair. For example, the Devon Rex may have very short, stubby whiskers or even none at all, and recently a breed with short, coarse, wiry hair and irregularly projecting crimped whiskers – the American Wirehair – has been developed.

Similar hairs to the whiskers, called carpal hairs, are present down the back of the forelegs, and are likewise very sensitive to touch.

Q *Why does my cat rub against things and people so much?*

A The reason is that the cat is marking the objects in his own territory which will enable him later to identify it and feel reassured at the familiarity of his surroundings.

There are scent glands on either side of the forehead between the eye and ear (temporal glands) and around the lips, particularly at the corners (perioral glands). These produce secretions which the cat smears on such things as doorways, stairposts and the legs of furniture as it rubs its cheeks against them. There are also scent glands on the tail (caudal glands) which deposit similar secretions as the cat brushes its erect and moving tail against a favourite object. Glands are also to be found around the anus and probably on the pads of the feet.

People who are favourably regarded by the cat are also similarly marked as it rubs against them with its cheeks and tail, often purring vigorously at the same time. This rubbing is the type of affectionate behaviour which a kitten shows towards its mother, but also it serves to identify that person as belonging to the special territory of the cat.

Q *Is it true that white cats are always deaf?*

A No, white cats are not *always* deaf, but unfortunately a significant proportion of them are.

The gene responsible for white coat colour is often linked to a gene responsible for malformation of that part of the inner ear (cochlea) which is sensitive to sound waves. This means that the condition is inherited and that it cannot be corrected subsequently.

With the exception of cats carrying Siamese and Burmese dilutions, *blue-eyed* white cats are usually deaf. Also, a white cat with only one blue eye will usually be deaf in one ear, though not necessarily on the same side as the blue eye. Although many white cats have blue eyes, the colour of a cat's eyes (by which we mean the colour of the iris surrounding the pupil) is inherited independently of the colour of the coat. Up to about three months of age all kittens have blue eyes; only afterwards do the true adult eye colours become apparent.

Totally deaf cats usually appear to be hyper-alert. To test for possible deafness, observe the animal's reaction to a sudden noise, such as a hand-clap or whistle, but, to rule out other factors, take care to do this out of the animal's sight, e.g. behind it, and not so close that it might react to any movement of the air. Stamping on the floor is unsatisfactory because the cat will feel the vibration even if it hears no sound. But bear in mind that kittens are born deaf because their ear canals are closed, although this condition is corrected after nearly two weeks. It is normal for young kittens not to be able to recognize or orientate towards sounds until they are three to four weeks' old.

Q *Why is a cat's tongue rough?*

A The surface of the cat's tongue is covered with numerous horny projections, the filiform papillae. These are arranged to point backwards, i.e. towards the back of the throat. It is these papillae which give the characteristic rough feel to the cat's tongue. Because of them, the tongue can be used as a rasp to remove flesh from bones, and they are also important in grooming, enabling the cat to remove loose hairs from its coat.

The presence of the papillae also accounts for the tendency of cats to

36

swallow needles. A playful cat may be attracted by the thread attached to a needle and, having begun to play with the thread, then finds that it becomes entangled in the papillae. The thread cannot be moved forwards because the papillae point backwards but, by gulping, it is possible for the cat to move the thread backwards. So gradually the thread is taken further and further into the mouth, drawing the needle with it. Eventually thread and needle can only be freed from the tongue by being swallowed. The needle may penetrate the wall of the throat, or somewhere further down the digestive tract, but it is usually swallowed blunt end first. Quite often a cat is lucky and the needle passes right through the digestive tract without causing problems. (Undoubtedly, the same explanation will serve for some cats' tendency to swallow similar materials such as string and tinsel.)

There are also other types of papillae (vallate and fungiform) on certain areas of the tongue. These contain the tastebuds able to detect different types of taste, although sweet tastes cannot be discerned by the cat.

Q *Do cats chew their food? Can my cat survive without his teeth when he is old?*

A Cats don't chew their food as we do. The natural function of their teeth is to serve as a means of killing their prey and of cutting it up into pieces small enough to swallow.

The large canine teeth ('fangs') are used to kill the prey by a bite to the neck with the two opposing teeth on the top and bottom jaws, penetrating one of the joints between the victim's neck vertebrae to sever the spinal cord. Then the premolar and molar teeth along the sides of the jaw are used to cut up the prey into pieces or strips which can be swallowed. Especially important are the largest of the teeth (the carnassials) which have a scissor-like action as the jaws close. The small incisor teeth at the front of the jaws can be used for pulling flesh off bones as well as for carrying objects, e.g. prey and kittens. (And of course, all the teeth, but especially the canine teeth, are used for purposes of attack and defence.)

Cats fed on canned or home-cooked diets, or even on raw meat which has been well cut up into tiny pieces, have no need to use their teeth at all. As a result of this lack of wear, tartar accumulates on the teeth initiating a dental disorder (see page 103) which may end in the teeth loosening and dropping out, or having to be removed. But of course if the cat needs only to swallow the same precooked, soft food, it will certainly not require its teeth, and indeed there are many old cats who have lost all their teeth and yet eat normally and remain quite healthy. So the presence of teeth is not essential and digestion will proceed normally with or without them, although of course a cat without teeth is not so well-placed to defend itself.

Obviously, it is preferable to prevent the cat from losing its teeth. This may be achieved by feeding it chunks of whole meat to tear at or dry foods, or by giving some large, hard biscuits or a hide chew (available at pet shops in various shapes). All of these will provide good dental exercise and reduce the possibility of dental disorders developing later.

Q *How will my cat's body change as it gets older?*

A The aged cat is less active and less adaptable than formerly. The reduction in the amount of muscle on its frame means that it has less strength and stamina; it moves more slowly and is less agile. Any severe loss of fluid (e.g. due to vomiting or diarrhoea) takes longer to correct, and temperature regulation is less efficient so that exposure to cold can easily result in hypothermia (abnormally low body temperature). The healing of damaged tissues takes longer and the senses of smell, taste, sight and hearing are all impaired to some extent.

The elderly cat is also less interested in what is happening around it, preferring to remain inactive for longer periods. It resents alterations to its daily routine and will not readily accept changes in its food or surroundings.

Renal disease, dental disease, and the occurrence of tumours (growths) are all common in old cats. Some cats lose the ability to pass motions, others are unable to control the sphincters of the bladder or anus resulting in incontinence. The skin is less elastic and, because the cat is less interested in grooming, discharges from the eye and ear can accumulate and have to be cleaned away by the owner.

Old age, however, should not be regarded as a disease but merely as a state in which, unfortunately, the cat has decreased powers of survival and of adjustment to change.

Q *My cat has been neutered and I've noticed it has a lot of loose skin underneath. Is this normal?*

A Yes, it is quite normal for both male and female cats that have been neutered (i.e. castrated and spayed respectively) to develop this sagging, freely-moving skin on their lower abdomen. A lack of the normal sex hormone causes an increase in the amount of subcutaneous tissue which attaches the skin to the underlying abdominal muscles. In castrated males it also markedly increases the flexibility of the skin. The similarity of response in both males and females is probably due to the fact that both the male hormone, testosterone, and female hormone, oestrogen, have a similar steroid structure.

Q *If my cat badly injures one leg, could he manage with three? Would it be kinder to have him put down?*

A Amputation of a limb may be necessary if it has been extensively injured or, less commonly, if it is diseased (e.g. affected with gangrene or a malignant tumour, i.e. cancer). If the animal is otherwise relatively healthy, the continued presence of the limb could jeopardize its future because the complications which would ensue would eventually involve the rest of its body.

Successful amputation is relatively straightforward and after a brief period of adjustment the cat will again be doing all the things it did before. Obviously, the fact that cats normally walk on four legs makes it easier, compared to ourselves, to compensate after losing one. They may have difficulty jumping and climbing but they remain remarkably sure-footed and usually will not attempt anything outside their capability.

It is usually the owners who wish the cat to be put to sleep rather than to have an amputation performed because they 'don't like the look of the cat' with only three legs. The cat, however, in common with other domestic animals, is more objective. Almost certainly, such animals spend little time in thinking that they *used* to have four legs or that other cats still have four legs, but rather they get on with living their lives and making the best of them.

Q *Is it true that there is a bone in the penis of the cat?*

A A bone (os penis) *can* develop inside the penis of some male cats, but it is not always present. When it does develop, it is not formed until well after puberty. It results from the fibrous partition between two columns of spongy tissue (corpora cavernosa) in the penis becoming slowly converted into bone, i.e. ossified. The bone is only about $\frac{1}{4}$ inch ($\frac{1}{2}$ cm) long and is shaped like a long tapering cone with its apex near the tip of the penis. If it has any purpose, it must be to help support the penis during mating.

A similar bone in the penis of the dog is much better developed and always present. Both are examples of bones which can form in soft tissues unconnected to the rest of the skeleton; a further example is the two small bones which develop in the heart of cattle.

Q *Is it true that a cat's penis is barbed?*

A The penis of the cat is unusual in being covered in about 120 barbed spines, or papillae, pointing towards the base of the penis. They disappear two to four months after castration. Deflection of these papillae during mating produces sensations which probably stimulate the discharge of semen (reproductive fluid). With repeated mating the papillae may pick up hair from the hind-quarters of the female. This can accumulate as a ring of hair around the base of the penis which has to be removed before further successful mating is possible. It is also thought that the sensation produced by the barbs as the penis is withdrawn stimulates the vagina of the female and induces ovulation.

Q *It has just occurred to me that my cat must be quite elderly. How long can I expect him to live?*

A Most cats will live between twelve and fifteen years. Naturally enough, it is always the exceptionally long-lived cats that one hears about, but these animals, living between twenty and twenty-five years or more, are certainly out of the ordinary.

Entire female cats usually continue to come into heat and to mate until near the end of their lives (e.g. twelve years' old), although there are fewer kittens in a litter after they reach the age of eight, and after eleven years' old many matings are unproductive. Tom cats, however, generally continue to mate successfully and to sire offspring up to fifteen or sixteen years' old.

Q *Why do Siamese cats have dark faces and dark tips to their ears, legs and tail?*

A The typical pattern of markings shown by Siamese cats (and also by breeds such as the Balinese, Birman and Himalayan) is due to regional variations in skin temperature. At the extremities of the cat's body the skin temperature is normally slightly lower than elsewhere. When the hairs grow at this lower temperature, they contain more of the dark pigment melanin and thus appear darker.

If part of the skin of the trunk is cooled more than usual, any new hairs which grow there will also be darker. This is seen around operation wounds (such as spay wounds) and may be due partly to interference with the blood supply but more likely due to clipping of the existing hairs which reduces insulation and increases heat loss in that area. Where Siamese cats are kept in very cold environments, the whole trunk will appear darker than usual. Conversely, in tropical countries, the normally dark extremities (known as 'points') are lighter than usual because they are warmer. The same effect, though localized, is seen when a dressing is kept on a limb for a long period; the increased warmth in the covered part causes new hairs growing there to be less heavily pigmented than those surrounding it.

4
Understanding Your Cat's Behaviour

Q *Why do male cats spray urine?*

A The spraying of urine on vertical objects, primarily by tom cats (un-neutered males), is a method both of marking their territory and of advertising that they are 'available' for mating. The urine of cats contains various chemicals known as pheromones which act as scent markers.

This scent-marking of his territory, and particularly its boundaries, helps the male to familiarize himself with his environment, and reassures him when he re-encounters the scent later. It also informs other males of his existence. However, it is not an effective deterrent in preventing 'trespassing' by other cats; rather, it serves to indicate that they should proceed cautiously to avoid unwanted meetings. Usually any 'interloper' will sniff at the mark and then stroll on apparently unconcerned, often after putting his own mark near it.

During the breeding season, the characteristic pungent scent of tom cat urine attracts sexually receptive females. The increased level of male hormone (testosterone), plus the increase in anxiety and excitement at this time, contribute to an increased frequency in spraying, both indoors and outdoors. Indeed, with male cats used for breeding (stud toms), spraying indoors is so commonplace that the animals are almost always kept in special quarters away from the owner's residence.

Spraying is more likely to occur when there are several male cats in a household or neighbourhood, and particularly when a cat is introduced to a new territory. It is often performed at certain times of the day. The male first examines the object (shrub, fence, wall, etc.) and then turns his rear towards it. With his back partly arched he raises his tail, makes two or three paddling movements with his hind legs and then quite accurately sprays urine backwards over the area in a fine jet to a height of one to two feet.

Males which have been castrated, before or after puberty, (the onset of sexual maturity is usually between six and nine months' old), are less likely to spray but *may* do so, particularly if they feel threatened, for instance by new cats appearing in their territory.

Entire (unneutered) females may also spray urine. Some normally do so during the breeding season when their urine contains the pheromones attractive to the male; (pheromones of both males and females are sexually attractive to the opposite sex). Other females may spray if their hormone balance is disturbed, for example by drugs to prevent or delay oestrus ('heat'). For anatomical reasons these females squirt the urine out in a series of droplets rather than a fine jet.

After spraying it is common for the animal (male or female) to smell the area. Often it will rub its face in the damp patch and then by further rubbing of the face transfer the scent to other objects in turn. Males may rub their hindquarters on the marked area or make agitated clawing movements whilst smelling the mark.

Most of this marking by urine-spraying fortunately takes place outdoors. But spraying indoors is a problem that can arise in males and females both entire and neutered if they feel that their territory is being threatened or if they become frustrated. This type of emotional disturbance can be triggered off by the arrival of a new member of the household (e.g. another pet or a baby) or even by a new piece of furniture or carpet, or by overcrowding, (e.g. six or seven cats in the same household), or by some change in its environment, such as moving house. Some cats may also spray urine at any visitors to the house. And as mentioned previously, spraying indoors by entire males and females can be a particular problem during the breeding season.

At times a cat will begin to spray, or urinate normally, on carpets, furniture or bedding, apparently out of resentment, e.g. at being scolded or being prevented from doing something it wishes to do, or even being fed food it doesn't like.

Q *I am feeding my cat regularly. Why does he have to kill birds and raid neighbouring fishponds?*

A Like all members of the cat family (*Felidae*), the domestic cat has a natural and strongly developed hunting instinct. This hunting, or predatory, behaviour still persists in animals which are receiving adequate regular meals, although having stalked and caught their prey there is not the same incentive to either kill or eat it. Cats which are kept to control rodents used to be fed only minimally to encourage their hunting, and these cats when hungry would usually consume their prey entirely. However, good 'mousers' are often more efficient if they are fed regularly; the lack of the *need* to kill appears to reduce anxiety and increase efficiency.

Cats are best adapted by nature to the catching of small rodents, but in urban areas these may be very few and then the cat resorts to hunting small birds. In fact, they will often attack anything not larger than themselves, such as fish, snakes, frogs and toads, squirrels (as soon as they are on the ground) and, in rural areas, young rabbits. They will also prey on insects such as flies and grasshoppers. Cats hunt on their own and there is no good evidence of co-operative hunting. If the hunting instinct disturbs you, I'm afraid you shouldn't keep a cat.

Q *How did my cat learn to hunt?*

A Usually, the first prey-catching movement is made at about three weeks' old. This is a tentative forward grope with one paw, which is the way an adult cat will investigate any new small object. The instinctive movements of hunting, i.e. lying in wait, chasing, stalking and pouncing, appear soon afterwards, but at first they are performed clumsily. They are practised in playing with litter-mates, but the movements are linked in a random fashion, along with other play movements, and not until later do they become arranged in the correct sequence for hunting.

Undoubtedly, the ability to hunt is learned chiefly from observing and interacting with the mother cat. The presence of kittens intensifies the mother's hunting instinct, and dead prey animals are brought to the litter when the kittens are about four weeks' old and eaten in front of them by the mother with growling noises. At first this behaviour frightens the kittens, but later they are attracted to it. At about six weeks of age the mother brings the first live prey to the kittens, by which time their hunting movements have been perfected – apart from the vital killing bite which requires special learning.

The stimulus for a kitten to kill appears to be elicited by the presence of live prey, and also by the rivalry between itself and its mother or litter-mates to be first to catch the prey. The peak time to learn to kill is at nine to ten weeks of age. If the mother cat doesn't bring live prey to the kittens in the critical period between six and twenty weeks' old, they either do not learn to kill, or only learn to do so very laboriously in later life. Cats, unlike many other animals, learn a lot by watching the behaviour of other animals that are learning a task and in the wild kittens accompany their mother on hunting expeditions both before and after weaning. Only with the onset of puberty does the group disperse to lead isolated lives.

Q *All right, I can understand why my cat hunts, but why does he have to play with his prey? It strikes me as rather cruel.*

A The so-called 'playing' with prey animals appears to be due to the cat's anxiety as to how the prey will respond. It is a pattern of behaviour that is shown by kittens, by all cats deprived of live prey for some time and by cats playing with various substitute objects. The normal hunting movements of carrying and tossing are performed in an exaggerated fashion and in random order, without any attempt at a killing bite. The cat may appear to play 'catch' with a mouse by delivering blows alternately with right and left paws and then, as the mouse moves, by rapidly approaching it, grasping it with both paws and finally picking it up in the jaws. The mouse is then gently put down and the process repeated. Similarly, the cat may draw a mouse near with its paws and, after lifting it in the jaws, toss it upwards or to one side, and continue to repeat this behaviour. Cats deprived of prey often show similar behaviour with a substitute object such as a toy mouse, a ball of wool or paper, or even a person's foot or ankles, or with stones and lumps of earth.

Often, between periods of this active 'play', the cat shows more restrained behaviour in which it gently taps the prey, afterwards recoiling in fright, especially if the prey moves. The cat may even lie on its side for a while, keeping the prey in view, and lick the inside of its forelegs.

This apparently cruel behaviour by the cat seems to be attributable to its worry about having to hunt and kill the prey, and is a means whereby it can discharge its pent-up nervous energy.

Q *Why does our cat bring his prey home? Is he trying to give us a present?*

A The bringing home of dead, or even live, prey animals by female cats, and sometimes neutered males, is a modification of the mother cat's normal behaviour in bringing dead, and later live, prey to its kittens. In fact, it is a practical demonstration of the cat's concern for the well-being of its owner. The cat usually 'calls' its owner to inspect the prey, just as the mother would coax its kittens. It is not so much asking for praise for being a good mouse-catcher, but rather it is wanting the owner to show an interest in the prey it has brought home, as it would expect its kittens to.

Q *Why do my cat's teeth 'chatter' when he looks out of the window?*

A Cats who are near to prey but unable to catch it (e.g. birds out of reach on a branch or seen through a window) often show 'teeth-chattering'. The corners of the mouth are pulled back and the jaws come together with a rhythmic smacking noise. The same behaviour can be seen in cats chasing frustratingly elusive substitute-prey objects, such as soap bubbles or rays of sunlight. It should be interpreted as a sign of frustration.

Q *I am very fond of birds as well as cats. Is there any way I can stop my cat from hunting?*

A The fact that a cat which is not hungry indulges in killing birds, and may bring dead or live rodents back home, greatly distresses some owners. Although cats can learn to hunt later in life, hunting is normally learned from the mother at an early age. Consequently, the kittens of a non-hunting mother cat are less likely to become hunters, both because they may not be taught it and also because they may inherit a genetic make-up which precludes hunting.

The castration of male cats does *not* reduce their predatory instincts.

Tying a bell to the collar ('belling the cat') is sometimes done so that the potential prey will have warning of the cat's approach. However, many cats learn to move so stealthily that the bell does not ring until it pounces on its prey.

Some owners try aversion therapy to discourage hunting. After concealing themselves, they dangle a dead bird (perhaps a previous victim) on a string and, when the cat attacks it, the unseen owner squirts the cat with water. The intention is that with repetition the cat will come to associate hunting with an unpleasant shock and so will be effectively discouraged.

Although it is believed that the majority of birds caught by cats are young, old or sick individuals, and that in order to keep the bird population in an area constant, around three-quarters of those hatched have to die, this may be of little consolation to the cat owner. Such preventative measures as the careful siting of nesting boxes and bird tables (away from hiding places and easy vantage points), the secure fixing of nesting boxes and the attachment of an anti-climbing device to a bird table may be the best that can be achieved.

Cats who as kittens were reared alongside other species such as mice usually make no attempt to hunt them, i.e. they do not regard these species as natural prey. However, since this rarely happens, it is prudent to ensure that cats do not have access to any other smaller pets such as rabbits, guinea pigs, hamsters, budgerigars and, of course, tropical and cold water fish.

Q *Does my cat need to sharpen his claws? I am rather worried about our new furniture.*

A The claws of the cat are used to obtain a grip in climbing as well as for attack and defence and in order to be fully effective they need to be kept needle sharp. The claws can be retracted into a sheath to prevent undue blunting when they are not being used, but those on the front legs especially still need to be sharpened from time to time. The claws, just like human finger nails, consist of compressed layers of horny cells and they grow continuously from the base. Periodically, a worn outer claw is pulled off by scratching to expose a new, very sharp claw growing beneath it. The old, shed claws can often be found at the base of scratching posts.

The cat does this sharpening by crouching or standing on its hind legs and dragging its protruded front claws down a roughened surface which will allow the claws to cut in. Many cats use a tree trunk or post in the garden for this purpose. This behaviour also serves to mark the cat's territory, and male cats may make these movements after first having sprayed the tree trunk or post with their urine. A display of claw sharpening appears to be intimidating to any watching cat who might consider invading that particular territory. It is also probable that the cat applies scent from glands in its pads to the scratched surface, which assists in marking the territorial boundaries. Possibly, the height of the mark informs other cats about the size of the animal which made it, although there isn't general agreement on this point.

This claw sharpening and territorial marking is perfectly natural behaviour for the cat. Unfortunately, some cats may select items of furniture for this treatment and can inflict severe damage on such objects as table legs, doors, upholstered chairs and sofas, curtains, carpets and even the wallpaper and plaster on the walls. Such behaviour appears more likely to occur in animals that do not have adequate access to trees or posts outdoors. At times, but fortunately not often, cats may even inflict such damage quite deliberately to show their displeasure, for example after being scolded.

Q *How does my cat indicate its moods?*

A A cat is able to communicate its moods to other animals and to humans by the posture and movement of its body – in particular the position of its tail and ears, the appearance of its eyes and the sounds it makes.

A contented cat will have relaxed muscles and it may just sit quietly, though its erect ears ('prick ears') indicate that it is alert and carefully watching what goes on. Contented cats tend to wash themselves with long, slow licks. Washing with short, sharp licking movements occurs when the cat is upset about something and its body is more tense.

Pleasure at seeing the owner is often indicated by standing with the head lowered, the hind quarters raised and the tail held straight up and often with the tip bent slightly forwards and moving slowly from side to side. In this posture the cat moves slowly, rubbing its cheeks, whiskers and tail against the owner and often winding between the owner's legs or jumping on to his lap. Purring is the usual accompaniment. This behaviour is strikingly similar to that of the sexually receptive female cat who crouches with her rear end held high and her tail drawn to one side. As mentioned previously (page 30), purring is usually an indicator of pleasure and the cat may at the same time make rhythmic treading movements with its feet, similar to those made by kittens whilst feeding.

When a cat is upset (either frightened or angry), its body muscles are tense. In the presence of a strange cat or other animal, e.g. dog or human, the cat will remain motionless while it assesses the situation, keeping its eyes fixed on the stranger.

If the cat is very anxious and afraid as this stranger approaches, the pupils of its eyes open wide (dilate), and its eyes dart rapidly from side to side looking for an escape route. It may adopt a submissive posture, crouching down with its ears flattened sideways across its head, its chin drawn in and tail held low. This submission may have the effect of appeasement if the aggressor is a cat, who then withdraws without attacking. If the aggressor comes nearer, a submissive cat will roll on its back, but a paw will be raised and will ultimately be used to defend itself. Or

46

the cat may try to make a run for it. But if it finds itself cornered it will be obliged to adopt a defensive posture. In this it combines signs of fear (dilated pupils and flattened ears) with those of aggression (growling and bristling of the hair). The cat growls, hisses and 'spits', displays its canine teeth and arches its back. It tries to stand sideways on to the stranger and raises the hair on its back and tail, all to make itself appear larger and more threatening. The tail is usually held upright. (Of course the flattened ears of the submissive and defensive postures should not be confused with the permanently forward-flattened ears of the Scottish Fold breed.)

If all these warning signs are ignored and the strange animal approaches closer than a yard (1 m) into what is called the 'flight distance', when there is no escape route, the cat will attack. It holds its tail straight out behind, crouches down and, with claws extended and fangs bared, leaps out.

However, the cat may adopt a dominant, aggressive stance from the start. In this offensive mood (e.g. in tom cat duels), the pupils of the eyes are constricted and the cat will attempt to 'stare out' his opponent. He faces the stranger with head stretched slightly forwards, his ears erect and his back stretched out straight (not arched). The hairs on the tail bristle only moderately and the tail is held in a characteristic 'straight down' position with the tip often flicking from side to side. He moves very slowly nearer his potential adversary, growling and howling, and salivating so much that he is obliged to swallow. Eventually the two cats are only a short distance apart. Then after a long period of facing each other, during which the tail movements become more violent and the howling rises and falls, one cat may suddenly attack the other with a bite and the fight begins.

As well as the sound of purring and what are called 'strained intensity' sounds, i.e. those of fear and anger, hissing and growling, cats can make many other sounds. Up to sixteen distinct sounds have been distinguished. There is a trilling sound used for greeting and by mothers to encourage kittens to suckle, and a variety of 'miaows' (vocal patterns) used in conjunction with a questioning look to ask for things or to indicate anticipation, pain or disapproval. And in the breeding season, the caterwauling of males and the yowling of females may shatter the quiet of the night. Most of these adult vocalizations can be produced by cats after three months of age. Some breeds, particularly the Siamese, are extremely vocal, whereas others such as the Abyssinian are naturally much quieter.

When feeling ill and wretched, the cat keeps its tail low, has a miserable facial expression and spends a good deal of time hunched up, often not even bothering to eat or wash itself.

Cats in an agony of indecision about how to behave in a perplexing or frightening situation may start to groom themselves, just as humans may scratch their heads or bite their fingernails; an example of so-called displacement activity.

A cat that wants something from its owner will usually continue to look directly at him or her, often 'miaowing' at the same time, until it gets what it wants or is shooed away, or else gives up. However, cats themselves have a dislike of being looked at directly. If a cat that is being secretly observed suddenly becomes aware of the fact it will stop whatever it is doing and will re-continue its activities only in an obviously self-conscious and more hesitant manner.

Q *Sometimes, when my cat smells objects or other cats, he seems to be attracted, and yet by the way he turns up his nose he finds the smell unpleasant. Why is this?*

A This reaction, which is known as flehmen, occurs when a cat is strongly attracted to a scent. It is most commonly seen when a tom cat smells a female in heat or her urine, but it is also shown by neutered males and females, for example when smelling the anal region of strange cats.

The animal extends his neck and lifts his lower lip producing a grimace suggesting that he finds the smell disgusting. But in fact by doing this he is constricting the nasal chambers ensuring that when he inhales, the scent particles (pheromones) are drawn through a duct leading off the roof of the mouth into a special pouch, the vomeronasal organ or Jacobson's organ. Here they are detected by special sensory cells which connect with the brain. This organ is possessed by all mammals, except man and certain other primates, and results in a greatly enhanced sense of smell, particularly for perceiving those odours which act as sexual attractants.

Q *Is it normal for my cat to sleep for a large part of the day?*

A Yes it is – in fact cats normally spend almost two-thirds of each day sleeping and they are only awake for just over a third. Sleep occurs most readily when there is fatigue after severe muscular exercise and, like many animals, cats will often sleep after a large meal. (Indeed, immediately after feeding is a good time to photograph a cat because of this natural inclination to rest.) Warmth is also important in inducing sleep, compensating for the slight fall in body temperature which occurs.

Sleep is recognized as being important in maintaining and restoring the normal function of all body tissues, especially the nervous system, and without sleep animals become irritable and ultimately severely ill. However, because cats prefer the hours of twilight and darkness for many of their activities, the hours when they wish to sleep often do not coincide with our own.

Q *What does it mean if my cat twitches and makes running movements when asleep? Is he having a fit?*

A No, he is certainly not having a fit. This behaviour is quite normal and occurs during periods of deep sleep. As in man, it is now recognized that there are periods of light sleep and of deep sleep, the latter accounting for around a quarter of the total sleeping time in the cat.

When a cat first goes to sleep, it is usually curled up into a ball and there is incomplete muscular relaxation. However, after ten to thirty minutes this initial phase of light sleep gives way to a period of deep sleep in which the muscles are fully relaxed, and the animal now lies on its side. At this time, although the eyes are closed, there are bursts of rapid eye movements (REM sleep), together with more obvious movements of the limbs, paws, tail, ears and whiskers.

In man dreaming occurs during this type of sleep, which is believed to be a state in which the brain is 'programmed' with information about recent events; the information is being transferred from a temporary memory store to the main banks of data. This would explain why the young kitten (with so much information to store) enjoys only deep 'dreaming' sleep for about the first month of life. After that it then gradually develops the adult sleeping behaviour.

In the cat each period of deep sleep lasts six or seven minutes, and in a long session of sleeping there may be a number of such periods.

Q *My cat always asks to go out at night. Is the cat a nocturnal creature?*

A The cat is not predominantly a nocturnal animal but two important activities do frequently take place at night, namely hunting and mating.

In the case of hunting, this is so because the small mammals which the cat is best adapted to catch, e.g. mice, are usually themselves most active in the hours of darkness. Mating almost always takes place at night because cats dislike being observed, and are inhibited, particularly in towns, by the daytime noise and bustle. The cat is able to perform these activities very effectively at night because it is able to rely much more than ourselves on its well-developed senses of smell and touch (e.g. through its whiskers) for information and communication, as well as its excellent twilight vision.

Cat owners know that cats frequently ask to go out at night, particularly a female that is on heat, or a tom cat that knows there are females on heat in the neighbourhood. This was the origin of owners 'putting out the cat' and then locking the door just prior to going to bed in order to avoid being disturbed later. However this routine is *not* recommended because the cat may be shut out in very cold or wet weather with disastrous effects on its health. Much better is to fit a cat door (cat flap) which permits the cat to come and go as it pleases. If necessary, the cat door can always be bolted shut to prevent this free entry and exit.

Q *Do cats sometimes pretend to be ill to gain attention?*

A Certainly, some cats that crave extra affection learn that if they damage themselves by biting or chewing at part of their body, often the tail, in the presence of the owner they will obtain attention and sympathy. In the absence of an obvious cause (such as flea infestation) for this behaviour the possibility of simulated illness should be borne in mind. In one reported case, the cat mutilated its tail so badly that amputation was necessary, but even afterwards the animal continued to bite the stump. Only when the owner responded to these 'displays' by leaving the room each time did the behaviour cease.

Other cats may realize that, following a fall or road accident, their lameness provokes a sympathetic response from the owner. Accordingly this 'sympathy lameness' reappears later, whenever the animal wishes to get extra attention from the owner, particularly when it-feels that it is in competition with other members of the household for that affection. Similarly, a cat that has recovered from a serious illness can be disappointed to discover that it is no longer being fussed over as much, and it may learn to be dejected in order to regain this extra care.

Sometimes so much frustration (i.e. behavioural stress) develops in a cat, for instance when a newcomer or visitor, animal or human, invades its territory and competes for affection, that it may trigger off definite physical signs of illness, such as not eating or vomiting. Such signs can appear in situations of overcrowding, or if the owner holds a party, or if the cat is transferred to a different environment. In these cases the animal is *not* pretending; the anxiety state has indeed produced the illness, but as soon as the stress is removed the abnormal signs will either improve or disappear entirely.

Q *Is a cat's sense of hearing more developed than ours?*

A In contrast to humans, cats have much more acute hearing and are able to produce and detect ultrasonic sounds. The human ear can detect sounds with wavelengths up to about 20 KHz; wavelengths greater than that are said to be ultrasonic. Because of the structure of its inner ear the cat is able to detect ultrasonic sounds up to a frequency of 60 to 65 KHz (including those high pitched squeaks of rodents that are inaudible to humans). However, the cat is rather less sensitive to the lower frequencies, being able only to hear sounds with a minimum wavelength of 30 Hz compared with the human lower limit of around 20 Hz. As with all species, the acuity of hearing diminishes with age; old cats may be almost completely deaf.

Q *Do cats have a good sense of smell?*

A Compared with ourselves, cats have a greatly heightened sense of smell. In relation to the total brain size, that part of the brain concerned with smell (olfaction) is much greater in the cat than man. This allows the cat to readily determine the identity of individuals and to detect their previous presence in an area by the scent markings (pheromones) they have left behind. Males can also discover whether a female cat is in heat, and therefore likely to permit mating, by detecting certain sex pheromones which appear in her urine and vaginal secretions.

Q *Why is my cat so attracted to cat-mint (cat-nip)?*

A The plant *Nepeta cataria*, known as cat-mint or cat-nip, contains a substance called nepetalactone which is attractive to all members of the cat family. Somewhere between half and two-thirds of domestic cats appear to be attracted to cat-mint. But very few kittens under two months of age are attracted to, or even able to tolerate, the plant.

Typically, a cat will sniff at the plant, or lick or chew at the leaves, and then exhibit a pattern of behaviour the intensity of which varies with the individual. Some cats just stare into space or shake their head; others rub their faces on the plant and some will roll on the ground. This behaviour generally lasts for five to fifteen minutes, but the same response cannot be produced again for an hour or more.

Because nepetalactone is related to marijuana and other hallucinogenic drugs, it is possible that the cat's response is similar to the sensations enjoyed by humans with these drugs. Alternatively, it may be that this substance closely resembles one of the chemicals that appears in the urine of male cats and which is responsible for the rolling and rubbing behaviour of female cats in heat. If so, it appears to produce an exaggerated stimulus, since cat-mint causes this response in females that are not in heat, as well as in males.

Perhaps it is simply that the smell of the plant, or its extract, produces a pleasant sensation by heightening the sensitivity of the skin in the head region, thereby prompting some cats to rub their heads on the plant or on the ground.

Whatever the exact cause, cat-mint is certainly very popular with many cats and has prompted manufacturers to produce play articles, such as toy mice, stuffed with it or scented with the volatile oils from it.

However, the over-frequent use of cat-nip, for example to make it possible to handle otherwise unmanageable show cats, can result in an unpleasant change in the cat's personality.

The plant known as common valerian (*Valeriana officinalis*), and especially its dried root, has a similar, though not so marked, effect upon cats.

Q *Why does my Siamese cat appear to enjoy chewing at my woollen sweater?*

A This habit of sucking or chewing woollen articles is common in certain strains of cats, particularly of the Siamese breed. In these individuals the behaviour usually begins around puberty (though in orphaned or under-nourished kittens it often follows weaning) and in most cases lasts only for a period between a few months and a year. But unfortunately, there are some cats that persist in this undesirable habit.

It is attributed to a combination of persistent juvenile behaviour and boredom; such animals may groom themselves excessively and suck at their own tails, nipples or paws (self-sucking).

The presence of lanolin in the wool appears to trigger their response; they are very relaxed and contentedly suck at the wool whilst 'kneading' it with the feet – just as a kitten sucks at its mother while it simultaneously 'kneads' the mammary gland.

Some cats progress to similar behaviour with other natural and even man-made fibres and some chew off pieces of the material and swallow them. This practice can lead to the material obstructing the stomach or intestines and having to be surgically removed. Some cats even suck and chew at their owners' hair or skin, nuzzling into the throat or armpit regions.

To curb this behaviour suggestions include applying pepper or mustard powder to garments that are sucked, and fitting an Elizabethan collar to cats that regularly self-suckle (p. 201). But regrettably, in some animals the habit is not easily broken whatever training method is adopted.

Q *Sometimes, after I have been stroking my cat for several minutes, it will suddenly attack me and then run off. Why does this happen?*

A This behaviour, which can occur in either sex but particularly in males, probably represents the natural switch from a submissive to a defensively aggressive role which was referred to earlier. In most cases the cat is lying on its side, with one foreleg raised, having its abdomen stroked. This is the typical posture adopted by a cat being approached by an adversary. If you then continue to stroke the cat it may feel that it is being attacked. Its natural instinct is to lash out with its claws, or even to bite as a defensive reaction and then to run away. This is a fairly common occurence in cats and the only solution is to appreciate why it happens, to recognize the early warning signs and then to avoid overstimulating the cat.

On very rare occasions an older cat may become suddenly and violently aggressive without any obvious reason. Such cases are usually due to some mental disturbance. The total unpredictability of its future behaviour, i.e. whether or when further attacks will occur, even if it is receiving medic-ation, makes it necessary to consider the wisdom of continuing to keep the animal.

5
Feeding
and Feeding Problems

Q *What sort of food is needed by my cat?*

A Basically, the diet of the cat *needs* to contain a high level of easily-digestible animal protein, together with some animal fat and small quantities of certain essential vitamins and minerals. In fact, the balance of nutrients should correspond closely to that found in the natural food of cats, which is small rodents. This means that the diet of cats must be based largely on animal tissues; for example, meat, fish, liver, heart, kidneys, etc.

Cats tend to regulate their intake of food according to its energy content. For example, the daily energy requirement of the average 7 lb (3 kg) pet cat is about 250 calories. After the cat has eaten food which will provide that amount of energy it stops eating. Therefore, if the diet you provide contains too high a proportion of fats or carbohydrates, which are rich sources of energy, the cat will finish eating before it has consumed sufficient protein. In other words it will satisfy its energy requirements and stop eating before it has satisfied its protein requirements.

However, so long as an adequate proportion of protein is provided, the *extra* energy which the cat needs can be supplied in the form of carbohydrates or fats which cost less to feed than protein. Indeed, there is a definite need for *some* animal fat, which may be part of an animal tissue (e.g. fat in meat) or else supplied separately (e.g. butter or bacon rinds). In contrast, there is no real *need* for carbohydrates, i.e. starches and sugary foods. Nevertheless, provided that the starches are pre-cooked (e.g. biscuits, potatoes, rice, breakfast cereal, etc.) carbohydrate foods can be used by the cat as a source of energy.

When it comes to the question of exactly *what* to feed, you may decide to prepare the cat's meals yourself from basic foodstuffs bought at the butchers, fishmongers or pet store, *or* to buy ready-prepared cat foods, *or*, best of all, you may decide to do both, giving a proprietary product one day and a home-prepared meal the next. Cats appreciate novelty in food, unlike dogs who will happily consume the same familiar diet day after day. After a period of being continuously fed one type of diet, most cats given the choice will change to a different diet, even though it isn't any more palatable. By feeding a variety of diets you are less likely to create a deficiency of some essential nutrients.

There are three main types of proprietary brands of cat foods: *canned 'wet' diets* with a moisture content of around 75–80%; *semi-moist ('soft-moist') foods* in sealed, plastic pouches containing 20–30% water; and *dry foods* containing 8–10% water.

Each type can be obtained 'balanced', that is containing protein, fat and carbohydrate in the correct proportions needed by the cat *plus* the necessary vitamins and minerals. Obviously, the less water in the diet, the less of it needs to be eaten to satisfy the protein and energy requirements. Always follow the manufacturer's directions about the manner of feeding and if you intend to feed it to pregnant or lactating females, or to growing kittens, check that it is recommended for that purpose. In the United States any cat diet described as 'balanced' (or alternatively 'complete' or 'scientific') has by law to be nutritionally adequate for the feeding of *all* weaned cats, but this is not yet the case in Britain. Furthermore, British pet food manufacturers advise feeding milk with some of their products to produce a completely balanced diet.

Q *Are commercial pet foods good for my cat?*

A There is often a feeling that proprietary foods are in some ways inferior to those prepared at home. However, the pet food industry is now a multi-million pound/dollar business with plenty of competition, and no reputable manufacturer would dare risk losing his share of the market by selling substandard products. The larger manufacturers conduct a lot of research, both into basic nutrition and into the quality of their products, and they take great pains to ensure that pet foods advertised as balanced diets do in fact contain all the nutrients known to be required and in the optimum amounts. However, there are two specific points regarding the cat: firstly, dog foods are not suitable for feeding to cats; the level of protein (and sometimes of fat) is often not high enough, and secondly, dry cat food may give rise to urinary problems, especially in males (see page 63).

Q *My cat won't eat tinned pet food. What other foods should I give him?*

A When making your own diets, the golden rule is to vary the type of foodstuff each day, ringing the changes between minced meat, fish, liver, chicken, rabbit, etc. with a small amount of added bread or cooked potatoes. Lightly boil the meat or fish and serve it with some of the cooking juices. In general, chicken and rabbit bones, if not splintered or jagged, can be cooked and served with the flesh to provide calcium and phosphorus. Some nutritionalists recommend pressure-cooking the bones and then mincing them before feeding them to the cat, but don't overdo the cooking of the flesh. If you don't like the idea of feeding bones at all, sterilized bone meal should be added at the rate of one-eighth of a level teaspoonful per 8 oz of food.

Table scraps of meat or fish, if available, can make up 25 to 30% of the diet. Eggs and cheese are other valuable sources of animal protein, and cheese also has a high concentration of calcium and phosphorus. The cat has a rather higher need than most animals for vitamin A, though this should be satisfied feeding a commercial balanced diet or a varied home-prepared diet.

Bear in mind that these recommendations are all based on the healthy adult cat. Cats suffering from various disorders may require some modification of their diet, i.e. an increase or decrease in the proportions of various constituents to compensate for changes which have taken place in the body.

Q *How often should I feed my cat?*

A The conventional recommendation has been to feed two meals a day, a small one in the morning and a larger one in the evening at about six o'clock. Surveys reveal that roughly 50% of owners do indeed feed their pet cat two meals a day. About 20% of owners give only one meal, another 20% give three meals, and the remaining 10% either feed four or more meals daily or else they vary the number of meals from day to day.

Cats allowed free access to canned, dry or semi-moist foods in feeding trials all took frequent, small meals of relatively constant size at roughly two hour intervals throughout both the day and night. And careful observation of pet cats shows that the meals served by owners are in fact often not consumed all at once but are eaten over a period of time, i.e. as a larger number of smaller meals. In addition, these meals may be supplemented by hunting and/or by food begged or otherwise obtained from neighbours and other sources. So, in summary, it has become clear that cats are essentially 'nibblers'.

These findings suggest that there is no need for hard and fast rules about feeding to be adopted; rather that it is preferable for owner and pet to develop their own mutually satisfactory feeding programme, provided that the minimum ration to satisfy nutritional requirements is supplied each day. It might be suitable for the cat to be fed at the same time, or possibly just before, the rest of the household; even to be fed *ad libidum*, i.e. to have food down all the time so that it can eat whenever it chooses. The latter regimen is ideal if someone cannot be present to feed the cat at regular times, but under normal domestic conditions only dry or semi-moist foods can be fed this way. 'Wetter' types of food quickly deteriorate if left down; they become stale, allow food-poisoning organisms to grow and attract flies. There are, however, some reservations about serving dry products exclusively, particularly to male cats (see p. 63).

If dry or semi-moist food is fed *ad lib* the feeding bowl should be replenished as necessary by placing the uneaten food on top of the new food in the bowl so that it is eaten in rotation. A special hopper feeder, which refills the dish automatically, can be bought at the pet shop. Fortunately, only very few cats fed this way will overeat, and therefore will subsequently need to have their intake rationed to combat obesity. In conjunction with *ad lib* feeding, some owners may prefer to feed one meal a day of some quite different food to provide variety; in such cases, the cat will naturally eat correspondingly less of the diet which is always available. This feeding of one varied meal a day is a good idea because cats appreciate changes in their diets, and feeding different foods minimizes the possibility that a diet may be deficient in some essential nutrient.

Female cats that are feeding kittens (lactating queens) and kittens that are just weaned both require about three times as much food as normal adult cats (i.e. non-lactating) on a body weight basis. This increased quantity simply could not be consumed at one time and therefore it *must* be divided into a number of meals per day, usually a minimum of three. Unless *ad lib* feeding is to be adopted, the number of meals for a growing kitten can gradually be reduced to a minimum of two a day at three to four months of age, and possibly to one a day at about six months.

Q *How much food does my cat need each day?*

A Most adult cats will require between 6 and 9 oz (170 to 250 g) of home-cooked 'wet' food or of a canned ('wet') diet per day depending on their size. The minimum amount of protein needed each day is reckoned at 5 grams for each kilogram of body weight. Since most 'wet' diets have about 10% protein this is equivalent to 50 grams of diet per kilogram. In other words, feed one-twentieth of the cat's body weight of diet each day for protein. (If a particular canned diet contains a lower percentage of protein, then correspondingly more of it must be fed.) Then another 2 to 4 oz (50 to 100 g) of food is required for energy. This means feeding altogether 6 to 9 oz (170 to 250 g) of a canned diet, *or* for a home-prepared diet 5 to 7 oz (140 to 190 g) of cooked meats, liver, chicken or fish with some fat, *plus* 1 to 2 oz (30 to 60 g) of cooked carbohydrate foods (breakfast cereal, potatoes, rice, biscuit). If the food is not particularly fatty, then add a little animal fat. Alternatively, about 2 to 4 oz (50 to 100 g) of a semi-moist diet will be needed each day, or 2 to 3 oz (50 to 85 g) of a dry diet.

The amounts required by lactating females and young kittens are considerably higher. A cat feeding four kittens needs around 18 oz (510 g) of meat per day; indeed, it is difficult to overfeed a lactating queen. Weaned kittens initially require about $3\frac{1}{2}$ oz (90 g) of 'wet' diet per day, rising to 7 oz (190 g) per day at ten weeks' old. The food requirements are also slightly increased for cats in the last month of pregnancy (see page 177). Also cats with higher energy requirements, owing to cold or increased exertion, will need more food.

Any food remaining in a can after feeding should be stored in the refrigerator and used as soon as possible as it will dry out on the surface. Partly full pouches of semi-moist food should be re-sealed and used in the near future.

Q *Why do cats go off their food?*

A A complete loss (anorexia) or partial loss (inappetance) of appetite can occur in association with illness. For instance, both in renal failure, where waste products accumulate in the blood, and in diseases causing fever the appetite centre in the brain is affected. In severe respiratory diseases the cat's ability to smell or taste its food may be lost, thereby severely discouraging eating.

Pain in the mouth or throat (for example due to loose teeth or ulcers) or pain elsewhere in the body (for example due to bone fractures) can also prevent the animal from eating. Some cats, mainly pedigree animals and frequently Siamese or Burmese can refuse to eat for several weeks after having recovered from a severe illness or major surgery.

Appetites may be lost, although usually only temporarily, following some psychological shock – perhaps moving house, being hospitalized or boarded, the arrival of a new pet or some other member of the household, continuous loud noises, or even simply altering the position of the feeding bowl. Or, the cat may feel full up all the time, as with 'hairball' (see page 101).

Many cats are reluctant to eat if they are being watched, especially by unfamiliar individuals, and those not used to being handled, such as farm cats, will not eat if they are approached to within the so-called 'flight distance', usually about six feet away. And, of course, tom cats can be distracted from eating by the presence in the neighbourhood of a female 'on heat'.

Finally, some cats develop an aversion to a certain foodstuff and may even prefer to starve to death rather than eat it.

Q *If my cat doesn't eat all his food should I remove the dish or leave it down?*

A Adult cats fed one meal a day can be trained to eat all their food within half an hour simply by removing any which remains at the end of that period. They are also more likely to finish their food quickly if there are other cats nearby (competitive eating). But as we have seen the cat's natural preference is to take a number of small meals a day, often consuming only part of the meal at once and returning to eat the remainder over a period of several hours. Provided that the food doesn't become spoiled (e.g. in very hot weather or due to the attention of flies), there is no reason why it shouldn't be left out for up to twenty-four hours. Foods with a high moisture content are most likely to go stale quickly; commercial dry foods and semi-moist products can usually be left down safely for *ad lib* feeding.

Careful observation of each cat's behaviour is helpful. If it is found that after a certain length of time following feeding any remaining food is rejected, then clearly it would be preferable to provide smaller meals at more frequent intervals.

Q *My cat asks for food all the time but she couldn't possibly be hungry. Is there something wrong with her?*

A It could be that the cat is simply demonstrating the type of behaviour mentioned previously – namely, the natural preference for frequent small meals. In that case switching to *ad lib* feeding of dry or semi-moist food should solve the problem but it would be prudent to keep a record of how much she consumes each day and to weigh her regularly. However, very few cats, compared with dogs, will eat excessively.

In general, unspayed female cats eat less than males, but there can be pronounced changes in eating behaviour and body weight related to the reproductive cycle. In particular, cats receiving drugs to suppress or postpone coming into heat often show a marked increase in their appetite and body weight. If this is not countered by reducing the food intake, such cats may easily become obese.

Increases in appetite associated with a below average body weight, particularly where weight continues to be lost, should be investigated by your vet. In adult cats such cases are hardly ever due to intestinal worms (though popularly believed responsible) but may be due to some impairment of digestion or absorption, or to some metabolic disorder (e.g. diabetes mellitus or hyperthyroidism) although such conditions are fortunately rare.

Q *Will I know if I am not giving my cat enough food?*

A If a cat fails to receive sufficient food from all possible sources, it will usually ask, even pester, you for more. However, a few cats may be greedy and therefore a more reliable sign is evidence of the cat's weight gradually decreasing. This is also more accurate than relying on the cat's appearance, which may show no obvious change in the early stages of weight loss.

Regular weighing, say once a month as a routine, but more frequently if an abnormality is suspected, will allow you to recognize a problem and correct it, if necessary with your veterinarian's help. Obviously, the effects of overfeeding can be also detected by routine weighing.

The weight of adult cats varies a little with the breed, though nowhere near so much as in dogs. In general, males weigh between $7\frac{1}{2}$ to 11 lb ($3\frac{1}{2}$ to 5 kg) and females $5\frac{1}{2}$ to 8 lb ($2\frac{1}{2}$ to $3\frac{3}{4}$ kg). Neutered animals often weigh slightly more than entire animals because of their greater tendency to lay down fat.

If a kitten is consistently underfed it will fail to attain both normal weight and size. In particular, the skeleton is very sensitive to a lack of food and so the kitten's growth will slow down and, in severe cases, may even stop. If underfeeding has occured over a long period, even though it is subsequently corrected, it is unlikely that the lack of growth will ever be made up. The affected animal will stop growing at the usual age, around ten to twelve months' old, and if it is undersized then it will remain stunted for the rest of its life. There are available growth tables showing the expected range of weight at different ages.

Adult cats that are seriously underfed, in addition to losing weight, have less energy and stamina, show a lifeless, dull coat and may be unable to mate and breed successfully. They may appear obviously thin, especially in the flank (just in front of the hindlimb), with prominent ribs and an evident loss of muscle mass from the head and the hindlegs. However, these changes are not easily seen in long-haired cats, although they can be felt. Poorly nourished animals of any age also have reduced resistance to infection from both micro-organisms, such as bacteria and viruses, and from the larger parasites, that is to say the worm and skin parasites.

Q *Should my cat's food be fed raw or cooked?*

A Long-term feeding trials have demonstrated that cats fed raw meat and milk show *marginally* better growth, development, reproduction and lactation than those fed cooked meat and milk. Nevertheless, it is *not* advisable to feed cats on raw meat foods because this is a major route by which cats become infected with the protozoan parasite *Toxoplasma gondii* which produces the disease toxoplasmosis. As well as destroying this parasite, cooking will also destroy any disease-producing micro-organisms and also any toxins formed by food-poisoning organisms multiplying on the food.

Certain carbohydrates called starches (found in biscuits, rice and potatoes) cannot be digested by cats unless they have been cooked. Eggs are a valuable source of first-class protein and also provide calcium and phosphorus. But raw egg whites contain avidin which is antagonistic to biotin (a member of the vitamin B complex) and also a substance (trypsin inhibitor) which interferes with protein digestion. Light cooking destroys both of these substances.

Cooking also improves the flavour of most foods. Gentle cooking is all that is required – boiling for a quarter of an hour for example. This will have no harmful effect upon proteins and there will be little change in most vitamins. Prolonged cooking, however, can destroy the B vitamins in particular. Consequently manufacturers of canned cat foods often add extra vitamin B to their products to ensure that a controlled amount survives the autoclaving stage, a sterilizing process similar to pressure cooking but with the food already contained in the can.

Q *Should my cat's food be served warm?*

A We all know that foods served warm have more flavour than when they are cold and that there are also improvements in texture; the food is softer and fats are smoother. Certainly for the cat the acceptability of canned food increases with its temperature, up to blood heat (around 140°F or 40°C) which is the temperature at which its natural prey would be eaten. Further increases in temperature beyond this point result in a sharp reduction in acceptability, and cats are very cautious about tackling any food much hotter than 122°F (50°C).

There seems little doubt, therefore, that your cat will enjoy its food more if it is served warm, and the food temperature can be critical in persuading a sick or convalescent cat to eat. Obviously, the warming of foods is only possible with those having a high moisture content. Attempts to heat up dry or semi-moist foods may result in them being burned and rendered quite unacceptable.

Q *Should I pander to my cat's likes and dislikes in food?*

A Certainly there is evidence that cats favour the high fat and high protein foods essential in their diet, but tests have shown that some foods which they find very palatable are not nutritionally adequate if used over an extended period. Unfortunately, the palatability of food is *not* a reliable indicator of its nutritional value.

Liver is a highly acceptable food, often preferred to muscle meat. Some cats develop a marked preference for it and will refuse other foods. But this should not be permitted because a diet consisting solely of liver will result in the excessive absorption of vitamin A, which would be followed by the development of serious and painful bone deformities which effectively cripple the cat. Usually it is adult cats who suffer, developing pain and stiffness in the neck and sometimes in the limbs. Liver in normal amounts is not at all harmful; it is simply that you can have too much of a good thing.

Next to liver, muscle meat is often the food most preferred by cats. Unfortunately, both liver and muscle (and also heart) contain relatively low levels of calcium and relatively high levels of phosphorus. All-meat diets which are not supplemented by the correct amount of calcium lead to the development of structurally weak bones and skeletal abnormalities. An example is the condition juvenile osteodystrophy which occurs in growing cats at three to six months of age, and especially in the Siamese. These kittens show lameness, especially in the hind legs, and their bones will readily fracture. Affected animals have a shortened body and neck with a relatively long, large head and are referred to as 'square cats'. Giving extra vitamin D (as contained in cod liver oil) only makes this condition worse. A diet rich in muscle meat is therefore definitely not a good diet. An acceptable compromise would be a diet containing five parts of fatty meat to one of liver, though additional calcium in the form of sterilized bone flour ($\frac{1}{8}$ oz (4 g) per day) or milk (7 fl oz (200 ml) per day) would also be needed.

In addition liver and other meat products are relatively low in iodine, although this deficiency is readily corrected if the animal also eats fish. On the other hand liver and muscle meat are rich in vitamin B_1 (thiamine) for which cats have a relatively high requirement.

Many cats find the small cans of special variety foods (tuna fish, beef, rabbit, etc.) highly palatable, as of course the manufacturer intends. But these speciality (or 'gourmet') diets are *not* intended to be *balanced* diets and should not be fed exclusively day after day, even though the cat expresses a clear preference for one of them. Some owners reserve these 'special' treats as a reward for good behaviour in training and *never* feed them at other times.

In summary, therefore, as well as owners sometimes feeding their animals on totally unsuitable diets, the cat itself does not necessarily know best when it comes to selecting his own diet.

Q *Recently my cat has just turned up his nose up at some foods he used to like. Why is this?*

A A cat may develop an aversion to some specific and perfectly palatable food; often one of which it was previously very fond. The aversion usually arises when a bout of nausea or gastro-intestinal illness follows the eating of this foodstuff. It appears to be a type of learning process to protect the wild animal from repeatedly ingesting a harmful food which would produce gastro-intestinal upsets. Such foods may be refused by cats for long periods, even though they are extremely hungry, in some cases to the point of death.

In addition, the cat's senses of taste and smell are very acute and adulterants in the food can be readily detected, particularly those with a bitter taste. This may deter him from eating certain foods. (Minute quantities of cat-mint (cat-nip) can also be readily recognized. Surprisingly though, cats have no well-developed sense of taste for sweet substances and cannot distinguish between a sugar solution and plain water.)

Q *Should I let my cat drink as much water as he wants?*

A The short answer is yes – unless he is vomiting.

In every case except one (a rare psychological disorder) cats drink to replace water which has already been lost from the body. If you do not allow them to make up for the loss, whether it has arisen normally or as a result of disease (e.g. vomiting and diarrhoea), they will become dehydrated. A total lack of water will cause problems (even death) much more rapidly than a lack of any other component of the diet such as protein or fat. Therefore a bowl of clean water must *always* be available.

Animals which continually have an excessive thirst are almost certainly suffering from some disorder that should be investigated by your vet. In these disorders the body loses water more rapidly than usual, i.e. cannot retain it, so that the cat produces more urine than usual. The cat often has difficulty in holding all this urine in its bladder over a long period of time, e.g. overnight, so that it frequently goes out to urinate or uses its litter box. Some owners mistakenly think that the answer to this problem is to withold water from the cat, not realizing that they will prevent the animal making good the heavy losses which have occurred and provoke the onset of dehydration, thereby making the illness worse. If the cat has an increased thirst always take it for veterinary attention.

Only withold water from an animal if it vomits. Vomiting is most often due to some irritation of the lining of the stomach which causes the stomach contents to be rejected. The loss of water and salts in the vomit makes the animal very thirsty so that it *wants* to drink, but the presence of water in the stomach provokes further vomiting. In this way a cycle of drinking and vomiting can develop which may lead to severe dehydration and collapse.

Therefore, after vomiting occurs, withold all liquids and food for at least two hours. Then give a small amount of water, e.g. a saucerful. If this is not followed by vomiting soon after, further small amounts can be given at hourly intervals, but if vomiting occurs wait a longer period (eight to twelve hours) before giving any liquids or food. If in the meantime further vomiting occurs, seek veterinary advice.

Q *My cat never seems to drink anything. Is this harmful?*

A If your cat is receiving a mainly 'wet' diet, then his low water intake almost certainly is not harmful. A low intake usually indicates that the normal body mechanisms for conserving water are working efficiently.

The water required to replace that lost from the body in the urine, expired air and the motions is obtained from three sources. Firstly, liquids that are drunk, secondly, moisture in the food and thirdly, 'metabolic' water. Metabolic water is water that is created within the body when food is oxidized to produce energy, and the amount produced is usually fairly constant.

Diets on the other hand can vary greatly in their water content. Canned foods will contain around 75% water, while at the other extreme dry foods may contain only 8% water. An adult cat of 7 lb (3 kg) receiving a 'wet' diet will only need to drink about 1 to 1¾ fl oz (30 to 50 ml) of water per day to make good its losses (i.e. around three tablespoonful); even less if the food has been boiled at home and served with some of the cooking water. If any additional liquid is required it could easily be met by a saucerful of milk (possibly being provided by neighbours) or water consumed by the cat outdoors e.g. from puddles or guttering. But on a dry diet, up to seven times this quantity of water would need to be drunk. Unfortunately, the cat often does not adjust its water intake sufficiently to compensate for alterations in the water content of its food. An important factor in the development of blockages in the urinary tract of male cats is their inadequate water intake when receiving a dry diet. Therefore a low water intake by a cat being fed on dry food *could* be harmful and should receive attention (see below).

However, regardless of the type of diet being fed, a bowl of clean water should *always* be available for the cat. As far as possible discourage drinking from other sources (the sink, toilet bowl, puddles) which could assist in the transmission of disease.

Q *My cat seems to prefer milk to water. Should I not bother giving her water?*

A Many cats *do* prefer the taste of milk to that of water, but this doesn't mean there is any *need* to provide milk. Milk consists mainly of water, though it is a useful source of calcium and contains other nutrients. But it supplies nothing that cannot be obtained more cheaply from other foods. A cat receiving a good balanced diet has no nutritional requirement for milk, so that if it is provided at all it should be given as a treat *after* the cat has eaten its normal ration. (There is, however, no truth in the statement that milk encourages worms!)

Perhaps surprisingly, many adult cats (including a high proportion of oriental breeds, particularly Siamese) are intolerant of cow's milk and get severe diarrhoea if they consume it. There are two possible reasons for this diarrhoea. Certainly many cats have a deficiency of the enzyme lactase needed to digest milk sugar (lactose). But some cats appear to be able to consume other types of milk (e.g. goat's milk, which also contains lactose) without getting diarrhoea, and it is probable that these animals have an allergy to the proteins in cow's milk. Clearly, if this intolerance is suspected it would be wise not to feed any milk or any other dairy products to your cat. And it may in fact account for why so many Siamese are unwilling to drink milk.

Milk should not be regarded as a substitute for water and, regardless of whether milk is also provided, a bowl of fresh water should always be available so that the cat can satisfy its normal water requirements.

Q *I have read a lot in the press about dry cat foods. Is it true that they are harmful?*

A Dry cat foods are usually well accepted by cats, contain adequate amounts of essential nutrients, give 'exercise' to the teeth thereby reducing the deposition of tartar and are convenient to feed in that they can be left down all day for *ad lib* feeding.

However, the feeding of dry cat foods has been associated with the

Signs of the feline urological syndrome

Licking the opening of the uretha which is situated at this point.

A male cat suffering from the feline urological syndrome (FUS) repeatedly licks at his penis, sitting in this characteristic posture to reach the area.

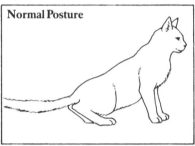

Normal Posture

A normal male cat adopts this stance to pass urine. In contrast to a cat with FUS, urination is accomplished rapidly and without undue straining or pain.

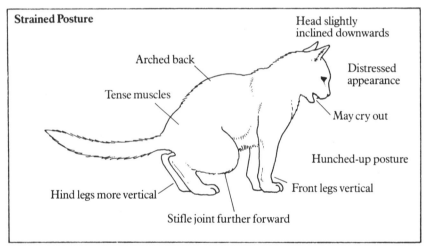

Strained Posture

Head slightly inclined downwards

Arched back

Distressed appearance

Tense muscles

May cry out

Hunched-up posture

Hind legs more vertical

Front legs vertical

Stifle joint further forward

A cat with FUS strains violently, though often ineffectually, to urinate. The reason is that his urethra is blocked by a gritty paste that was formed in his bladder. The signs listed distinguish straining from normal urination. Cats showing these signs must be treated promptly as FUS is eventually fatal.

formation of plugs of crystalline material in the urinary tract. Plugs of this paste block the urethra of male cats (the tube along which urine passes to the outside) as it goes through the penis. This condition is known as the feline urological syndrome; FUS for short. (Blockage is unusual in female cats because of their wider urethras, though cystitis can occur.) An affected male licks his penis and strains to pass urine. In the early stages he may pass a little, stained with blood, but when obstruction is complete no urine is passed and the cat shows signs of worsening renal failure, including depression, loss of appetite and vomiting.

In fairness it must be said that other causes of FUS have been suspected, the major one being viral infection and it seems probable that both diet and infection are important in producing it. Castration early in life was suspected, but is now known not to be the cause.

There seem to be two main ways in which dry cat foods can assist the development of FUS. One is by causing a reduction in the cat's water intake. The natural prey of cats (small rodents) contain about 70% of water, the same as most canned foods, whereas dry foods contain only 8 to 10% water. Careful measurements have shown that, even when ample fresh drinking water is available, the *total* amount of water taken in (both in the food and as liquid) by cats fed dry food is much less than that taken by cats fed canned food. The cat just doesn't adjust its water intake to the water content of the food. With less water being taken in, the urine becomes more concentrated, and this favours the precipitation of salts in the urine to form the crystalline plug.

Secondly, some dry cat foods used to contain a high level of magnesium salts. Eventually these salts appeared in the urine and contributed to the formation of the crystals, which are composed of magnesium ammonium phosphate (otherwise called struvite). Following an appreciation of the problem, the magnesium content of these foods has been reduced (generally below 0.15%). However, high magnesium levels are naturally present in certain foods, notably fish (particularly the oily varieties – sardines, pilchards and herrings) and beef. The levels in these foodstuffs can be three times those in fish roes, egg, tripe and canned cat foods.

Cats that have suffered from FUS in the past are best not fed on a dry cat food, but on a canned product, or food boiled at home, with some additional water (about two tablespoonsful) mashed into it. If dry food *is* fed it should be thoroughly soaked in water, milk or gravy to form a sloppy porridge before being presented to the cat. Extra salt should be added to all foods given to these animals (three to four good 'pinches' of salt each day) to stimulate the drinking of more water. Many manufacturers now routinely add more salt to their dry diets (up to $3\frac{1}{2}$%) to increase water consumption. Clean water (not just milk) should be available at all times. In some cases your vet will provide tablets for the cat to take to make its urine more acid, which helps prevent these crystals forming.

Regular exercise with plenty of opportunities to urinate also helps to reduce the chance of FUS recurring. Regular urination avoids large volumes of urine remaining in the bladder for long periods during which the salts are able to precipitate out. Obese, lethargic and elderly cats are less likely than others to exercise and urinate frequently, and it is recommended that these animals should *also* not be fed regularly on dry foods.

Q *Does my cat need extra vitamins and minerals?*

A Cats seem to have no specific need for vitamin K and can normally make sufficient vitamin C within their bodies; therefore these vitamins are not required in the diet. The cat's requirement for vitamin D in the diet is small when compared with that of dogs and humans. Cats differ from most mammals in not being able to convert carotenoids in plants (e.g. carrots) into vitamin A and therefore this vitamin *must* be supplied – for example in liver, kidney or fish oils. Overall, most diets will contain sufficient vitamins, with the possible exception of vitamin B, although some additional vitamin A should be provided for kittens in the form of cod-liver oil.

The minerals needed from the diet are present in most foodstuffs in amounts sufficient to meet the cat's requirement, although muscle meat and organ meat (liver, heart, kidney) are relatively deficient in calcium.

Cod-liver oil is a convenient source of the fat-soluble vitamins A, D and E, but because these vitamins are stored, i.e. accumulate in the body, too much can create problems. An excess of vitamin A (hypervitaminosis A) in the cat causes painful abnormalities of the spine and limb bones. Excess vitamin D can retard growth, cause malformed teeth and jaws and lead to changes in other organs. Greatly excessive quantities of vitamin E may also be harmful, impairing blood clotting, and too much vitamin K can cause jaundice. However, there appear to be no ill-effects from giving excessive amounts of the water-soluble vitamins, vitamin B (e.g. in yeast extract or tablets) and vitamin C.

Bone meal contains calcium and phosphorus which in excess can cause a variety of skeletal abnormalities and joint problems with lameness, especially in growing animals. Anaemia due to iron deficiency is an extremely rare occurrence in the cat and consequently there is no need for routine iron supplementation. Other supplements, such as seaweed powder to supply iodine, are unnecessary; fish is rich in iodine. The huge variety of commercial vitamin and mineral supplements are no more necessary, and no safer in excess, than the simple substances mentioned above.

Q *Is some supplementation of my cat's diet ever required?*

A Well, a reputable commercial diet fed according to the manufacturer's instructions will almost certainly supply adequate levels of vitamins and minerals and should not require any supplementation. In fact, precise amounts of vitamins B_1 and A are added to compensate for losses that occur during manufacture and storage. A varied and balanced home-prepared diet will also need no supplementation, though supplementation of an unbalanced home-prepared diet, such as one based primarily on muscle meat, *is* required, but only in respect of calcium, phosphorus and vitamin B. For an adult cat, sufficient calcium and phosphorus can be provided by adding to each 8 oz (250 g) of meat ⅓ oz (⅛ of a level teaspoonful) of sterilized bone meal (bone flour) or some alternative proprietary supplement. (Only sterilized bone meal must be used; not the unsterilized grade intended for use as a fertilizer in gardening.) Vitamin B should be provided by giving your cat two brewer's yeast tablets daily.

A home-prepared meat or fish diet for kittens, which is fed from when they first begin to take solid food up to six months of age, should be supplemented *each day* with ¼ oz (¼ level teaspoonful) of sterilized bone meal (bone flour), a half to one brewers' yeast tablet and one to two drops of cod-liver oil. Greater amounts than these could be harmful.

Q *Should I give my cat bones to chew?*

A Opinions tend to be divided on this matter. Certainly in the wild a cat will consume all of its prey with the exception of plucked feathers, hairs and some small pieces of bone. The majority of the bones are eaten and provide a valuable source of calcium. These bones, of course, are small and uncooked and seldom seem to cause problems by lodging in or piercing parts of the digestive tract.

If a cat is receiving a balanced commercial diet, or a bone meal supplement with a home-prepared diet, it will already be receiving adequate calcium and therefore will not actually *need* to consume bones. However, there is no doubt that many cats enjoy chewing bones and the exercise which it provides for the teeth is valuable in preventing an accumulation of tartar which may lead to periodontal disease, particularly if the animal usually receives a 'wet' diet. In practice bones seldom become wedged or splinter internally. Usually, any problems are associated with fish bones or with cooked bones, e.g. rib bones occasionally get wedged across the roof of the mouth between the large upper teeth, or a canine tooth may 'spear' a vertebra which the animal then has difficulty in dislodging.

Some nutritionalists actually advise feeding cooked bones with the muscle meat, e.g. in chicken or rabbit; others advise cooking bones separately (e.g. in a pressure cooker) and then mincing them before adding them to the rest of the food. Irregular bones are best avoided and it is always advisable to remove the small needle-shaped bones from fish.

However, the benefits of bones can be provided in other ways; bone meal is an alternative source of calcium, and dental exercise can be provided by chewing at a hard biscuit or a rawhide 'chew', or by the regular feeding of dry cat food. Any bone deliberately provided should preferably be uncooked, relatively large (e.g. part of a limb bone) and not irregular or easily splintered (so that chop and poultry bones are best avoided).

Q *Does it do my cat any harm to eat things he has caught such as mice, insects, birds and worms?*

A The hunting instinct is strong in cats but, although this constitutes perfectly natural behaviour, unfortunately their prey may be harmful in a number of respects.

The first of these is the transmission of parasites. As will be seen later (see page 154) there are a number of parasites of the cat which use another animal species in which to undergo part of their life cycle. When such an infected animal is eaten by the cat, the parasite(s) gains entry to the cat's body and can develop there. Mice and rats can act as hosts for the cystic stage of the tapeworm (*Taenia taeniaeformis*) and for larvae of the two roundworms of the cat (*Toxocara cati* and *Toxascaris leonina*). These roundworm larvae are also found in *other* species which may be eaten by the cat, such as earthworms, birds and rabbits.

Slugs and snails often carry the larvae of the feline lungworm (*Aelurostrongylus abstrusus*). Although at times they may be eaten by a cat, it is more likely that slugs and snails will be eaten by such species as birds, rodents, frogs or snakes and that the cat will, in turn, eat one of these. The lungworm larvae transfer from each of these species to the one that has consumed it, until they reach their final host – the cat.

Almost any animal species can carry stages of the microscopic coccidian parasite *Toxoplasma gondii* whose final host is again the cat. These intermediate hosts include birds, rodents, earthworms and flies, as well as all the meat-producing animals (cattle, pig etc.), and even man. There are other similar coccidia (*Hammondia*, *Sarcocystis* and *Levineia*) with simpler life cycles which again infect the cat through the eating of rodents, etc.

All of these parasites have developed life cycles which depend upon the cat's ability to catch and eat its prey so that they may spread and ensure their survival. Only the lungworm and *Toxoplasma* usually present any really serious health risks to the cat, but many of the parasites present public health risks.

Another hazard is that by eating rodents which are already dead or dying from the effects of rat poison (commonly warfarin) the cat itself can become poisoned. This is thought to be the most common way in which cats become poisoned by rodenticides. In general they are much more fastidious than dogs and are therefore less likely to consume rat or mouse bait directly, although at times this happens either out of the animal's inquisitiveness about the presence of the poison in its territory, or because it develops a liking for a particular poison and deliberately seeks it out. Examples of such 'addictable' poisons are the rodent poison alphachloralose, and metaldehyde which is contained in slug pellets.

Although not really to be regarded as prey, the wasps and bees which cats occasionally chase and catch in the mouth can of course produce a painful sting. If the tongue is stung it may swell and block the back of the throat, necessitating immediate first aid treatment.

Q *Is it an old wives' tale that feeding fish to a cat is harmful?*

A Well, so much fish has been fed to cats for so many years that it is difficult to believe that it *could* be harmful. Essentially fish is, of course, a valuable source of protein in the diet. But, perhaps surprisingly, there are some disorders of cats that can arise specifically from eating fish.

Firstly, several varieties of raw fish (e.g. herring and carp) contain high levels of the enzyme thiaminase which will destroy the vitamin B₁ (thiamine) present in other foods in the diet. Eventually the lack of this vitamin could result in the cat losing its appetite and showing nervous signs (staggering, trembling, convulsions). Cooking the fish destroys this enzyme.

Eating infected raw fish from certain areas can transmit specific disease-producing organisms to cats: the tapeworm *Diphyllobothrium latum* from freshwater fish in, for example, Northern Ireland, and bacteria from salmon and trout causing 'salmon poisoning' in the Pacific North-West of America. Again in North America and in South Africa the eating of crayfish can transmit a lung fluke *Paragonimus kellicotti* to the cat. And the livers of some marine fish contain substances which, if uncooked, will damage the nervous system.

In areas where the river water or sea water is heavily polluted with agricultural or industrial wastes, toxic substances can become concentrated via a food chain in the bodies of fish which are sometimes offered for sale. If eaten, raw or cooked, poisoning with herbicides, insecticides or one of the heavy metals (e.g. lead, mercury or cadmium) could follow.

A diet deficient in vitamin E and rich in unstabilized polyunsaturated fats can result in the fat-storing cells beneath the skin becoming inflamed (pansteatitis, or 'yellow fat disease'). Pressure on the skin causes pain and so the cat naturally resents handling. The diet most commonly at fault is one containing large quantities of canned red tuna fish, but other fish, particularly oily varieties, and even large amounts of horsemeat, are sometimes responsible. However today, sufficient vitamin E is added to most commercial tuna fish products to prevent this disease occurring.

On the credit side, one disease popularly thought to be due to feeding fish but now known not to be, is miliary dermatitis, or miliary eczema, previously called 'fish eczema' or 'fish eaters' eczema'. The multiple small skin eruptions, which eventually rupture producing crusty scabs accompanied by intense skin irritation, are in fact due to an allergic reaction to the bites of fleas (flea allergy dermatitis).

Q *Are cats ever allergic to certain foods?*

A Fortunately, true allergic responses to foods are uncommon in cats, though it seems that some cats are allergic to the proteins in cow's milk. Many reactions to foods are caused not by an allergy, but by an inability to digest or absorb a particular food, so that in *large* amounts the food produces diarrhoea or sickness. However, in the case of a *true* allergy even *small* amounts of that particular food will be sufficient to trigger the allergy, provided that a minimum of ten to fourteen days has elapsed from the time that type of food was *first* consumed by the cat. This is necessary for the cat's body to produce sufficient antibody to give a reaction. At other times the apparent food allergy is in fact a reaction to some disease-producing organism or to a drug.

Discovering the food responsible for an allergic reaction involves feeding a variety of different meals and noting the response. This can be a tedious process but when the causal foodstuff is absent an improvement is usually noted within three to five days.

Q *Is it all right to feed my cat on the special pet meat I can buy at the pet shop or frozen food store?*

A Frozen pet meat is quite acceptable but is should be allowed to thaw out before being cooked lightly (i.e. boiled for fifteen minutes) to allow the heat to penetrate all of the meat.

There are a number of pet meat preparations in which the meat is minced, mixed, compressed and presented in the form of a large slab. These foods contain a chemical preservative to discourage the growth of bacteria and moulds. At one time benzoic acid was widely used as the preservative but it was found that this accumulated in the body and caused cats to become hyperaesthetic (i.e. abnormally sensitive to stimuli, such as noise) and sometimes aggressive. If used at high levels it even produced convulsions and death. As a result reputable manufacturers switched to using sorbic acid as the preservative and at effective levels this appears to be entirely safe. As a general rule though, if a cat being fed this type of pet meat product should develop abnormal behaviour and nervous signs, it would be prudent to discontinue feeding this food until the matter can be investigated and the product declared safe.

Q *We are a committed vegetarian family. Can we feed our cat a vegetarian diet without harming her?*

A I'm afraid the answer must be no if you want your cat to remain healthy. The cat has a definite need for a high protein diet some of which, at least, must come from animal sources. This is because, unlike most mammals, cats cannot regulate the rate at which they break down and eliminate protein. Other mammals fed a diet low in protein will reduce the rate at which they break down the protein in order to conserve it, but this is not the case with the cat. It seems probable that, because cats in their evolutionary development were always strict carnivores feeding on a meat diet (i.e. one rich in protein), there was never any need for selection to be based on ability to conserve protein. Indeed, because meat is low in carbohydrate, it would be an *advantage* for cats to have an efficient mechanism that could break down protein in order to provide glucose to act as a source of energy.

There are, of course, many foods other than meat which contain protein and it is possible to maintain dogs in good health by feeding proteins solely of vegetable origin.

All proteins are made up of a number of smaller units called amino acids. Altogether there are twenty different amino acids and each type of protein consists of an arrangement of only some of them. In dogs and cats ten of the aminoacids are essential for the proper growth and functioning of the body (essential amino acids) and unless the diet provides all ten of these in adequate amounts then some nutritional disease will develop. Digestible proteins which contain all ten essential amino acids in the ideal proportions for use by the body are described as having a high biological value (high quality proteins or first class proteins). The best is egg protein, but most other animal-derived proteins (meat, liver, milk) also have a high biological value. However, proteins from plants (beans, cereals, etc.) are of lower biological value although still useful, but, if properly combined, all the essential amino acids can be supplied from plant sources.

In addition to these ten essential amino acids there is another one, taurine, which must appear in the diet of cats. This amino acid is necessary to prevent degeneration of the retina in the eye which would lead eventually to blindness. Most mammals, but *not* the cat, can make sufficient taurine within their bodies out of the other amino acids. Since only protein foods of animal origin contain sufficient quantities of taurine it is clear that to maintain good health at least some of the protein in the cat's diet *must* be of animal origin.

Secondly, let us consider the role of fats. Fats make food palatable, provide a source of energy and help transport the fat-soluble vitamins. In addition they supply substances known as essential fatty acids, which are necessary for nutrition because they are used in making new cells and in synthesizing prostaglandins (prostaglandins are vitally concerned in a number of body functions including blood clotting and reproduction). Of the three essential fatty acids, one, linoleic acid, is widely present in vegetable oils and most mammals have the ability to manufacture the other two essential fatty acids from linoleic acid. However, the cat does *not* possess this ability, and since the other two fatty acids are only found in animal tissues it is necessary that an adequate amount of animal fat must appear in the cat's diet. Also, we have already seen that the cat is unable to make vitamin A from plant sources; it must be available preformed in animal tissues.

Therefore, with a proven need for protein, fat and vitamin A of animal origin, a strictly vegetarian diet for the cat is out of the question.

Q *My cat seems very fond of chewing grass. Will it do her any harm?*

A Although cats are essentially meat eaters, they will eat a little grass from time to time if given the opportunity, especially young growing grass. It may be that the purpose is to obtain additional minerals or vitamins. For instance, cooked meat diets are often rather low in their content of folic acid, a member of the vitamin B group, which is present in grass. It also seems likely that it is eaten to provide fibrous bulk in the diet, possibly to avoid constipation. Certainly in the wild cats eat grass, and also the innards of grass-eating animals which they have killed. Some domestic cats will even eat other plants such as young runner beans, house plants or flowers in a vase.

Cats suffering from some alimentary disturbance will often consume a lot of grass and vomit afterwards, i.e. they use grass as a natural emetic. Presumably, they do this because they feel nauseous and wish to provoke vomiting in order to obtain some relief.

Therefore, although it's not absolutely essential, there certainly seems to be no harm in your cat eating grass, *unless* of course the grass has previously been treated with herbicide. It is, however, possible to purchase kits for growing a tray of grass indoors which avoids the dangers of toxic sprays and provides a convenient source of grass for urban cats, particularly those which need to be trained not to eat house plants.

Q *The vet has said that my cat is overweight and should be slimmed. How should I do this and how will I know when she is slim enough?*

A Obesity arises because an animal or, indeed, a human being, consumes more food than is needed to supply it with energy and the surplus food is then stored as fat.

Most cats refrain from overeating, though if the owner regularly provides more food than is required, particularly if it is highly palatable, overeating will be encouraged. Obesity is most likely to affect neutered cats where energy requirements, and therefore food requirements, are less than for entire animals. In general, if you cannot feel a cat's ribs it is likely to be overweight.

In theory the treatment of obesity is simple. If *less* food is provided than the cat needs to satisfy its energy requirements, then it will begin to reduce its fat stores. This body fat is used to supply the energy which is deficient in the diet. In practice, the cat may be supplementing its meals at home with food from elsewhere, either prey it catches or meals provided by kind-hearted neighbours.

To slim a cat, *ad lib* feeding, if practised, must be stopped and there must be no giving of titbits. And little if any milk should be provided because of its fat content. As far as possible other sources of food should be eliminated. Then the cat must be relatively underfed on its normal diet, provided that this has a balanced composition. One suggested regimen for doing this is as follows. Weigh the cat in pounds and then, having regard to its breed, age and sex, estimate what it *should* weigh if it were not overweight. If necessary your vet will help with this estimate. By subtracting one weight from the other find how much overweight the cat is, in pounds. Then multiply this number of pounds by 80. Lastly divide the figure you have just obtained by 100 if you feed a dry food, or by 85 for a semi-moist food or by 40 for a canned, or home-prepared, diet.

The final figure represents the number of ounces of *that* food that should be removed from the diet each day, i.e. the daily reduction that must take place.

Weigh the cat regularly (at least once a week) and, when it has reached the previously estimated *normal* weight, its diet should be increased again to prevent any further weight loss. Do this by restoring each day *half* of the number of ounces of food that you removed originally. This daily ration of food can then be fed continuously, probably for the rest of the animal's life, unless it becomes ill or pregnant or shows any further marked weight change.

Q *How can I tempt my cat to eat when she has been ill?*

A Animals may have to be coaxed to eat after a severe illness or if, for medical reasons, they have to be fed a special diet which is not very palatable. In particular, cats suffering from respiratory disorders need to be tempted with foods having strong, distinctive flavours and odours because otherwise they are unable to smell or taste their food. In general, the following should be tried:

1 Feed foods with a strong taste and odour such as sardines, kippers, herrings, pilchards, liver, salmon (tinned or smoked), shellfish, tuna fish, chicken fat, chicken livers, cooked rabbit and fried fish. Any discharge around the nose should be wiped away to enable the animal to smell the foodstuff. If necessary, an inhalant can be used to help clear the nasal passages.

2 Add to an existing diet such flavouring agents as the oil from a can of sardines, meat extract, yeast extract (e.g. Marmite), dairy cream, the juices from roast meat, gravies and meat soups. If the cat will not consume these voluntarily, smearing a little on the nose usually causes the cat to lick it off, thereby providing a first taste which stimulates him to take more. The addition of a pinch of salt to many dishes, including canned foods, will often enhance the flavour and stimulate the appetite.

3 Feed foodstuffs at blood heat rather than cold. All foods have more flavour when heated (which is why foods intended to be served cold, such as ice cream, require a disproportionately large amount of sweetening and flavouring).

In addition, there are available from your vet convalescent diets and food drinks specially prepared for cats, which are rich in nutrients and highly palatable.

Make sure that the feeding dishes are rinsed clean with absolutely no residue of stale food, disinfectant or detergent which could give an unpleasant taste or odour, and feed only a little food at a time.

Such foods as milk puddings, proprietary invalid diets, baby foods and chicken, although nutritionally excellent and therefore ideal for the feeding of sick or convalescent animals, have a relatively bland or insipid taste and it may prove difficult to persuade cats to eat them. Competition with another animal may sometimes provide the incentive to eat, though care should be taken to see that a weaker animal is not prevented from eating by a more dominant one. If the cat cannot be tempted to eat, so-called 'force-feeding' or artificial feeding (artificial alimentation) may be required as described on page 194.

Q *My cat drags her food away from the plate to eat it. Is there anything which can be done to make her eat in one place?*

A This is instinctive behaviour, resembling taking the prey somewhere quiet to eat it, and it arises frequently in cats fed with large pieces of meat. Quite a number of cats prefer to remove food from their dish and to eat it from a piece of paper placed alongside. If the food is moved no further, this may well prove acceptable to you.

The techinque recommended for training a cat not to remove food from the dish is simply to tell the cat firmly 'No', and then to pick up the food and replace it in the dish. This should be repeated as often as is necessary for the cat to get the idea. If this doesn't work, try serving a very sloppy diet with plenty of added gravy which it will be impossible to carry about.

One item to check is that the side of the feeding bowl is not so high that it touches the animal's neck and interferes with swallowing.

——6——
Handling a Cat

Q *What is the best way to pick up and put down a cat?*

A A basic fact when handling almost all animals (and people!) is to be firm, yet gentle, and to have a confident approach. This confidence certainly communicates itself to the cat who is much less likely to try to escape, or to scratch, if it feels secure. If it feels insecure it will use its claws to obtain a firmer foothold. If the cat is to be picked up, especially if it is a stranger to you, don't make a sudden grab at it. It will defend itself instinctively from what it believes is an attack, and you may get scratched or bitten. Rather, approach it quietly, talking to it and stroking it.

A cat should always be raised and lowered gently, firmly supported from underneath and *never* dropped from a height. Although it usually lands safely, the animal will be unwilling to repeat the experience and will come to resent handling. The cat will find it uncomfortable, even painful, if too much strain is put on one part of the body when being picked up and carried. Therefore don't (and don't let children) pick the cat up solely by the scruff, *or* by the front legs (or hind legs) alone, *or* using one or both hands around the abdomen (i.e. the soft 'middle' of the cat behind the

How to carry your cat

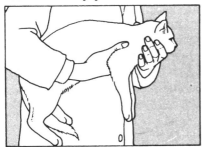

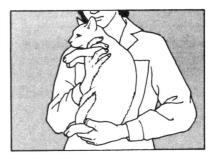

Place one hand beneath the cat's chest with your fingers between its legs. Close your arm into your side to support its rear end. Gently restrain its head.

An alternative way to carry a pregnant cat is in the 'sitting-up' position. One hand takes the weight of the body, whilst the other holds the front legs.

chest). Children in particular tend to squeeze a cat around its middle.

In an emergency it may be necessary to lift a rather wild cat by the scruff of the neck in order to secure it (see page 77) but this is a special situation and only occurs occasionally.

Q *How should I carry a pregnant cat?*

A Clearly, it is important to avoid putting pressure on the developing foetuses in the abdomen and yet to provide adequate support for the rear end, which is heavier than usual. Certainly, the cat should *not* be lifted with a hand beneath its abdomen. The same method as illustrated for a normal cat would be satisfactory.

Some breeders prefer to carry pregnant females with their body in a more vertical plane; one hand holding the front legs up and the other supporting the weight of the hind quarters, so that the cat is in a 'sitting up' position.

Q *Should I pick up kittens by the scruff of the neck?*

A A mother cat carries her young during the first weeks of life (principally the first three weeks) after picking them up by the scruff of the neck with her teeth. At this early age they are incapable of walking any distance unaided. The mother uses this method to retrieve kittens that have fallen out of the 'nest'. (Incidentally, she is attracted to such 'lost' kittens not by the sight of them, but by their cries.)

If the site of the 'nest' is changed, the mother will carry each kitten in turn from the old nest to the new in this way and, because cats cannot count, she will also return to the old nest after all the kittens have been moved to search for any that have been 'forgotten'. (Wild cats commonly change their quarters regularly to make if difficult for predators to find them.) Later, the mother will carry the kittens to somewhere outside the nest to begin toilet training.

After these first few weeks of life, picking up a cat solely by its scruff puts an undue strain on the neck muscles. It is better then to pick up a kitten in a similar way to an adult cat, i.e. to take the weight of the kitten on the upturned palm of one hand and to use the fingers of the other to hold the scruff and limit the amount of wriggling.

Kittens benefit from plenty of handling from an early age, certainly from around weaning (six to eight weeks' old) which encourages socialization with humans. However, very young children (babies and toddlers) *should not* be allowed alone with kittens and cats as they tend to make rapid grabbing movements which frighten the animals and encourage retaliatory defensive movements. Older children should be in a sitting position before being allowed to handle a kitten. As the kitten begins to wriggle or protrude its claws, children will invariably let go and drop it.

Q *You have suggested that I should weigh my cat regularly. What's the best way to do this?*

A In the early stages of kittenhood the kitchen scales may be used, *provided* that the scale pan is well washed afterwards. It should be protected with a polythene bag and a couple of paper towels in case of accidents; these won't alter the reading significantly. Later, the bathroom scales can be used, preferably with the cat inside a carrying basket, laundry basket or even a cardboard box to prevent him from repeatedly jumping off. Usually, the cat won't sit still long enough for you to be able to read the dial accurately. Weigh this container both with and without the animal and then find the cat's weight by difference. Alternatively, you could suspend a cat basket from a spring balance, again to find the cat's weight by difference. Or weigh yourself holding the cat and again without it.

Use the same scales each time if possible so that any error in the weighings will be consistent, allowing a meaningful comparison.

In all cases, if the needle on the dial of the scales fails to give a constant reading because of the animal's movements, note the upper and lower limits of the swing of the needle and use the point midway between them as the cat's true weight.

Q *What is the best way of handling a cat after a road accident?*

A Following its involvement in a road accident a cat, if still conscious, will be disturbed and frightened and will often run away blindly in an attempt to escape from the scene. The animal does not understand what has happened to it and reverts to defensive behaviour. Even when approached by its owner, it may prove aggressive and resent handling.

The approach to such a cat should be calm, quiet and yet purposeful. Leather gloves can provide some protection against scratches, but they should be sufficiently flexible not to prevent you from making firm grasping movements. A coat, or other garment which covers your arms down to the wrist, will prevent them being badly scratched. There is, however, no effective way to muzzle a cat.

It is useful to have the help of two or three sensible people, but noisy and hysterical onlookers should be asked to leave. Approach the animal slowly, making sure that it can hear or see you coming to prevent it flying into a sudden panic. Be very cautious if the animal is on a wall or projection above ground level, or if it is cornered, because it may then try to attack. By talking to the animal in a quiet reassuring voice, you may be able to get close enough to stroke it and very carefully pick it up. If you attempt this, it is best to make a few preliminary stroking movements and then to take a firm grasp of the cat's scruff and to lift it into some suitable carrying container placed nearby. Be prepared for the animal to struggle, and don't let go unless you absolutely have to because second attempts are usually much less successful. Watch the animal all the time.

If you find you are unable to gain the animal's confidence sufficiently to allow you to do this another technique to pick up an aggressive cat is to drop an old coat or blanket over the animal, to quickly tuck all the edges underneath the cat, and then to lift the whole bundle and quickly place it inside your container. If all else fails, you will need to telephone for professional assistance, e.g. from an animal welfare society, veterinary surgeon, police or, in some countries, a professional dog and cat catcher. Devices specially developed for catching stray animals will probably have to be used.

Of course, it is the less seriously injured cat, and sometimes the totally uninjured but very frightened cat, that presents the greatest problem. The seriously injured animal is unlikely to be aware of or to care much about your presence; indeed, it may be unconscious.

Some of the things not to do in this situation include chasing the cat (this will simply increase its fear), trying to tempt it with food or drink (after an accident eating and drinking is very far from its mind), shouting or making sudden movements, and taking hold of the animal by an obviously injured part. When the injured animal is within a secure container it should, as soon as possible, receive veterinary attention.

Q *Should I get a collar, lead or harness for my cat?*

A Collars and harnesses can provide some means of identification. This can take the form of a transparent name panel on a 'flea collar', or an engraved identity disk (or small tube containing your name and address on paper) attached to the cat's leather collar or harness. Unfortunately, if a collar gets hooked on to a branch as the cat climbs a tree, the animal can be left dangling from it and is gradually strangled. For this reason, only cat collars with an elastic panel in them should be used, the intention being that they will stretch sufficiently for the cat to continue breathing and to get its head free. Unfortunately, in struggling, the cat may turn round and round and use up the slack in the collar, so that eventually it is still asphyxiated. Some quick-release fastening, e.g. of Velcro, would clearly be an advantage to prevent this type of mishap.

An adjustable harness, securely fitted, is safer than a collar, although again it can get caught up and leave the cat stranded. Certainly, a harness is better than a collar when training a cat to walk on a lead (leash), as described on page 92. If walking on a lead is to be taught, the lead should initially be long enough to permit the cat some freedom to move around (six to seven feet), but as it becomes used to walking nearby (ideally alongside) this can be shortened. A light leather lead, or one of canvas or of cord (e.g. washing line), is suitable. Most pet shop leads are about four to five feet long. The clip at the end of the lead should preferably be of the bolt type rather than the spring clip type which sometimes becomes firmly fastened to an area of skin and can only be removed by being sawn apart. Chain leads and collars, e.g. 'choke' chains (check chains), are too heavy to be worn by cats.

The question of the value and advisability of flea collars is dealt with on page 151.

Q *Should a cat be handled after an operation?*

A Any operation wound will obviously hurt if the cat is carelessly handled within a week or so of surgery. Even if the wound is not touched directly, picking the cat up awkwardly, e.g. dangling from its front legs, will produce tension at the operation site and consequent pain. So that after an operation it would be better *not* to handle the cat unless it is really necessary, and then only to do so very cautiously, taking care not to pull, or put pressure on, the operation wound. (Of course, that is not to say that the cat itself might not be attempting the most difficult jumps and twists only a day or so after surgery.) Later, when healing is quite complete (three to four weeks after the operation) the cat can be handled normally again.

Q *Is it best to put my cat in a basket even when travelling by car?*

A Yes, any cat being transported should be in a securely-closed container, whatever the means of transport. Cats which are allowed to travel loose in a car may suffer impact injuries if the car has to swerve or stop suddenly. They can also cause accidents by distracting the driver's attention (e.g. by climbing onto the shoulder) or by getting under the driver's feet so that he cannot operate the brake pedal. And a cat that decides to make a dash for it through an open window, or as soon as a door is open, is often lost for ever in unfamiliar terrain.

Q *Is one type of cat basket better than another?*

A There are many types of travelling container which are suitable for transporting cats. The main requirements are that they should provide adequate ventilation, be comfortable and be secure. There are two basic designs of the traditional wickerwork cat basket: one is a rectangular box with a hinged lid, the other has a curved 'roof' and a wire mesh door at one end which allows the cat to see out. Some large baskets, with the lid or door left open, can even double as the cat's normal bed, which makes it easier to persuade the animal inside for the journey. However, wicker-work is difficult to clean adequately and the hinges and fastenings on some baskets are so loose that a determined cat could wriggle through the gap around the lid or door and escape. If you have such a loose-fitting door on your basket, it is advisable to tie the door and basket together at a number of points with pieces of string. Some cats even learn to put a paw through the wire mesh door and dislodge the wire pin which, on some models, holds the door closed; leather straps make a more secure fastening.

Another type of container is constructed of strong plastic-covered wire mesh, which also allows the cat to see out and to be seen. Both this type and the wickerwork baskets are very draughty so, if carrying them outdoors in windy weather, the walls should be lined with stiff paper beforehand. Rigid fibreglass and plastic containers are easy to clean and again some have transparent roofs or sides which allow the cat to view the outdoors. Whether this is desirable is open to discussion; some owners believe that their cats feel more secure inside a totally enclosed container.

Plastic carrying-bags with a transparent end panel and ventilation holes, and fastened by a zip, are much cheaper, though rather cramped for long journeys. And, of course, a very cheap, though impermanent, carrying container is a cardboard cat carrier, usually obtainable from your vet or from an animal welfare society. This can be re-folded flat for storage and may have a water-repellant lining but will not survive a good soaking in the rain. Some cats will also bite or claw the cardboard into shreds, especially if you misguidedly enlarge the ventilation holes beforehand. These carriers are therefore *not* recommended for long (especially unaccompanied) journeys.

In an emergency you can use a strong cardboard box with a secure lid and some ventilation holes punched in the sides, the whole box securely tied both front and back and side to side with string which passes all the way around. Strong shopping bags with zips are fine for carrying an unconscious cat, but conscious animals are often able to work a paw, or their head, through the small gap which has to be left for ventilation and to force the zip back sufficiently to escape.

Inside a cat basket a piece of towel or other soft material (even a wad of newspaper) can be used as bedding, but not a large cushion which will take up most of the space. Newspaper, of course, has the advantage that when it is soiled, and this may happen with fear or on a long journey, it can simply be thrown away or burned. In very cold weather a wrapped, *warm* water-bottle could be provided.

Normally food and water should not be placed inside the container; it will usually be spilled and if the cat eats during the journey it may be sick. Exceptions to this rule are rail, sea and air journeys of more than twelve hours, when the animal is contained in a special box or crate. For air travel these containers are made of plywood or fibreglass for lightness. For cats they need to have minimum dimensions of 26 inches by 18 inches, and to be 18 inches high (66 cm × 46 cm × 46 cm). They must have a solid, impervious floor and adequate ventilation holes, food and water containers and a toilet tray for unaccompanied travel. Animal baskets or crates should always be stowed away from particularly noisy areas, and whenever possible pregnant cats should not be transported.

At the end of any journey the carrying container should be opened slowly, especially if it is of the type which does not permit you to see the cat from outside. Do this preferably in a closed room; in a strange environment, and after the excitement of the journey, some cats will leap out and rush away to hide. On the other hand, some cats may be very reluctant to leave the comparative safety of the basket and will need plenty of reassurance as they are lifted out.

Q *Should my cat have a sedative before it travels?*

A Not as a general rule. Sedatives are best reserved for those cats that become distressed by travelling, and even then only when they have to undertake a long journey. Most cats will accept travelling by car or public transport with only the occasional vocal complaint about the bumps and jolts along the way. Sedatives should be reserved for those cats who are known to become extremely anxious and excited when travelling and for those who suffer from true travel sickness.

Travel sickness is a response to the motion of a moving vehicle (cars, buses, planes, boats) which continually stimulates the organs of balance in the animal's inner ears and which in turn stimulates the brain i.e. that part of it known as the vomiting centre. Usually the cat is initially very quiet, and then may salivate, retch and even vomit. Fortunately, recovery takes only a few minutes after the movement ceases.

The anxious cat becomes very excited, shows dilated (i.e. wide open) pupils and also salivates. Excessive salivation and panting are in fact features of both extreme anxiety and true travel sickness.

Sedatives given by mouth (i.e. as tablets) to control nervousness or motion sickness begin to exert their maximum effect within one or two hours. When injected, they are effective within twenty to thirty minutes, though faster if given intravenously. Their effect lasts for around six hours, but some degree of sedation, with a lowered body temperature and reduced ability to respond to stimuli, lasts for at least twenty-four hours. Obviously, it would be preferable for the cat to endure a half-hour journey than a complete day's hangover, unless there is some very good reason.

To minimize the possibility of excitement, a cat can be trained beforehand to accept travel in a car. It is firstly fed titbits in the car, then spends short periods in a travelling basket in the motionless car, and eventually it is taken for short drives.

To minimize the occurrence of travel sickness, don't give any food to the cat for six to eight hours before the journey, and no liquic for one to two hours beforehand. Make sure that the basket is well ventilated and that the ventilation holes are not blocked by surrounding cases, bags, or outdoor clothes, especially when travelling by car. As a general rule, it is inadvisable to give food or drink on a journey of less than twelve hours.

7
Housing and Training

Q *What basic behaviour should I expect from a properly trained cat?*

A By the time a cat is adult it should have been trained:

1 To be clean in the house and use a litter tray if necessary.
2 To sleep in its own bed.
3 To come in, answer to its name and know the meaning of certain 'command' words.
4 Not to scratch the furniture, carpets or walls.
5 Not to claw or climb the curtains.
6 Not to climb on to furniture or food preparation surfaces.
7 Not to steal food from plates.
8 Not to eat flowers or houseplants indoors.
9 Not to be unduly aggressive.

Training should start at an early age so that the cat doesn't develop bad habits that may prove difficult or impossible to eradicate afterwards. It is important to realize from the outset that either you or the cat is going to be the dominant personality. If you allow it to be the cat you will almost certainly regret it later.

Toilet training, under the mother cat's supervision, will start as early as three weeks' old; the other training from around six to eight weeks, the start of the important socializing period of a cat's life. During this period cats will adjust naturally to the presence of people and other pets, to being handled and to the normal noises of the household. Kittens which are not adequately handled and trained during the early weeks and months of life will usually be difficult to handle when they grow older, particularly by strangers or outside their normal environment. A name should be chosen and spoken whilst the kitten is being stroked and played with so that it begins to associate the name with itself.

Q *What general methods can be used to train a cat?*

A In training it is important to be firm but fair. With your eyes on the kitten, speak your command words in a firm voice, and at the same time

82

show the kitten what action is required or *not* required of him. For example, 'Down' as the kitten is lifted from the chair into which it has climbed, 'Out' as it is placed outdoors in toilet training, and the multi-purpose 'No' when it is caught doing something undesirable, like scratching the carpet, and is removed to prevent it from continuing.

It is, of course, not only the word but the manner in which it is spoken and the whole attitude of the owner which helps to convey its meaning to the cat. Keep to the same routine, always using the same word for the same activity and say it as if you mean business. Later, if the cat ignores you, it is important to correct its behaviour immediately. Otherwise, it can easily develop into the equivalent of an awful child who blithely does whatever it wants whilst its parents lamely and ineffectually beg it to stop. Undesirable behaviour *must* be checked as soon as it appears; habits that appear cute in a kitten, like scratching or climbing up clothing, are not so amusing when they persist, as they will, in the adult cat.

Feeding the cat before meals are prepared for the human members of the household will discourage stealing and begging for food. Cats can be rewarded for their good behaviour by receiving extra attention and affection from the owner, or by being given a favourite titbit, or even by being allowed outdoors or to sit in some favourite place. Never feed the cat directly after it has behaved badly because this is likely to be mis-interpreted as a 'reward' and will thus encourage further similar occurrences.

When an older cat misbehaves, the punishment should be related to the problem. Hitting the cat with a rolled newspaper is effective if it scratches, bites or growls, since this is how another more dominant cat would deal with it. However, to prevent other types of misbehaviour, hitting, shouting or throwing things, although temporarily effective, may result in the cat fighting back or rushing away and in the long-term continually avoiding you.

A cat appears to associate the punishment more with the person delivering it than with the behaviour that caused it. Consequently, some form of aversion therapy is required, i.e. in which the punishment is directly associated with its behaviour. Comparatively harmless but unpleasant shocks delivered remotely, i.e. without, or apparently without, human involvement, are very effective. Spraying with water from a water pistol or dropping a bunch of keys are useful procedures, but ideally the cat must not see you doing the spraying or dropping. This also requires someone to be present whenever the cat is *likely* to misbehave.

A truly remote method is to protect areas where the cat may misbehave with crinkled aluminium foil to give an unpleasant feel and sound. Balloons, which hopefully will burst, and mousetraps (arranged *upside down* after being set), which when disturbed will go off, will also provide a nasty shock. Often only two or three such deterrent treatments are necessary for the cat to abandon its undesirable behaviour.

Drugs are not able to help correct behavioural problems, with the exception of progestagens and cyprodione which are effective in controlling urine spraying, roaming and fighting in a high proportion of tom cats.

Q *How can I persuade my cat to use a litter tray?*

A Cats are naturally clean animals. The toilet training of cats is made relatively easy because, after the first two to three weeks of life, it is a natural instinct for kittens to urinate and defaecate in loose, sandy soil. Before this age the mother cat keeps the nest clean by consuming these waste materials when she licks each kitten. Indeed, it is the stimulation of the mother licking the anal region which causes urine and motions to be passed.

This maternal behaviour ceases when the kittens are around three weeks of age and they begin to struggle out of the nest. If a litter tray is provided nearby, many will find it and use it instinctively. Often the mother cat will pick up each kitten in turn and carry it to the tray; alternatively, you can place them there yourself. The arrival of fresh food in the stomach stimulates a reflex movement of material through the bowel (the gastro-colic reflex) so that the best time to do this is immediately after each meal.

The cat's natural instinct is also to dig a shallow hole in which to defaecate, and to cover the excrement by scratching the litter backwards with its paws. In the wild this behaviour serves to conceal the animal's presence.

The scent of previous eliminations encourages the kitten to return to the same spot. It is advisable to confine a kitten to the room containing the litter tray until he has become accustomed to using it, and not to change the tray's position within the room. Cats like privacy when using the tray and therefore a dimly lit secluded area, out of the reach of young children, is preferable.

If a kitten uses the wrong spot, immediately place it gently but firmly into the litter box and clean the soiled area, ideally with white vinegar or with diluted bleach if the floor covering will withstand it. *Don't* use ammonia, which often encouages further urination there. By eight weeks old kittens should be almost completely house trained.

It is advisable to provide a litter tray at night even when a cat is adult, and cats without access to a garden will require one permanently. Cats that are ill may also need to use a litter tray, and this arrangement allows the motions to be inspected and, if required, collected for examination.

Once a kitten is accustomed to using a litter tray it can, if necessary, be trained to urinate and defaecate outdoors. This is best done during dry weather. On successive days the litter tray is moved progressively nearer to the external door and eventually just outside it. Some already-soiled litter should then be placed in the garden and the kitten carried to it after feeding. A day or so should produce the desired result. (Using this type of 'successive approximation' training it is even possible to train a cat to defaecate and urinate in the household toilet. Whether this is desirable remains a debatable point.)

If a cat accidentally passes a motion on to the edge of its litter tray, it will attempt to cover it by pawing and scratching at the area *around* the tray, even though there is obviously no litter there. This is an example of the deeply-rooted type of instinctive behaviour referred to as 'displacement activity'.

Q *My cat seemed perfectly house trained but recently he has been soiling indoors in different places. Why has he forgotten his training?*

A In some cats the training to go outdoors or use a litter tray breaks down and they begin to pass urine and motions elsewhere indoors. Sometimes it is due to poor control of the bowel or bladder, due either to old age or illness, but fortunately this is relatively uncommon. Often the behaviour is due to a dislike of the smell of an imperfectly or infrequently cleaned tray, of a deodorized litter, or of some disinfectant used in cleaning. It can also arise where there is overcrowding (too many cats in the household), or simply if one cat objects to using the same box as another (often a newcomer).

At times, the problem follows household changes, such as moving house, the arrival of new pets or children, or simply altering the position of the litter tray. And sometimes it is just that the cat doesn't care to go outside in wet weather. It could even be that he has become tired of being caught when using the litter tray – to be played with or given medication.

In all these instances the corrective measures are fairly obvious, but there remains the problem of re-training the cat to use the tray and not some other area in the house. Firstly, the soiled area should be thoroughly cleaned, ideally with bleach or with white vinegar. Then its further use for elimination may be discouraged by one of the following:

1 Prohibiting access to the area.
2 Feeding the cat at that spot, since most animals will not eliminate in feeding areas.
3 Covering the area with aluminium foil or plastic sheeting. If, as is hoped, the cat prefers not to walk on this, it should be left down and only gradually removed, a piece at a time, over several weeks.

If persuading a cat to use the litter tray becomes a real problem, the animal should be confined with the tray to a small room with an easily cleaned floor, e.g. the bathroom or cloakroom, and only allowed out into other areas of the house when the tray is being used regularly. Alternatively, an extra litter box can be placed at the spot where the cat has been in the habit of urinating. When it has begun to use this new box, it can be moved little by little (a few inches a day) back to the original site, and the cat fed in the place where previously it had been urinating.

85

Some cats insist upon using a plant pot as a litter tray; this can be countered by covering its surface with gravel or spraying the plant and the soil surface with white vinegar or cat repellant.

Q *What type of litter tray should I buy for my cat?*

A The litter tray's minimum dimensions should be 12 inches by 8 inches and $2\frac{1}{2}$ to 3 inches deep (30 cm × 20 cm × 6.5 cm), though a little shallower for kittens. Those made of plastic are best for routine use, though disposable litter trays of cardboard are available for temporary use. Metal trays which will neither rust (like those made of ferrous metals), nor chip (like enamel dishes), are also suitable. Some types are fitted with a cover about 8 inches or so high, with an opening in one side through which the cat can enter. This completely encloses the litter tray and enables the cat to perform in privacy. It also avoids the scattering of litter and prevents other pets such as dogs from interfering with the tray.

The scattering of litter can be a problem. It can, however, be reduced by standing the tray on an easily cleaned floor, e.g. vinyl or ceramic tiles and not on a carpet, and by placing newspaper under and around the tray to minimize the sweeping up. A container with deeper sides (e.g. a large plastic washing-up bowl) could be used for adult cats.

Suitable materials for use as litter include sand or sandy soil (though this can become muddy and messy), peat or processed tree bark, torn-up newspaper or kitchen towels, wood chippings or shavings, or commercial litter which consists of granules of dried clay (fuller's earth). Commercial litters are very successful, but some contain deodorizers which may discourage some cats from using them (e.g. those containing chlorophyll), or dyes which may stain the fur of white cats. Sawdust is not recommended as it may be eaten by kittens, it clings to the paws and haircoat causing long hair to matt up and is also spread throughout the house. Peat may also cause long hair to matt up. Some people feel that the use of newspaper may encourage the cat to urinate on newspapers elsewhere in the house. Changing the litter is made easier by spreading it to a depth of at least one inch (2.5 cm) on sheets of newspaper laid at the bottom of the tray. Sprinkling the litter with garden soil may simplify re-training the kitten to use the garden at a later date.

Q *How can I dispose of soiled litter?*

A It is *always* desirable to *burn* cat litter to prevent the spread of the infective stages of the common feline parasites (*Toxocara cati* and *Toxoplasma gondii* – see page 165) to other cats and to other species, including man. Some types (soil and clay) are not intrinsically flammable and will therefore need to be added to an existing fire. Other methods of disposal *will not* necessarily destroy these infective stages, merely transfer them elsewhere. The eggs of *Toxocara* are very resistant to disinfectants and other chemicals and therefore it is unlikely that they will be killed by chemical treatment before or after disposal.

Therefore, if the incineration of refuse is customary in your area, place the discarded litter and faeces into a plastic bag, seal it and dispose of it with your other rubbish.

If incineration is difficult to arrange then small amounts of soiled litter can be flushed down the toilet (this is the method often advocated by the manufacturers of commercial cat litters), though large amounts may block the toilet. Some local authorities dump the treated sewage at sea so that environmental contamination is minimal; others spread it on the land, thereby encouraging widespread contamination. It is *not* advisable to place soiled litter on a compost heap.

The soiled litter should be removed from the tray each day (use a special scoop) and replaced by fresh. At least once a week (more often if used by more than one cat) the whole trayful should be disposed of and the tray itself cleaned. Always wear rubber gloves when doing this and do not allow the tray or soiled litter near food preparation areas or kitchen sinks.

Wash out the tray thoroughly with hot water and detergent, either outdoors or in the bath, and then disinfect and deodorize with diluted household bleach. When it is dry, refill and replace it. It is recommended to use a deodorizer around the tray, and some form of fly repellant in warm weather.

Q *How can I stop my cat from spraying indoors?*

A The reduction of any territorial threat, for example by reducing the number of cats in the household, is often sufficient to stop spraying.

And moving the animal's feeding bowl to the spot where spraying occurs will sometimes deter this behaviour. Shouting or hitting the cat when it is discovered spraying *may* be effective but it is thought that in most instances the cat does not associate his behaviour at the time with the way you are treating him. He simply feels that you are being unkind and responds by keeping away from you rather than by not spraying.

The reception of an unpleasant shock when he begins spraying, especially if it *seems* to have no direct connection with yourself, is much more likely to deter him. Throwing some noisy object like a bunch of keys to land near the cat has already been recommended, as has spraying him with a water pistol (squirt gun) or best of all throwing a glass of water over him. Although these responses may seem extremely unkind, they do mimic the type of natural 'disincentives' by which cats learn to avoid indulging in certain behaviour.

Some cats will only spray one or two places regularly. Hanging a piece of aluminium foil in front of them, which will produce an unpleasant rustling sound if sprayed, may discourage the cat. In the case of tom cats, treatment with one of a number of natural or synthetic female hormones may, although not always, control the problem. The castration of adult males also produces a marked decrease in this behaviour (in around 90% of cases) as well as reducing other forms of typical male behaviour – fighting and roaming.

When spraying (or any undesirable urination) occurs indoors, thoroughly wash the affected area as soon as possible three or four times with diluted bleach (to those surfaces that will stand it) or with white vinegar. Don't use ammonia because this tends to encourage further urination in the area. If the surface is absorbent (e.g. a carpet or upholstery) soak up as much urine as possible with paper towels before washing, and also blot up the remaining liquid each time you wash it. Afterwards, the wet area of carpet should be covered with cornflower or baking powder (bicarbonate of soda) and left to dry. When thoroughly dry, the powder can be vacuumed up. It is important not to leave any residual odour because this acts as a 'mark' and encourages the cat to spray or urinate in that place again. Spraying is the usual means by which a male cat scent-marks its territorial boundaries.

Motions are also deposited as a marker at the boundary of the cat's territory. These are not covered by the cat, in contrast to what usually happens to those passed within its territory. The cat may also deliberately defaecate in a very prominent and undesirable position indoors if it feels threatened, and make no attempt to hide it.

Q *We are shortly moving house. What is the best way of introducing our cat to his new home?*

A Some cats form a very close attachment to their territory, so much so that when the owner moves to a new house the cat may leave this new home and return to its old territory. This is particularly likely to occur when the two homes are less than a mile apart, but with tom cats who roam over a much wider area, even up to ten miles away. On the other hand, many owners move house a number of times and never experience this problem. This suggests that in these cases there is a much stronger bond between the cat and the owner, or that the cat is much less familiar with the surrounding area. (Indeed, some cats normally confined to a flat may even have difficulty in finding their way back to the correct floor of the apartment block.)

Among the methods suggested to prevent cats wandering back to their old territory is the dubious remedy of putting butter on their paws. The intention is for the cat to be so occupied with licking off the butter that by the time it has finished the urge to return to its former abode has disappeared. But the most successful is simply to confine the cat to his new home for a week (using a litter tray) so that his attachment to it grows and displaces his longing for his previous domain. Then, when the time comes to let the cat out for the first occasion, do it just before feeding, or ideally when he is asking for food, to ensure his rapid return. On subsequent days, the cat can be let out progressively earlier so that there is a longer interval between being let out and being fed.

When a cat is first introduced into an unfamiliar room it will insist on exploring the room thoroughly, walking all around the perimeter and sniffing as it goes. Even when there is another cat in the room, it is the room that has to be investigated first. A cat usually spends most of its time in what is called its 'resting area'. This may be the whole house, part of the house, just its bed or even an area outdoors such as a shed or outhouse. Then it also has a 'territory' immediately surrounding the resting area which it defends against other cats and the boundaries of which it marks with scratches and, particularly in the case of tom cats, with urine. In addition, there is what is sometimes referred to as a 'home range' which is a larger area containing frequently visited areas for hunting, sunbathing and keeping watch. Within this area the animal travels along a network of paths.

The home range of domestic female cats in rural areas is about one-third of a square mile ($\frac{1}{2}$–1 km^2) though inevitably it is smaller in urban and suburban districts. The home range of male cats is several times larger, especially during the mating season. The home range may overlap with the ranges of neighbouring cats and cats watch carefully to ensure they do not meet others on their travels. If another cat is observed he will wait until the other has moved away sufficiently before he recommences his journey.

Q *We are thinking of installing a cat door. Is it difficult to train a cat to use one?*

A A cat door or flap is a small light-weight 'door', approximately 6 inches square, fitted into an opening in one of the external doors which ideally gives access to a garden. It allows the cat free entry and exit to relieve itself outdoors and to take exercise. It is also possible to fit a cat door into a wall but, because this involves considerably more work, this is unusual.

The opening should be three to four inches above the ground and situated well away from the bolts used to fasten the main door. If necessary, baffles can be fitted around it on the inside to further frustrate would-be burglars. Don't be tempted to make the opening too large; children and small adults have been known to enter, uninvited, through an opening measuring 12 inches by 15 inches (30 cm × 40 cm).

Two main types of cat door are commercially available, both of which are hinged at the top. One can be pushed open from either side, the other always opens outwards and therefore can only be *pushed* open from the inside. The latter type is designed to keep out stray cats who do not know how to open it from the outside. Consequently your cat will need to learn how to lift the flap in order to re-enter the house.

Some cats learn almost instinctively how to use these doors, but if training is necessary then it is best to begin at about three or four months of age. Initially, the hole can be left without the door fitted, or with the cat door permanently fastened open with string or wood blocks, so that the cat gets used to going out (to explore and play) and to come back in (for food and sleep). Calling him from first one side and then the other may help to persuade him to use it. Then the flap can be gradually lowered on successive days to reduce the opening, so that eventually it has to be pushed or lifted with a paw for the opening to appear.

Q *Do cat doors have any disadvantages?*

A Apart from the risk from burglars, there are two problems which can occur with cat doors. One is the problem of draughts, which can be solved by a magnetized strip being fitted to the flap so that a firm push is required before it swings open. The other is the problem of unwanted cats entering the house. Sometimes they come after food; making a practice of not leaving food down may stop this. If your cat is an unspayed female, males will certainly be attracted when she is in season. Therefore, it is important to have a bolt fitted to the inside of the door which will enable you to keep your cat in, and others out, whenever this is necessary. The absence of any locking device is the disadvantage of another type of cat door which has a circular opening covered by a series of overlapping flexible plastic triangles hinged at the circumference. To pass through, the cat pushes its head at the centre, where the apex of all the triangles meet, causing them to bend outwards (or inwards) and allowing the animal to pass through. The type of flap that requires the cat to learn how to lift it may deter many strays, but there are also sophisticated types with a battery-operated lock that only open when activated by a magnet on the cat's collar. In theory these allow only the resident cat to enter, but there has been a report of a cat wearing this device and learning to stand near the flap, thereby allowing it to be opened, so that its 'guests' can enter before it also passes through!

Q *How can I keep my cat off certain areas of the garden?*

A The Roman philosopher Pliny in his *Natural History* advised placing bunches of rue (*Ruta graveolens*) around domestic dove-cots to keep cats away from them. Since it appears that cats dislike the plant and will avoid it, it might be worth planting it to see what effect it will have.

An unpleasant smelling substance, e.g. one containing oil of citronella, smeared on plants and shrubs may prove a deterrent. And covering the area with fine wire mesh or nylon netting a few inches above the ground is often effective, though unsightly. Growing seeds can be protected by surrounding or covering the area with prickly branches or leaves, e.g. of gorse, rose or holly, though obtaining sufficient of them may present problems. Another suggestion is to lightly dab the cat's gums with lemon juice or vinegar and then to spray the leaves of plants in the area with a dilute solution of the same liquid.

Several balloons, firmly pegged down, can be used to provide aversion therapy: the noise as they burst discourages further invasions. Alternatively, a loud electric bell or horn placed in the area and sounded by remote control when the cat approaches can cause it to avoid the spot.

Q *Our cat ripped our old sofa to shreds. Now that we are buying some expensive new furniture, is there any way we can stop him from damaging it?*

A Cats often like to lie on chairs, sofas and other furniture and may adopt favourite pieces as part of their own territory. Many owners will not object unduly to this, provided that the furniture is not damaged or covered with cat hairs. If you do wish to avoid this behaviour it is best to train the cat from an early age only to use its own bed. Most owners, however, will object when the cat begins to deliberately damage furniture and carpets by scratching at them. As was mentioned in an earlier section (page 45), this is natural behaviour on the part of the cat, both to keep its claws sharp and to mark its territory. Once a cat has chosen an object or area to scratch it will usually not readily change.

To prevent or minimize damage indoors, cats should be trained to use a scratching post or board. This is a piece of log or board arranged vertically upright measuring 6 to 8 inches wide (15 cm to 20 cm) and 2 to 2½ feet high (60 cm to 75 cm) and for the cat to use it, it must be stable, preferably fixed onto a firm base or fastened to the wall. It is best kept in the room where the cat sleeps as scratching is often performed upon waking. Ideally this board should be introduced while the cat is still a kitten so that it gets into the habit of using it. Commercially-produced posts may have a covering of cardboard, canvas or carpet, and some are scented with cat-mint (cat-nip) to increase their attractiveness. Fastening a piece of old carpet to a leg of the kitchen table has been suggested but this *may* simply condition the animal to damage furniture. Pieces of carpet may also harbour fleas.

The key to effective discouragement from scratching is a sudden shock. This could be given by simply throwing a magazine, bunch of keys or coat-hanger near, but not at, the cat, or even by spraying him with a water-pistol. Less effective is to point at the cat and tell it loudly and firmly 'No' as soon as it begins to scratch the furniture or even adopts the posture to begin scratching. Whatever discouragement is adopted, the cat should then be taken to the scratching post and its forelimbs moved in the normal claw sharpening movements to demonstrate how you wish it to behave. If an animal has been in the habit of clawing a particular piece of furniture, that item should be moved and the scratching post substituted in the same position – then the training procedure should be adopted. In time the scratching post can be *gradually* moved to a more convenient position in the room. With carpet clawing, the scratching post should be placed in the most frequently damaged area. In this case the post should remain there and not be removed subsequently.

If you cannot always be present other techniques have to be adopted. Many cats dislike smooth textures and covering a piece of furniture with plastic sheeting may discourage the cat temporarily. When buying furniture upholstered in fabric, it is worth bearing in mind that cats find loosely woven material much more satisfying to scratch at than thick, tightly woven material. Since cats dislike unstable objects, a deterrent can be to drape the item of furniture which is frequently damaged with a loose cover which will move if the cat attempts to scratch at it. Alternatively, the cat's attentions may be discouraged by building alongside the scratched area a 'booby trap' of precariously balanced books or feeding bowls which will topple over if disturbed, or by placing some small object under one leg of a table so that it rocks if touched. And if the cat has to be left unobserved, it is best placed in a room where scratching has not previously been a problem.

Q *Can my cat be trained to walk on a lead?*

A Many cats can be trained to walk on a lead (Siamese and other oriental cats in particular), preferably starting when they are kittens. A lead can prove a great asset in allowing safe exercise for the cat during long journeys (if you just let him loose he will probably run off and become lost) and in hazardous urban areas. Cats won't walk to heel in the way that dogs will, but they can be trained to walk alongside you.

The cat should wear a harness rather than a collar. Collars tend to be easy for the cat to slip through, and in any case pressure around the neck makes a cat reluctant to move. Certainly a 'choke' chain as used on dogs shouldn't be used with cats. The harness should be capable of adjustment and fitted so that it is tight enough to prevent the cat wriggling free. Then a lead of light leather, canvas, nylon or cord, six to seven feet long, is attached to the harness.

The keynote of training is to have a number of short training sessions and not to attempt too much at one time. At first, training should be performed indoors, the cat simply dragging the lead around without you holding it. Later, he should be encouraged to walk with you holding the lead; wherever he wants to go at first, but later where *you* wish to go. He should be checked from dashing ahead or pulling back by a pull on the lead. If he is stubborn, don't drag him along – rather try to cajole him into walking a few more steps. A reward can be given afterwards in the form of a little favourite food, but *only* if he does what is asked of him. Some trainers recommend using a long stick such as a garden cane, not to hit but to push the cat gently and persuade it to move into a position nearer to you. Whether the cat walks on your right or left side is unimportant, but the *same* side should be adhered to.

When he is able to walk alongside and to change direction when you do, he can be taken outdoors, though he will need to be reassured frequently about his safety. Do this by picking him up every few seconds at the start and gradually the periods on the ground can become longer.

With a policy of gentle persuasion, rewards for good behaviour and reassurance, it should be possible to train your cat to walk on a lead by your side. However, don't be tempted to let the cat loose if things are going well; without restraint any sudden startling noise or movement could send him scuttling away.

Q *How should I arrange to board my cat while I am on holiday?*

A Like so many other things, the best boarding catteries are often recommended by word of mouth. Or you might ask your vet if there is a cattery he could recommend. You should then approach the cattery owners or manager to make the necessary arrangements. Do this as soon as you have decided on your holiday dates because the best catteries are always fully booked during the most popular holiday weeks (just like good hotels). And, like good hotels, good catteries tend to charge rather more. A good cattery will insist that your cat is fully and recently vaccinated, to protect both itself and the other boarders, and *will demand proof* in the form of vaccination certificates. You may thus need time to arrange for a vaccination course to be completed. Vaccination is required against feline enteritis, and sometimes feline influenza as well.

Catteries vary widely in quality (even though in Britain they must all be licensed by the local authority) and if you want to inform yourself about the type of establishment ask for an appointment to view the accommodation before making a definite booking. A well-run cattery will have nothing to hide.

Q *How can I judge whether a cattery is a good one?*

A The way in which the establishment is managed is reflected in its general hygiene, i.e. the smell, the cleanliness of the cages, the condition of the food and water bowls and the toilet tray, and the appearance of the attendants. Note whether the cats are boarded individually or two or more to a cage or chalet, and decide whether they look contented and well-cared for. If the cattery looks sub-standard and poorly run, try elsewhere. Even if you are satisfied, check that the accommodation you have seen is where your cat will be housed; sometimes second-rate accommodation is tucked out of sight.

Some catteries will ask about each cat's preference for food, though it is surprising how often a boarded cat will eat with apparent relish foods that are refused at home. Certainly, if there is definite evidence of an allergy or intolerance to certain foods, this should be mentioned.

Two types of cat are unpopular in a cattery; one is a tom cat, because of its smell, and the second is a sick cat, because it represents a source of infection for all the other cats. If you have a cat that has to receive regular medication during your holiday period, the cattery should be informed as soon as possible; some are willing to give treatment or to arrange for their local vet to visit, but some are not. There are, however, some veterinary surgeons who run boarding catteries and who may be able to accept a sick cat for regular treatment whilst you are away.

A familiar cushion or blanket left with your cat can help him to avoid feeling totally abandoned. But because old cats, like old people, don't adapt well to new surroundings and new ways of doing things, elderly animals are best not boarded unless boarding has previously been a regular occurrence and the cattery is familiar to them. Most cats will quickly adapt to their new circumstances but these older animals may become very withdrawn and depressed, and even refuse food.

Finally, it should be appreciated that outbreaks of disease can occur even in the best run catteries, despite all possible precautions. Unfortunately, this is inherent in any establishment where a number of cats are brought together. If you avoid the use of a cattery altogether you will reduce, though certainly not eliminate, this particular risk.

Q *We are going on holiday soon but our old cat hates being boarded out. Is there any alternative?*

A Obviously, the cat mustn't simply be abandoned to find its own food when you go away. If it is moved to someone else's house, it often escapes back home where there is no-one to feed or care for it.

The best alternative to boarding (from your cat's point of view it is probably preferable) is for a friend or relative to visit your home twice a day to feed and look after your cat in its own familiar environment.

8
Grooming Your Cat

Q *Is it ever necessary to bath my cat and if so, how often?*

A Many cats are never bathed throughout their lives and as a general rule a cat only *needs* a bath when its coat gets particularly soiled – with mud, dirt, urine or diarrhoea, for example. This is not to say that the cat does not need regular *grooming*, but actual bathing is seldom required. However, if the coat becomes very dirty many cats may refuse to clean it, which is not surprising in view of how it must taste. Most cats dislike being bathed but will accept it if handled gently but firmly, especially if it is first done when they are young.

Sometimes there are medical reasons for bathing. Treatment for fleas can be given in the form of a shampoo containing an insecticide (see page 150). Bathing may be necessary to remove toxic and corrosive materials such as tar, paint and diesel oil from the coat. This may require the use of a liquid detergent. Often vegetable oils or other solvents are used to soften or dissolve these substances and then have themselves to be removed. In such circumstances veterinary attention should always be obtained as soon as possible. Many organic solvents are themselves irritant or corrosive and should *never* be used on cats, e.g. paint stripper, turpentine, paraffin (kerosene) and petrol (gasoline).

Cats that suffer from 'stud tail' will need, at least initially, to have their tail washed with shampoo or soap and water. There are numerous large sebaceous glands on the upper surface of the cat's tail along its length (collectively called the supracaudal organ) and, particularly in confined animals, the waxy secretion that these glands produce can accumulate. As a result there is matting of the hair and crust and scale formation on the skin. The condition occurs most frequently in uncastrated toms and is therefore known popularly as 'stud tail', although it is also known in castrated males and in females. This greasy material must be washed away, followed by daily combing and cleaning of the area with a pad soaked in alcohol, e.g. rubbing alcohol, surgical spirit (although this is slightly greasy it contains 2% castor oil) or cologne. A cat will usually begin to clean itself more thoroughly and so avoid a recurrence of the condition if it is allowed more freedom and consequently increased access to fresh air.

Bathing removes natural oil from the coat and it will take several days for the coat to regain its natural gloss and bulk, usually described as 'body'. Owners who exhibit their animals at cat shows often bath them as part of the preparation for the show (especially in the case of white and chinchilla cats), but this should be done several days, ideally two weeks, beforehand to permit the recovery of the coat and the return of the natural oil. There are also preparations which can be sprayed onto the coat to give extra gloss and thereby overcome the dulling effect of bathing.

Just before a pregnant female cat (expectant queen) gives birth, cat breeders often wash the skin and nipples and also clip away the hair in that region to make it easier for the kittens to feed. This is especially useful in the case of the long-haired breeds.

Q *Is it true that a cat which has been bathed will never wash itself again?*

A No, there is absolutely no truth in this statement, though naturally a cat with residues of soap or shampoo in its coat may at first be reluctant to lick at it. However, a coat covered in diesel oil, foul-smelling mud or other obnoxious matter is even more unpleasant, and will often effectively deter the animal from cleaning itself.

Washing normally takes place after sleeping or eating. The cat first licks around its mouth, then at all the areas it can possibly reach, manoeuvring into very strange postures to do this. Finally, to clean the areas that can't be reached with its tongue, it licks a paw to dampen it, and then rubs the paw over its head and ears and down the face. A considerable quantity of saliva is used each day in the washing process.

Smearing a little butter onto the coat is one way in which you might be able to provoke a lazy cat into grooming itself. Kittens start to groom themselves, and each other, at about three weeks of age, and can do so very efficiently by six weeks' old.

Q *Is it possible that my cat could be washing herself too much?*

A Some cats, particularly Siamese and Abyssinian, undertake *excessive* licking, even chewing, of the skin, and this results in hair loss, inflammation and ultimately raised, firm, moist lesions, typically on the abdomen, back or hind legs. This condition (lick granuloma) should be treated by your veterinarian.

Q *What should I use to bath my cat?*

A As a rule it is best to use a baby shampoo which will not irritate the eyes. However, the mild detergents in baby shampoo are unable to remove heavy grime or grease and if that is necessary a reputable non-medicated shampoo should be used. Shampoos are either soap or detergent based and may contain various additives. Soap shampoos often have lime-dispersing agents added to avoid leaving a dull film on the hair when used in hard water. Detergent shampoos may incorporate lanolin, glycerine or various oils to make the hair glossier and easier to comb.

In the absence of a shampoo, a tablet of ordinary unmedicated toilet soap such as you would use to wash your own skin, or even mild soap flakes, could be used, but these are often more difficult to apply and may sometimes irritate the skin. Soaps and shampoos should always be thoroughly rinsed from the coat.

At times special medicated soaps or shampoos may be recommended or even provided by your vet, but otherwise medicated products are best avoided – especially any containing cold tar or carbolic. *Never* use detergent liquids or powders intended for washing clothes, nor dish-washing liquids. However, when cats are covered in oil or creosote, the application of diluted dishwashing liquid (50/50 with water), or of a detergent gel intended for removing grease from the hands (e.g. Swarfega), may be the only way to shift such tenacious materials.

Bath oils and protein-containing 'body-builders' are usually of little value, though hair conditioners (creme rinses) can be useful after shampooing in preventing 'fly away' hair. The positively-charged particles that conditioners contain neutralize the negative electric charges which dry hair picks up, especially after extensive brushing, and which cause adjacent hairs to repel each other.

Q *I'm sure he's going to hate it, but how should I go about shampooing my cat?*

A It is more convenient to carry out the bathing where there is a fixed sink or bath and ideally where a shower attachment is already provided or can be attached to the tap. A shower makes it much simpler to wet and rinse the coat but be careful that the water is only lukewarm. A warm utility room or bathroom is preferable to the kitchen, unless the sink area can be thoroughly washed down afterwards and before any food or cooking utensils are placed in the sink or on the draining board.

If a shower attachment is not available, fill the sink or a couple of bowls or buckets with lukewarm water (for rinsing) and have a small (one pint) plastic jug standing by. If there is no sink a baby's plastic bath makes a good substitute. Because cats like to feel secure, it helps to place a piece of rubber sheeting or an old towel where the cat is intended to stand, either on the bottom of the sink or on the draining board. You will also need the shampoo, diluted with a little warm water, a towel and/or hair dryer (or fan heater) and a clean comb and brush. It is also preferable to have someone to assist you if possible.

Plug the cat's ears with small pieces of cotton wool to prevent water entering (but use pieces large enough to be pulled out easily with your fingers afterwards) and have a firm collar around the neck. Or make a temporary collar by firmly knotting (not too tight!) a piece of strong gauze bandage to give something to hold onto in case a soapy cat should start to struggle.

Then, with the cat either standing on the draining board or at the bottom of the sink, wet the coat all over with water from the shower or from the jug. Hold the cat firmly by its scruff or its collar and press it downwards if it begins to struggle. Downward pressure is most effective in restricting movement of the cat. Then pour on the shampoo and rub it all over, trying to prevent it from going into the eyes or mouth. Some medicated shampoos need to be left on for fifteen to forty-five minutes to act on the skin. The instructions you have been given should be followed, but in all cases the cat must be kept warm and prevented from licking off the lather during this time.

Then spray or rinse liberally to wash away all residues of lather from the coat until the hair in all regions feels 'squeaky' when rubbed between fingers and thumb. Once they are already wet, many cats allow themselves to be immersed with just the head above water. So for the final rinse you could fill the sink and gently lift the cat into it.

After rinsing, squeeze as much water as possible from the coat, then lift the cat on to a towel and wrap the towel around to soak up as much water as possible. Dry the coat as quickly as possible and do not allow the cat to get cold, particularly not to go outside (though this would be inadvisable anyway if the cat is to be shown).

Some cats can be persuaded to allow a hair dryer or fan heater to be used (despite the noise), but take care not to get these so close that they begin to burn the animal. Otherwise, towels alone can be used but avoid rubbing too vigorously. Comb and brush against the natural run of the hair as it is being blown to make it fluff up. If there is real difficulty experienced in drying the cat, it can be placed in a wickerwork basket and positioned some distance in front of a fan heater. Quick drying is important to avoid chilling, especially in the short-hair, single-coat cats.

Q *Are dry shampoos advisable for cats?*

A Dry shampoos are essentially powders which are made to be dusted into the coat and then completely brushed out (an upwards and away from the body brushing action is required). They are a mixture of absorbent materials such as talc, boric acid and mild alkali, intended to remove both grease and dirt. A number of proprietary brands are available. Those who show cats professionally often use talcum powder or cornflour on cats with light-coloured fur, and fuller's earth on those with brown fur.

The effect can be pleasing if the application and removal is done thoroughly. However, if the coat is very dirty or greasy, these powders will not clean it effectively. Some breeders rub warm bran into the greasy coat to absorb the grease and then brush it out, but this is still not as good as bathing. The application and removal of the powder can be tedious, and on black cats any residual powder looks like dandruff. Powders also tend to make the coat dry and can irritate some cats, making them dribble and their eyes run. Finally the extensive brushing necessary to remove the powder increases static electricity in the coat making it 'fly away'.

All in all, dry shampooing is not very effective and not recommended for cleaning, even though it is often adopted for show purposes.

Q *Will bathing get rid of fleas?*

A Bathing a cat with a conventional shampoo, that is to say one which does not contain any specific antiparasitic agent, will *not* be sufficient to eliminate an existing flea problem. As is mentioned later (page 149), the successful removal of fleas depends upon treating both the infected animal(s) and the surroundings with an insecticidal preparation. At any one time there are usually far more fleas in the surroundings (e.g. the bedding and around the sleeping area) than on the animal.

Shampoos are available which contain insecticides and, providing these are used as directed on adult cats, *not* kittens, they should be safe. After the cat's coat has been soaked with water, the shampoo is vigorously rubbed into it all over for five minutes, avoiding the mouth and eyes. Then, after the specified time interval (which varies with the active ingredient), the shampoo is rinsed out using running water, e.g. from a shower attachment, for at least five minutes so that *no* residue remains in the coat. Otherwise, the cat is likely to ingest it whilst cleaning its coat subsequently. Bathing with an insecticidal shampoo may sometimes be recommended prior to treatment with an antiparasitic powder or aerosol spray.

An insecticide-impregnated soap is also available with which to lather the coat. It is generally more difficult to use and, because in order to be effective the residue is best not completely rinsed out, it is more difficult to avoid the cat licking in the insecticide. This soap is generally less effective than a shampoo at getting rid of fleas.

There are other points which should be clarified. Bathing cannot be relied upon to *drown* the fleas. Many of them will simply hop off the animal as it is wetted, and can therefore hop on again later. Even if they did drown, there would be plenty of other fleas in the surroundings able to take their place. Also, because of their great mobility, combing the coat to get rid of fleas is likewise useless. The only advantage of combing is that by parting the hair it is easier to demonstrate the presence of fleas or flea dirts.

Bathing a cat in a disinfectant solution, and washing the surroundings with disinfectant, will *not* remove fleas. Disinfectants are not formulated for this purpose and certainly flea eggs are able to withstand treatment with any of the disinfectants that you would be prepared to use on your floors and carpets. The ability of disinfectants to destroy organisms of all kinds is seriously over-estimated by most members of the public, largely as a result of misleading advertising. The pine oil disinfectants, sold under many brand names for household use, have particularly low activity and are not taken seriously as disinfectants by the experts in hospital hygiene. Other antiseptics (skin disinfectant solutions) sold for the bathing of wounds also have a disturbingly low activity against most organisms. Disinfectants are more likely to upset your cat by their unpleasant smells, by being licked from the coat, or even by causing a skin reaction, than to contribute to the successful removal of fleas.

Q *What types of brushes and combs should I buy for cat grooming?*

A A natural (pig) bristle brush, although more expensive, is undoubtedly better for the coat than one with nylon or other synthetic bristles; these can cause heavy charges of static electricity to build up and lead to breakage of the hairs. A narrow brush with long bristles is often easier to use than one with a broad head. Wire brushes tend to pull out the hairs by their roots, though a rubber brush is valuable for removing dead hairs which, if swallowed, would cause hairball.

Brushing is valuable in giving a sheen to the coat, but combing is more effective in ensuring that all dead hair is removed. A steel comb is usually better than one of plastic or bone, provided that the ends of the teeth are rounded so as not to scratch the skin. In general, two different spacings of teeth are required; a wide spacing for preliminary combing (especially in long-haired breeds) and a medium spacing for thorough combing. These different teeth spacings may be arranged at either end of a long comb. However, a comb with a handle is often easier to use so either two combs are needed or one which is double-sided. In addition, a fine comb can be used around the face and even all over on the short-haired breeds.

The teeth of the comb should be inserted down to the skin for the combing to be effective. A carder or slicker brush (a square brush with a short handle and numerous fine wire angled teeth) may be helpful in removing matted hair from long-haired animals but is by no means essential.

With grooming, as with many other tasks, there is a happy medium; it needs to be done thoroughly all over, but forcing the comb out through matts will tug out living as well as dead hairs. Excessive brushing will cause many hairs to break.

Provided grooming begins at an early age and is continued regularly (daily if possible), most cats will tolerate and often enjoy it. It is important not to stand any nonsense or the cat may believe that if it struggles enough you will stop. Grasp it gently but firmly by the scruff and carry on until the job is finished. Usually it is best performed with the cat standing on a bench or table top to catch the loose hairs.

Q *Can any special grooming be done purely for show purposes?*

A For show purposes the sheen on the coat of short-haired breeds is improved by a final smoothing over with a chamois leather or even repeated hand stroking. Exhibitors of long-haired breeds often wipe the fur with a cloth lightly dampened with a very dilute solution of household ammonia (six drops in half a pint) and finish off by 'polishing' the fur with a piece of silk or velvet wrapped around their hand.

Q *Do all breeds of cat need grooming?*

A The answer is yes, except for the few hairless cats like the Sphynx and some extreme types of Rex cats. Although the need for regular grooming is greatest in the long-haired breeds, all cats, whether show animals or household pets, need daily grooming to make them look their best and to prevent other problems developing. (Incidentally, talking about the absence of hairs, you may notice that all cats lack eyelashes.)

Cats can be classified for grooming purposes into the following groups:
1 Short-hair, single-coat breeds (e.g. Siamese, Burmese, Rex and British Shorthair) which need to be first combed and brushed *against* the hair to remove dead hairs, and finally brushed *with* the 'lie' of the hair.
2 Short-hair, double-coat breeds (e.g. Abyssinian, Russian Blue and American Shorthair) which have, in addition to the long guard hairs which give the coat its colour, a dense short undercoat. Grooming is the same as for the single-coated animals, but should *not* be overdone as it can destroy the coat.
3 Long-haired breeds (e.g. Persian, Himalayan, Turkish (Angora)) which need careful and extensive combing and brushing; the fur around the head and shoulders being finally brushed upwards to form a frame around the face.

Most short-hair cats have a coat about $1\frac{3}{4}$ inches (4.5 cm) long, whereas in the long-hairs it can reach 5 inches (13 cm) or more. Regular grooming (particularly combing) removes from the coat the loose hairs which are naturally shed by all animals. If these are not combed or brushed out, the cat will remove them as it washes itself. The cat's tongue is covered with numerous spiky processes (papillae) which give the cat's tongue its rough, rasp-like feel. The loose hairs are thus combed out by the tongue as the cat licks. But because these processes point backwards, it is difficult for the hairs to then pass forwards off the tongue. It is much easier for the hairs to pass backwards as the tongue is pushed out so that they gradually work back into the throat and are swallowed.

These swallowed hairs accumulate as solid, sausage-shaped masses in the stomach, commonly known as hairballs or furballs, and in ungroomed long-haired cats this can be a regular occurrence. A cat with a hairball in the stomach can feel hungry and yet full up at the same time. It consequently makes frequent trips to the feeding bowl but eats very little on each occasion. Often the hairballs are got rid of by being vomited up, but sometimes they pass into the intestines and can cause a blockage. It may be possible for the cat to get rid of this after a dose of liquid paraffin which lubricates its passage (being mineral oil it is not digested); otherwise surgical removal becomes necessary.

A neglected long-haired cat can also get hair entangled behind its lower canine teeth. The cat cannot dislodge this although it paws at its mouth and salivates excessively. Eventually this 'rope' of hair digs into the gums.

All of this can be avoided if the hairs are regularly removed each day by combing.

Q *Are there any other reasons for cat grooming?*

A Daily combing and brushing also avoids matting of the coat in areas which it is difficult for the cat to reach; between the shoulder blades, behind the ears, and under the chin, legs and tail. Again, this problem is especially likely to occur in long-haired breeds. If any matts are discovered, it may be possible, if they are small, to tease them apart by pulling sideways on them with the index finger and thumb of both hands (trying not to pull on the skin), and then to comb them out. It is best to cut off larger matts, but be careful. Use blunt-ended scissors, not those with sharp points which can easily penetrate the skin. And it is best to work the teeth of a comb between the matt and the skin first and then to cut over the top of the comb. Whatever you do, *do not* wet the coat to try to remove these tangles; this really makes them set as a solid mass. (So all matts must be removed before a cat is bathed.) In a much neglected long-haired cat with extensive matting of the coat the only solution is for a veterinary surgeon to give a general anaesthetic, and to comb and clip the matts out with electric clippers. (In Britain clipping the fur would debar the cat from being shown under the rules of the Cat Fancy.)

Last, but not least, regular grooming of the cat allows you to discover signs of flea infestation (small gritty flea dirts or the fleas themselves, see page 149) and of other skin disorders like wounds, abscesses and painful areas which are often indicative of bites from other cats.

Q *When should I first start grooming a kitten?*

A Grooming should start when cats are around four months' old to get them used to being handled. At the other extreme it is particularly important for elderly or ill cats who are unwilling or unable to groom themselves.

Q *Is it ever necessary to clean a cat's teeth?*

A Cleaning a cat's teeth is unusual, but if the cat will allow you to do it, it can be useful in preventing or minimizing the accumulation of tartar.

The build-up of tartar (dental calculus) on the teeth is responsible for most of the dental problems of cats; they don't often suffer from pitting of the tooth enamel (caries) which is the main problem for humans. The teeth most commonly affected are the upper and lower canines, the premolars and the first upper molars.

Tartar forms naturally from the growth of oral bacteria on the teeth, from the trapping of food debris (plaque) and the precipitation of salts, principally calcium hydroxyapatite, from the cat's saliva. In cats who use their teeth a lot frequent rubbing on the tooth surface minimizes tartar formation. Therefore cats who catch and eat their own food (mice and birds) usually have little tartar, and the same is true of cats fed on large chunks of meat and dry cat food or given meaty bones from which to tear the flesh. Unfortunately, the teeth receive little wear if the cat is fed soft foods, such as tinned pet foods, fish or finely chopped or minced meat, and cats regularly fed this way soon accumulate tartar.

Tartar is deposited first where the tooth is rubbed least – where it meets the gum. This rough material traps further bacteria and food and irritates the gum, which becomes inflamed (gingivitis) and causes a bright pink or red line above the teeth. The tartar at first looks like a yellowish-grey upper rim on the teeth, but in time large masses accumulate which if not removed can eventually become larger than the tooth itself. As more and more tartar is deposited, the inflammation gets worse. As the gum swells away from the tooth, the roots are exposed and bacteria are able to get into the tooth socket. Ultimately, this can result in massive infection, a loosening of the tooth and sometimes even abscess formation. This condition, known as periodontal disease, is very common in cats.

The irritation produced can cause excessive salivation and old cats often sit with long 'drools' of thick saliva hanging from their mouth and wetting the hair on their chest. Their breath has a foul smell (halitosis) and the pain of a loose tooth may prevent them eating except very gingerly or on one side of the mouth; sometimes not at all. Often they rub or paw at their mouth.

To remove tartar (by cracking it with dental forceps and using a dental scraper or ultrasonic scaler) and any loose teeth requires the use of a general anaesthetic. Obviously, it would be better to avoid tartar accumulation, ideally by changing the diet and providing vinyl chew 'toys'; but there are some owners who also regularly clean their cats' teeth.

A small, soft child's toothbrush, moistened and dipped into tooth powder, is probably best. Cats seem to object more to toothpaste because of its flavour and the detergent content which makes it froth in the mouth. A good alternative is to use moistened sodium bicarbonate (baking soda) powder or hydrogen peroxide. The noise of electric toothbrushes renders them unsuitable.

The cat should be held by its scruff on a table, ideally in a sitting position with his feet held by a helper. The brush should be moved firmly, but not

How to clean your cat's ears

1. *Place the cat on a working surface and gently but firmly hold its scruff. If the animal is difficult to restrain you will need someone else to help you.*

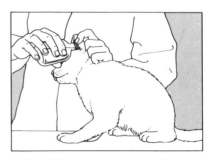

2. *Carefully pour lukewarm oil into the cat's ear canal until it is almost full. On no account use hot oil because this will cause severe scalding.*

3. *Gently massage the base of the cat's ear between your forefinger and thumb, so that the oil will soften accumulated ear wax and loosen any other debris.*

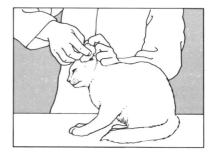

4. *Wrap a piece of cotton wool (known as cotton in North America) around your forefinger, and gently wipe out all surplus oil from the ear canal.*

5. *Using one or more flexible cotton buds, carefully clean all the folds of the ear canal. Don't probe too far down or you might damage the cat's ear drum.*

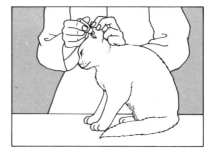

6. *If your vet has supplied eardrops, place 3 or 4 drops down the canal and massage the base of the ear. Finally, wipe any spilt oil from the cat's coat.*

too vigorously, up and down and from side to side. Clean both top and bottom teeth at the front and the back, paying particular attention to the teeth at the back of the mouth at the point where each tooth meets the gum, but stop if any bleeding occurs. If the cat will not permit the use of a brush, a finger wrapped in soft rag may be used, though take care not to get bitten.

Daily cleaning is preferable for preventing the recurrence of calculus, but weekly brushing is probably adequate.

Q *How can I clean my cat's ears?*

A Though not often needed, there are three main reasons for cleaning a cat's ears: to remove an accumulation of natural wax, particularly if the cat is to be shown (this is especially common in Rex cats); to remove dust or water from the ear; and as part of the treatment for an ear condition, usually ear mite infection.

It is a good idea to check the inside of a cat's ears during grooming, or if the cat is regularly seen to be shaking, rubbing or scratching its ears. Cats' ears are seldom acutely inflamed but if they are the canal below the ear flap appears reddened, is painful when handled and may be full of moisture (exudate or pus). There may even be a foreign body in the ear canal (e.g. grass seed or piece of twig). In these cases it is best that you seek veterinary advice before attempting any cleaning.

Ear mites (*Otodectes cynotis*) are the most common cause of irritation and inflammation (otitis externa) of the ear in cats, especially the young, and, as described later (page 115), they cause the formation of dark wax and greyish crusts in the ear canal. This condition requires treatment with ear drops which contain a drug (an acaricide) to kill the mites. These are best obtained from your veterinary surgeon. But before each application, it is important to clean as much debris as possible from the ear canal to allow the drops to penetrate. *Never* put any form of powder into the ear; it tends to set like concrete and completely blocks the canal.

First, stand a small bottle of olive oil or liquid paraffin in a bowl of hot water until it is lukewarm. Do not heat it in a saucepan; it can get far too hot and scald the ear. Have some cotton wool handy and some cotton buds. Then place the cat on a working surface and if possible have someone else to help you restrain it. Grasping its scruff with your left hand (if right-handed), turn its head so that the ear is uppermost. Fill up the ear canal almost to the top with warm oil, and then gently massage the base of the ear with your fore-finger and thumb to loosen the debris. Wipe away excess oil with a swab of cotton wool wrapped around your finger. Repeat as necessary. During the application or removal of the oil it is usual for the cat to shake its head violently, so perform this cleaning somewhere where oil splashes can be tolerated. Then clean out all the remaining oil and debris by carefully using one or more of the cotton buds. Clean around all the folds of the ear but don't push too hard. Finally, you should apply the ear drops (usually from a squeezy plastic dropper bottle) and wipe any spilled oil from the cat's hair. If necessary repeat this procedure for the other ear.

Q *Should I ever clip my cat's claws?*

A Clipping cat's claws is usually necessary only if the claws have grown too long. This won't happen in cats that get plenty of exercise, stalking around the neighbourhood and climbing trees, because their claws are continually being worn down. In cats which are unwilling or unable to exercise sufficiently, due to old age, illness or simply because they are kept indoors most of the time, the claws can grow far too long and begin to catch on carpets and soft furnishings. A cat may even chew at these long nails to remove the frayed outer cuticle and expose a new claw underneath.

In old cats, the dewclaws on the inside of the front legs just above the paws never receive any wear and may grow so much that they turn a complete circle and begin to enter the skin again.

It is a good idea to check the length of the claws periodically. Bear in mind that those of the hind feet are naturally shorter than those at the front. If the claws are unpigmented (i.e. transparent), the pink quick which contains the blood vessels can be seen inside and normally reaches almost to the tip of the nail. If the nail extends beyond the quick, it is too long and either yourself or your veterinary surgeon can clip away the surplus, taking care not to cut into the quick which will cause bleeding. If the claw is pigmented (i.e. black), the quick cannot be seen and where to cut has to be judged from experience. Remember that there is a slight increase in the length of the quick as the claw grows longer, so that to cut back a very long claw to a 'normal' length may damage the quick; it is better to leave the nail a bit longer than usual and to trim it again a fortnight later.

The cat should be restrained on a table top by a helper and the claws of each foot trimmed in turn. Place the index finger of one hand on the pad below and behind the claw, and the thumb on the skin above the claw and by exerting gentle pressure between them the nail will be retracted and held firmly for clipping. Use a large pair of nail clippers with spring handles, not the folding type used for cutting finger nails. The design with two separate blades is often easier to position than the guillotine type. Never use scissors which will split and splinter the nail. Afterwards, any rough edges can be smoothed with a nail file or an emery board.

Make a clean cut straight across the nail, not one which slants. If by any chance some slight bleeding should occur, rapid clotting can be aided by holding a styptic pencil on the bleeding point; you could also apply a small piece of cotton wool or some inert powder, e.g. talcum powder or flour. Pushing the nail into a bar of soap will often control slight bleeding too. If there is more severe bleeding a pressure pad should be applied (see page 212) and veterinary attention obtained.

The only other reason for clipping a claw is if it has been fractured and the broken end is dangling from the rest of the nail. Ideally, this part should be clipped off completely and any haemorrhage controlled as before.

Clipping the claws merely to blunt them and so prevent the cat from damaging the furniture is often futile. The cat will usually sharpen them again at the first opportunity.

Q *I read somewhere that cat owners sometimes have their cats 'de-clawed:' Is this operation advisable if the animal is destructive?*

A Veterinary removal of the claws (onychectomy) is a painful mutilation which cannot be recommended under any circumstances. Cats with their nails removed are deprived of an important defence mechanism and have difficulty in climbing. Many continue to behave as if they were still able to sharpen their claws, and some undergo a profound personality change following surgery. The operation is very seldom performed in Great Britain, though more often, I am sorry to say, in North America. Any cat which has been de-clawed is automatically disqualified from cat shows under the rules which are in force in most countries. The operation is often performed at three to four months' old but if not properly performed one or more claws can grow back. If the only way you can tolerate a cat is after this dreadful mutilation, then you should not keep one at all.

Q *Do my cat's eyes ever need cleaning?*

A A small amount of dried exudate ('matter') often accumulates at the inner corner of the eye and should be wiped away with a piece of moistened cotton wool; never use it dry because this will stick to the eye surface.

In long-haired breeds of cats, it is common to get an accumulation of brownish matter at the inner corners of the eyes and permanent runs of tears down the face (see page 119). This matter should be bathed away with lukewarm water or boric acid solution (two 5 ml teaspoonsful of crystals in half a tumbler of warm water), and your vet consulted if it persists.

9
Signs of Illness

Q *What signs and symptoms are the most serious and require immediate professional attention?*

A In human medicine the term *symptoms* is usually reserved for sensations apparent only to the patient (i.e. which are purely subjective) such as feeling dizzy or having a painful knee; whereas *signs* are features which can be detected by an external observer, including the doctor. In veterinary medicine the inability of patients to communicate means that strictly speaking only signs are available for diagnosis; any sensations that are felt but produce no external manifestation remain hidden from us.

The following signs would indicate a real emergency that should receive immediate attention:

1 Severe bleeding.
2 Serious difficulty in breathing.
3 Collapse (i.e. being unable to stand).
4 Unconsciousness.
5 Fits (convulsions).
6 Shock (the signs of shock in the cat are essentially the same as in humans). There is rapid, shallow breathing (panting), the lips, gums and tongue appear pale, greyish and cold, the paws feel cold even in warm surroundings, and the animal often shivers and may vomit.

The necessary first aid treatment when any of these extremely serious signs appears is described in Chapter 14, but professional help should be obtained as soon as possible.

Accidents often produce severe injuries that should receive attention with the minimum of delay, for example:

1 Penetrating fractures (where the broken bones have been forced through the skin).
2 Paralysis.
3 The protrusion of internal organs (either through a natural opening or through a wound).
4 Severe burns or scalds.

Swift action is necessary on other occasions:

1 If you know or strongly suspect that your cat may have eaten some poisonous substance.

2 If it has or might have been bitten by a poisonous snake.

3 If it strains continuously (which includes a cat having difficulty giving birth).

4 If it is suffering from heat stroke (having been confined in an overheated area such as a car parked in direct sunlight), or from hypothermia (i.e. exposure to extreme cold).

Q *As animals can't communicate their feelings in words, how would I know if my cat is suffering?*

A In acutely painful conditions the cat resents being moved (including being lifted) and will flinch, cry, or even attempt to bite or scratch when the painful area is handled. In many illnesses the cat does not experience any severe pain but nevertheless is obviously feeling unwell or uncomfortable.

The general signs of illness to watch for are as follows:

1 General lack of interest in what is happening around it and in going outdoors – the cat appears depressed, dejected and listless.

2 Lying in its bed and sleeping much more than is usual.

3 Loss of appetite, with later loss of weight and possibly increased shedding of hair.

4 Failure to groom itself, or to sharpen its claws.

There may also be other specific signs, often developing later in an illness:

1 Vomiting and/or diarrhoea.

2 Sneezing and/or coughing.

3 Discharges from the eyes and/or nose.

4 Difficulty in eating, e.g. dropping food from the mouth, gulping and drooling saliva.

5 Protrusion of the third eyelids ('haws').

6 Repeated licking, biting, rubbing or scratching, especially at a particular part of the body.

7 Lameness.

8 Remaining in an unusual posture for long periods.

9 Laboured breathing.

10 Distension (i.e. swelling) of the abdomen.

Precisely what constitutes suffering is obviously open to individual interpretation, but an animal showing any of these signs must clearly be experiencing some discomfort. And the longer the signs persist then the more significant they become. It is worthwhile remembering, however, that it is normal for a female cat in heat to go off her food and to make calling noises suggestive of extreme pain, although in fact she is perfectly healthy.

Q *Should I always take my cat to the vet at the first sign of illness?*

A Generally speaking yes, and certainly if it is causing you anxiety. Most owners would prefer to know what, if anything, is wrong with their cat as soon as possible, and most vets would sooner that owners brought their animal for examination even for some trivial condition rather than to let a major illness go untreated.

Sometimes it is very clear from clinical signs that the animal is ill; for instance, when there is a sudden change in temperament from an active, inquisitive cat to one that is listless and interested only in sleeping; *or* where blood is being passed (in the motions, urine, or vomit); *or* where there is frequent sneezing with running eyes and nose.

At other times, when the cat appears normal in all respects save one, it can be difficult to decide whether this indicates the start of an illness or not. An isolated bout of coughing, or even vomiting, is not unusual – for example from a small hairball. Temporary lameness may simply be the result of minor bruising after jumping, nor is a day's inappetence uncommon, especially if the cat has been fed elsewhere. If the signs persist, certainly for longer than twenty-four hours, it would be wise to obtain a professional opinion. The *more signs* of illness there are (from the list in the previous question), the *more severe* they are, and the *longer* they persist, the more likely it is that the condition is of significance and should receive attention. Sometimes quite serious injuries can produce few signs; for example, after a road accident there may be very little to see except some damage to the claws, some dirt and oil on the coat and pallor due to internal haemorrhage. Whenever you are in doubt about the importance of changes you notice always ask your vet for advice.

Q *What signs indicate good health in the cat?*

A The healthy cat should appear alert and interested in what is happening around it, moving its eyes and ears in response to movements and sounds. It should be reasonably active and keen to explore its territory out-of-doors. The cat should present a sleek, well-groomed appearance with a clean glossy coat and bright, sparkling eyes which have no evidence of discharge at their corners. The skin should be elastic and unbroken, and the ears clean. The body should be firm and well-muscled, and warm to the touch. A healthy cat will almost certainly be observed grooming itself.

The animal should be neither thin nor overweight, and its movements should appear easy and supple without signs of pain or stiffness. The tongue and gums should be pale pink and the teeth clean and white.

The cat's appetite should be good, but not ravenous, and its thirst should not be excessive. There should be no difficulty in picking up or swallowing its food. Urine and motions should be passed without straining, and be normal in appearance (i.e. no abnormal colours or blood, the stools formed rather of a soft or liquid consistency).

Breathing should also be easy, without coughing, wheezing or exaggerated movements of the chest, and not unduly rapid (i.e. panting). Finally, the pulse rate and the temperature should be normal if taken; around 120 pulses per minute and 101.5°F (38.5°C), though both are slightly raised in very young animals.

Of course, for a cat to be completely healthy *all* of these signs should be present. However, it is not unusual to find cats that appear healthy in all respects save one; very thin cats who are still extremely active, or cats with skin disorders whose appetite and other behaviour is perfectly normal. But even a single abnormal sign should be investigated. Some signs popularly supposed to be reliable indicators of good health, namely purring and a wet nose, may in fact occur both in healthy cats and in those suffering from an illness.

Q *Should a healthy cat have a wet nose?*

A This certainly seems to be the case with most normal healthy cats. However, there is no evidence that the skin on the nose contains any special moisture-producing glands. The moisture on the nose seems to come from the cat licking its nose from time to time, but mainly from a watery secretion produced by glands in the lining of the nasal chambers which appears at the corners of the nostrils and spreads over the surface of the nasal skin. The prime functions of this nasal secretion are to increase the moisture content of the air inhaled and improve the sense of smell.

Cats that are dehydrated as a result of illness or a lack of liquid to drink, particularly those with obviously high body temperatures (e.g. in fevers), characteristically have a dry nose. Three factors may be involved:
1 Dehydrated cats produce less secretions, including both saliva and nasal secretion.
2 An increased body temperature will increase the evaporation of moisture from the nose.
3 The cat that is unwell neglects its normal habits, including grooming and licking its nose.

However, a dry nose is not reliable as a sign of illness; a cat that has been lying in front of a fire or radiator will also have a dry nose. (But if the dry nose is accompanied by other abnormal signs, such as listlessness and a lack of appetite, then it would be sensible to seek your vet's advice.) Conversely, a wet nose can be found in an animal with fever if it has recently had its nose in the water bowl. (Incidentally, the ridges on the nose pad form a pattern as unique in each cat as a human fingerprint.)

Q *Do healthy cats normally shed hair?*

A Yes, they do. Normal hairs undergo a cycle of growth, unlike the claws which grow continuously. Firstly, there is a period when the hair grows by the multiplication of cells at the bottom of the hair follicle deep in the skin; this phase is called anagen. This is followed by a period when the growth stops and the hair is retained in the follicle; this phase is called telogen. These non-growing or dead hairs, called 'club' hairs, are less firmly anchored than the growing hairs and consequently are more easily removed. Removal may be by grooming or simply by friction from sitting or lying. Eventually the cells which produce the hair begin to multiply again and a new hair is formed. This new hair grows up the follicle, alongside the old club hair if this is still present, though as the new hair emerges at the surface the old hair becomes detached and is shed.

In the cat, as in the dog and man, the growth of hairs is not synchronized, i.e. they are not all at the same stage at the same time. Adjacent hairs can be at any stage in the growth cycle – the so-called mosaic pattern of growth. However, in the cat the greatest activity (i.e. the most shedding of old hairs and growth of new ones) occurs in the late spring when the hours of daylight markedly increase. The periodicity of light has more influence than the environmental temperature. The underhairs (secondary hairs) often undergo a period of subsidiary growth activity in the late autumn (fall). Growth activity is minimal during the winter months.

The *rate* at which hairs grow in the cat averages one hundredth of an inch (0.25 to 0.3 mm) per day, and is also least in the winter and greatest in the late spring. The sex of the cat and whether it has been neutered have little effect on either the growth cycle or the growth rate. However, in generalized disease or ill health the total number of hairs in the resting phase increases so that increased shedding of hair can be a sign of illness. Also, in some hormonal (endocrine) disorders, many hairs enter the resting stage at the same time and are therefore shed simultaneously. Severe damage to hairs, for example by ringworm, may cause them to break off, leaving a stubble.

Q *My cat drools saliva a lot. Is this normal?*

A Cats with a severe dental problem (see page 103) or with a foreign body stuck in their mouths usually salivate profusely, as do cats poisoned with organophosphorus compounds (e.g. certain weedkillers or an overdose of some preparations to kill fleas). However, in all these instances the animals will show other abnormal signs; pawing at the mouth and loss of appetite with oral disorders; vomiting and trembling with organophosphorus poisoning.

Perfectly healthy cats will produce large amounts of saliva, which drips from their mouths, if they are frightened or excited. The panic that seizes some cats when they are handled, for example to give a pill, causes stimulation of that part of the nervous system called the parasympathetic nervous system and the cat proceeds to drool. (The problem can also occur with some tablets which contain bitter ingredients protected by an outer coating. If such tablets are broken or crushed before being given to the cat, they will produce spectacular frothing at the mouth which is very distressing to the cat.)

A cat will also salivate profusely in a hot environment and spread saliva over the coat with its tongue. The resultant evaporation of the saliva from the coat removes heat from the body (latent heat of vaporization) which serves to cool the body and thereby helps maintain a constant body temperature. This process achieves the same effect as sweating in humans; sweating is not important in regulating the body temperature of the cat.

In some cats, salivation on being stroked can often occur in conjunction with purring, head-rubbing and treading (kneading) movements of the feet. This is an indication of the cat's delight at seeing you. Excessive salivation is also a feature of a display of aggression, most commonly preceding a cat fight.

Q *What does it mean if my cat is always scratching himself?*

A Scratching is the cat's response to an itch in the skin, otherwise called pruritus. Itching can have a number of causes: allergic reactions, inflammation due to chemicals on the coat, the bites of insects or arachnids (e.g. fleas or ear mites), infection with bacteria and foreign bodies in the skin. All of these cause the release of proteolytic enzymes which attack nerve endings in the skin and trigger the release of electrical impulses that then pass via nerves to the brain. Although both are unpleasant, itching and pain are regarded as separate sensations. In the cat, scratching is *most commonly* due either to the irritation of ear mites (see page 115), or to flea infestation (see page 149).

It is, of course, important to establish the true cause and then to remove it if possible. Consequently, your veterinary surgeon should be consulted at an early stage.

Scratching, and also biting and chewing, can result in extensive self-mutilation, and while the cause is being brought under control it may be necessary to administer internally, or apply externally, drugs to control the itch. It may even be necessary to protect the area which is being damaged, for example by fitting an Elizabethan collar (page 201). Sometimes firm pressure, or the application of heat or cold, will relieve the itching, at least temporarily. Scratching can be made worse by boredom or depression, so that whenever possible a scratching animal should be distracted, for example by being fed, played with or being allowed outdoors.

Q *The cats in my neighbourhood are always fighting. How would I know if my cat had been bitten?*

A Bites are usually found on tom cats. They occur out of inter-male rivalry for mates and for territory. But occasionally castrated males, and sometimes even females, get into fights and are wounded. In a fight, the parts of the body which usually get bitten are the front legs or head as the two adversaries face each other, and the tail or hind-quarters as one cat turns to run away. However, when two cats are rolling on the floor in a fight almost any part can get bitten. Occasionally, female cats can develop an abscess on the neck from the over-enthusiastic gripping of the skin by a male as he mounts her to mate.

Typically, a cat bite is produced by the two long canine teeth (the top and bottom teeth on one side of the jaw) penetrating the skin and under-lying tissues. These teeth are sharp and narrow and so the wounds that are created on the skin surface are very small, bleed very little and soon close over. They are also well hidden by the hair coat. Any blood is usually soon removed when the cat retires afterwards to literally lick his wounds. Therefore, unless there is some very obvious sign after the fight such as a torn ear, you may be unable to tell that your cat has been fighting. However, a cat can remain excited for a long time after a serious fight and attempts on your part to soothe the animal may be rewarded by quite serious bites or scratches.

One or two days after the fight has occurred you may notice some of the following signs:

1 Your cat limps on one leg or is unwilling to move a particular part of his body such as the neck or tail.

2 He flinches, cries or becomes aggressive when you touch a particular part of his body.

3 He loses interest in food and only wants to rest.

These signs are due to a developing abscess at the site of the bite. Bacteria from the biting cat's mouth and on the bitten cat's skin and hair get pushed deep down into the subcutaneous tissue by the long teeth. The surface of the skin closes over and starts to heal because the punctured wound is so small, and the bacteria deep in the tissues begin to multiply and produce toxins. These toxins cause inflammation at the site and they are also carried in the blood to other parts of the body. In severe cases, their effect on the brain is to produce a loss of appetite and listlessness, usually with a rise in body temperature.

To confirm that a bite is responsible, examine the area very closely. Somewhere there will be two tiny wounds about $\frac{1}{2}$ to 1 inch (1.25–2.5 cm) apart; on a limb or on the tail the wounds are usually on opposite sides. You may feel them first as two small, rough scabs and on parting the hair you see two scab-filled wounds with a tiny dot of dried blood in the centre.

As a result of the continuing battle between the bacteria and the body's defensive white blood cells, pus is gradually formed (this consists of dead and living bacteria, dead and living white blood cells and inflammatory exudate) and the resulting lesion is called an abscess. As the abscess becomes well-defined the inflammation and the pain become less, though bacterial toxins are still being absorbed, so that there may still be a poor appetite and general lassitude. However, these signs are not always present.

It may be possible to feel the abscess as a soft fluctuating mass beneath the skin and eventually, if left, it would burst, usually on to the surface as the skin is gradually eroded from beneath. This discharge of a mixture of pus and blood is sometimes the first thing that an owner knows about the affair. Some abscesses can be enormous and damage a lot of skin which then sloughs away.

At whatever stage these bite wounds are discovered, veterinary attention should be obtained. Treatment may be with hot bathing (hot fomentations), surgical excision of the abscess and/or antibiotic administration (injections, tablets or creams) depending on the stage of the process. Once the abscess has been opened or has burst and then been cleaned, the aim is for the wound to heal. This should happen from the deepest part outwards so that the skin is the *last* to knit together. Otherwise, the infection will be locked in again and further abscesses will develop as a result. Initially the application of hydrogen peroxide and later regular bathing and the insertion of anti-bacterial creams into the wound help to achieve this.

Bacteria from bite wounds can also spread to other parts of the body; bites in the chest region may give rise to pus in the chest (pyothorax). Of course, abscesses can also arise for reasons not associated at all with bites, e.g. an infected tooth socket, which necessitates removing the tooth and draining the abscess.

Q *My cat keeps shaking his head. Is there anything wrong with him?*

A For the majority of cats it signifies that one or usually both ears are infected with ear mites (*Otodectes cynotis*), a condition referred to popularly as 'ear mange' or sometimes 'canker'. (Canker has nothing to do with cancer, despite the similarity of spelling.)

The mites are so small that with the eye alone they can hardly be distinguished inside the ear canal. However, with a magnifying glass they can be seen as small, whitish specks moving slowly over the lining of the canal. Veterinarians usually use a combined magnifying glass and light source, an auriscope or otoscope, to view the ear. When some of the wax from the ear is placed under a microscope the mites can be easily identified.

Ear mites do not penetrate the skin but live and breed on the surface, grazing on the dead skin cells and possibly sucking lymph from the skin vessels.

Although many cats can have a small number of ear mites and show no obvious signs of discomfort, in some cats their activity produces considerable inflammation and irritation of the outer ear (otitis externa). This causes the cat to shake, rub and scratch its ears almost constantly. The cat often inflicts dreadful damage upon itself with its claws by ripping at the ear flaps and the skin of the head behind them, often causing wounds and bleeding. This continuous rubbing can often cause all the hair to be removed from the skin behind the ear and from between the ear and the eye. Also a blood blister (haematoma) may be formed in the ear flap which should be drained surgically, otherwise the flap will distort into a 'cauliflower ear' in healing.

In response to the irritation in the ear canal, a large amount of dark brown wax is formed which dries into crusts in the ear.

In most cases the ear mites are easily eliminated by cleaning the ears and applying a parasiticidal preparation, usually as ear drops, for a few days. Both ears should be treated and, because the mites are readily transmitted between animals, *all* the dogs and cats in the household should be treated simultaneously, whether they are showing signs yet or not. Mites can also travel to other parts of the body and so it is a good idea to treat the whole body with a parasiticidal spray or powder.

Much less common is bacterial infection in the ear, or objects such as grass seeds or grit in the canal. These can also cause an irritation which gives rise to head shaking. To identify the cause the cat is best examined by your veterinary surgeon who can supply the appropriate medication.

Q *My cat's gums and lips look very pale; does this mean that he is suffering from anaemia?*

A No, not necessarily. In many cats the gums, lips and palate (which are the most easily examined mucous membranes) together with the inner lining of the eyelids and the tongue may appear a very pale pink. But in most of these animals laboratory tests establish that there is actually no anaemia, i.e. no deficiency of red blood cells or of the red oxygen-carrying pigment (haemoglobin) which the cells contain. Clearly, pallor of the mucous membranes is a normal feature of many cats.

Apart from anaemia the other important cause of extreme pallor of these membranes is shock. This usually follows some form of injury and is accompanied by other signs which are so obvious (extreme weakness, panting, cold paws even in warm surroundings, trembling and often loss of consciousness) that it is usually easy to diagnose.

In anaemia the lack of haemoglobin to carry sufficient oxygen to the tissues causes the animal to tire easily and to breathe rapidly even after only mild exertion. In severe cases the heart beats rapidly even when resting.

Q *What causes anaemia in cats?*

A Three main causes of anaemia are recognized. One is the severe loss of cells due to bleeding (haemorrhagic anaemia) which can occur suddenly if a major blood vessel is severed. Less obviously, a slow but persistent loss of blood can produce this type of anaemia, e.g. from a heavy infestation with blood-sucking parasites such as fleas, or from poisoning with the anti-

116

coagulant rat poison warfarin which both damages the blood vessels and prevents the escaping blood from clotting.

Haemolytic anaemia arises from the destruction of red blood cells within the circulation. This can be caused by the blood parasite *Haemobartonella felis* or by bacterial toxins, or by such poisons as lead, phenol and chlorate and the drugs phenacetin and sulphafurazole (sulphasoxazole).

Finally, anaemia may be due to a failure of the red bone marrow contained within certain bones to produce sufficient replacement cells to keep pace with natural losses (hypoplastic anaemia). Because each red blood cell survives for about ten to eleven weeks it can take a long time for this defective production to result in discernible anaemia. It can develop if the cat is deprived of adequate amounts of the raw materials necessary for the production of red blood cells such as iron, protein, and vitamin B.

Damage to the bone marrow can also be responsible for hypoplastic anaemia; rarely this is due to bone marrow tumours or excessive doses of radiation. In the cat the most likely cause of bone marrow damage is drugs. Cats have greater difficulty than many other species in detoxicating many drugs, i.e. breaking them down in the liver to harmless substances which can be excreted. They are therefore particularly at risk from any toxic side-effects which a drug may possess. Drugs known to damage the bone marrow in the cat include the antibiotic chloramphenicol, insecticides and aspirin. In fact, aspirin has two effects which in combination produce anaemia very rapidly. It causes ulceration and haemorrhages in various organs, particularly the intestines, and because of the effect on the bone marrow the blood cells that are lost cannot be effectively replaced. Aspirin also has toxic effects on the liver and is extremely harmful to cats. A daily dose of half a 300 mg tablet will kill most cats in two to three weeks.

Q *If my cat should be involved in an accident, how would I know if he were dead or just unconscious?*

A The important distinguishing features are that in unconsciousness breathing and the beating of the heart are both present; in death both will have stopped.

An unconscious cat can resemble a dead animal in that there may be no movement for a long period, and during this time it may not respond to such stimuli as noise or pinching. In both conditions, the muscles relax, i.e. become limp, and relaxation of the sphincters of the bladder and anus may permit urine and motions to be passed. Bear in mind that in death the eyes do not close automatically; they may remain open just as they might in unconsciousness, so this cannot be used as a distinguishing sign.

However, two signs are characteristic of death. Firstly, the body will *gradually* become colder (how cold depends on the temperature of the surroundings), and within three to seven hours the muscles become rigid (rigor mortis), a sure sign of death.

How to find your cat's heartbeat

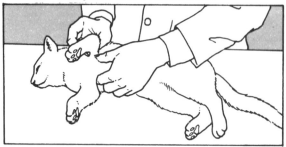

Place your hand around the lower part of the chest – between, or just behind, the forelegs. If fingers and thumb are on opposite sides the heartbeat should be felt between them. If not, alter their position slightly and feel again.

Your cat's third eyelid

Normally the third eyelid (or haw) stays at the inner corner of each eye. But when a cat is debilitated its eyeballs sink further back so that these eyelids pass over the front of the eyes. As weight is regained they return to the corners.

Q *A skin has suddenly appeared across both my cat's eyes. It looks so frightening. What does it mean?*

A This skin or membrane is in fact a third eyelid (called the nictitating membrane) which is well developed in the cat and can be seen in the inner corner of the eye as a small pink flap. Popularly, it's called the 'haw'. Although the condition does look alarming, the movement of this membrane across both eyes does not signify a loss of sight or some other eye disorder, but a generalized loss of condition.

Fat is laid down in the body mainly beneath the skin and around the kidneys, but there is also a pad of fat at the back of the eyeball where it lies in a socket in the skull, the orbit. This pad of fat, which is semi-liquid at body temperature, helps provide protection for the eyeball if it should be pushed back on to the underlying hard bone of the skull, i.e. it cushions the impact of blows to the eyeball. However, when the animal is debilitated (following diarrhoea or some other disorder associated with loss of weight and condition) the reserves of fat begin to be broken down to provide essential energy. The reduction in the amount of fat in the orbit allows the eyeball to sink further into the socket. This 'sinking' of the eyeball permits the third eyelid to move further than usual across the front of the eye. When the animal gains weight and replaces its fat reserves the eye moves forwards again and the third eyelid is pushed back into its normal position at the inner corner of the eye.

With debility then, both eyes are affected in this way, though not necessarily to the same degree. Where there is a membrane across only one eye it *may* be due to a more serious condition involving nerve damage or the growth of a tumour, or there might be a foreign body (e.g. a grass seed) in that eye, and therefore advice should be sought immediately.

Q *My cat seems healthy but has two wet streaks down his face. It looks as if he has been crying. Why is this?*

A Humans have the distinction of being the only species to display their emotions by crying (and incidentally by laughing as well), so although your cat won't be happy about this condition, it isn't crying that is responsible. However, these wet streaks *are* due to tears (lacrimal fluid) overflowing down the face. On white cats this condition (epiphora) produces a characteristic ginger-brown stain.

Where this is a long-standing problem, unassociated with any irritation or inflammation (such as with injuries, foreign bodies in the eye or respiratory diseases), it usually arises because the ducts (naso-lacrimal ducts) which normally drain the fluid from the surface of the eye are unable to take all, or any, of the fluid. It occurs especially in cats with flattened faces, such as Persians.

Lacrimal fluid is continuously secreted by a gland above the eyeball for the purpose of washing away micro-organisms and dust from the surface of the eyeball, aided by the occasional wiper action of the eyelids in blinking. In normal cats the fluid then passes down the naso-lacrimal ducts into the nasal chambers, but if the ducts become blocked, or if the bulging of the eyeballs prevents the fluid reaching the duct opening, as in flat-faced cats, it has no alternative but to flow down the front of the face. Blocked ducts can sometimes be unblocked, but this is a time-consuming procedure necessitating a general anaesthetic.

---- IO ----

Infectious Diseases
and Vaccination

Q *What are the important infectious diseases of cats?*

A Infectious diseases are, by definition, specific diseases caused by micro-organisms (bacteria, viruses, fungi and protozoa) – popularly called microbes or germs. They are far too small to be seen by the naked eye. The important infectious diseases of cats are indicated in the table on page 121. This importance is not necessarily because the disease commonly occurs, although some do, but also because of the severity of the illness and its public health significance, i.e. the risk of it being transferred to human contacts. More information about these diseases is given later in the chapter.

The other diseases listed are either uncommon, or else produce only mild signs of illness, if any.

Viruses You will see that most of the important infectious diseases are due to viruses. The common condition, feline urological syndrome, which was mentioned on page 64, is placed in square brackets in the list because, although an important condition, it is not clear how significant viruses are in its causation. Certainly, current veterinary opinion regards dry cat food as being at least as important, if not more so, in its development than viral infection.

Reoviruses, though isolated from cases of feline respiratory disease, do not appear to play a major role in the condition. Aujesky's disease (pseudo-rabies) is seen in North America and most other countries, particularly in rural areas, but not in Britain or Australia. It affects the brain of many species including cats, but not humans. It is generally believed that most cats become infected by eating already infected rats. An infected cat becomes excited, mews persistently, salivates but cannot swallow, and frequently shows signs of intense itching, often scratching an area raw. Death invariably occurs within thirty-six hours of these signs appearing, whether treatment is given or not. In many respects the disease resembles rabies, though it runs a shorter course and attacks on humans are not a feature of it.

Table I Infectious Diseases of Cats

VIRAL DISEASES
* Feline infectious enteritis (FIE) = feline panleukopenia (FPL)
  Feline respiratory disease (FRD) = feline influenza (cat 'flu)
  * Feline viral rhinotracheitis (FVR)
  * Feline calicivirus disease (FCD)
    Feline reovirus infection
* Feline leukaemia
* Feline infectious peritonitis (FIP)
* Rabies
* Pseudorabies (= Aujesky's disease)
* [Feline urological syndrome (FUS)]

FUNGAL DISEASES
* Ringworm (= dermatomycosis)
  Candidiasis (= moniliasis)
  Mycetoma (= maduromycosis)
  Cryptococcosis
  Blastomycosis
  Coccidioidomycosis
  Histoplasmosis

BACTERIAL DISEASES
* Feline infectious anaemia (FIA) = feline haemobartonellosis
* [Trench mouth (= Vincent's stomatitis)]
  Feline respiratory disease (FRD) = feline influenza (cat 'flu)
      Feline pneumonitis
      Mycoplasm infection
  Tetanus
  Tuberculosis (TB)
  Salmonellosis
  Nocardiosis
  Actinomycosis
  Listeriosis
  Pseudotuberculosis
  Feline leprosy

PROTOZOAN DISEASES
* Toxoplasmosis
  Other forms of coccidiosis
  Giardiasis
  Entamoebiasis

---

* Asterisks denote most common or most serious diseases
[ ] Diseases in square brackets are often not regarded as infectious diseases, though there are grounds for including them

Bacteria There are a very limited number of bacterial species which produce specific diseases in the cat and these are shown in the table. A further small number of other bacteria (of which staphylococci, streptococci, pasteurellae, *E. coli*, *Proteus* and *Pseudomonas* are the most important) are responsible for causing a variety of diseases at different sites of the body (e.g. pyodermas, arthritis, enteritis, mastitis, pharyngitis, otitis, etc.). In terms of the total number of animals affected with disease, this latter group is far and away the most important, but the disorders which they produce are not classified as infectious diseases. In general they are regarded as normal inhabitants of the body (especially on the skin and bowel) which only cause disease when its defences are impaired.

Feline infectious anaemia (otherwise called feline haemobartonellonis) and trench mouth (or Vincent's stomatitis) are two common conditions with specific causes. Trench mouth (so-called because the condition was common in soldiers in the trenches during World War I) is due to a combination of spirochaete and fusiform bacteria, and produces inflammation of the gums (gingivitis) and a painful mouth with halitosis. Untreated, it can result in destruction of bone and loss of the teeth. It is reputedly more common in the Siamese breed. (The condition is placed in square brackets in the table because it is not often classed as an infectious disease, although it seems appropriate to include it here.)

Mycoplasms and *Chlamydia* are bacterial agents that may sometimes play a part, though a relatively minor one, in the development of feline respiratory disease (cat 'flu). (At times, mycoplasms may also possibly cause abortion in cats.)

Tetanus (lockjaw) is a rare condition in the cat, as are the chronic conditions of nocardosis, actinomycosis (both of which chiefly affect the lungs), listeriosis and pseudotuberculosis.

Tuberculosis (TB) is also rare in cats in those countries where the general incidence of the disease in man and animals is low. However, cases do arise, usually due to drinking infected 'raw' (i.e. untreated) cows' milk, but sometimes caught from owners. Feline salmonellosis is an unusual, though highly contagious, disease causing gastro-enteritis and fever. Cats suffering from tuberculosis or salmonellosis can transmit these diseases to humans, and they represent a considerable public health risk.

Feline leprosy is an uncommon, chronic disease reported from most countries and caused by a bacterium similar to that responsible for tuberculosis. It produces multiple, soft nodules in the skin which are painless but which frequently ulcerate.

Fungi The most widespread fungal condition of the cat is undoubtedly ringworm, which affects the hair, skin and nails. Candidiasis, due to a yeast (*Candida albicans*), very occasionally produces lesions on the skin and in the mouth. The other fungal diseases mentioned occur principally in certain regions of North America. They are rare, and all develop slowly.

Cryptococcosis principally affects the respiratory and nervous systems, mycetoma affects the skin and nose and the other three listed generally involve the respiratory tract, causing wasting with a chronic cough and high temperature.

Protozoa Of the parasitic protozoa which may infect the cat, few produce any ill effects. However, toxoplasmosis can result in severe illness at times, affecting both the cat and other species which may become infected.

Q *Can I clear up a point. When you speak of infection is this the same as a disease?*

A No it is not, and it is very important to appreciate the difference. *Infection* denotes that the particular micro-organism has become established in, or on, the cat's body. However, this does not necessarily result in disease; indeed many micro-organisms (called *commensals*) normally live on the skin, throughout the alimentary tract, and in the outer parts of the respiratory, urinary and reproductive systems without causing disease. Only if the animal's normal defence mechanisms are damaged or weakened (e.g. due to starvation, cold or previous illness), allowing these commensals to invade other areas, will they then produce disease. Even when *known disease-producing* organisms (pathogens) are present in the body they do not *always* cause disease. Individuals who can harbour pathogens *without showing signs of the disease* are known as carriers.

The *incubation period* of an infectious disease is the interval of time between the organisms responsible becoming established in the body (infection occurring) and signs of disease appearing.

Carriers are of two types: firstly, there are those individuals who have had a disease and have shown the usual clinical signs (i.e. the signs typical of that disease). *But,* even after recovery, they do not completely rid themselves of the organism responsible, either for a long time or in some cases, ever. These are called *convalescent carriers.* For instance, approximately 80% of cats that recover from feline rhinotracheitis become carriers of that virus.

Secondly, there are some infected individuals who *never* show clinical signs of the disease. These are called *healthy carriers,* or alternatively *immune carriers.* These animals have a natural resistance (innate immunity) to the particular pathogen and are not themselves affected by it. For example, some cats show no obvious evidence of ringworm infection.

Q *My neighbour has advised me to have my cat vaccinated against feline infectious enteritis. How important is this disease?*

A Well, your neighbour is quite right to advise vaccination because this is a very serious cat disease common in all countries. The virus is highly contagious and cats usually develop signs within a week to ten days of becoming infected. Infection occurs either by direct contact (i.e. with already infected cats) or indirect contact (meaning contact with objects infected with the virus). Some recovered cats can act as carriers and continue to excrete the virus for some while afterwards. Fleas can also transmit the disease from one cat to another. The virus is one of a group (parvoviruses) that are very resistant to destruction; they will withstand most disinfectants, except aldehydes and the hypochlorite bleaches, and can survive in the surroundings for more than a year. The virus is, however, killed by boiling.

Sometimes the virus causes sudden death, leading to the suspicion that the cat has been poisoned. This occurs primarily in young cats, who are always more seriously affected by infectious diseases. In general, however, it causes an acute disease attacking the rapidly multiplying cells of the intestine and the bone marrow. This accounts for its two common names of feline infectious enteritis (FIE), enteritis meaning inflammation of the intestine, and feline panleukopenia (FPL), panleukopenia being a generalized reduction in the number of white blood cells which are produced by the bone marrow. The latter name is more commonly used in North America.

Q *How would I know if my cat had got feline infectious enteritis?*

A The cat develops a high temperature accompanied by lethargy and a loss of appetite, plus severe frothy vomiting, and later diarrhoea in which blood often appears. The fluid lost in the vomit and diarrhoea leads to dehydration, which can be demonstrated by a loss of skin elasticity; when a fold of skin is drawn up and released, instead of 'flowing' back into place, the skin fold remains stiffly standing up and only slowly subsides.

Characteristically, the cat hovers over its water bowl, but seldom tries to drink, and it often cries with abdominal pain. Treatment requires intravenous fluid replacement, and, in severe cases, even blood transfusion. There are no anti-viral drugs readily available, but antibiotics are given to prevent secondary bacterial infection. All infected bedding should be destroyed, the surroundings well disinfected, and any incoming cats isolated. Hyperimmune serum is useful in preventing the development of the disease in cats that have been in contact with clinical cases but which are not yet showing signs themselves.

Most untreated cats will collapse and die within three to five days, so that survival beyond five days is an optimistic sign. However, even cats that recover may have permanent intestinal damage resulting in frequent bouts of diarrhoea. Infection in females in early pregnancy can lead to abortion or resorption of the foetuses. Infection just before birth, or just after can interfere with the development of the cerebellum (the part of the brain responsible for controlling balance) so that affected kittens stagger about and may tremble (juvenile ataxia due to cerebellar hypoplasia). This may not become apparent until about four weeks after birth because before then all kittens seem badly co-ordinated. Because of these dangers, pregnant females should not be vaccinated with *live* vaccines.

Where a cat has died from the disease, other animals should be excluded from the premises for six months, and even then not allowed entry unless vaccinated.

Q *Is cat 'flu the same as human 'flu?*

A No it is not, although the disease known popularly, especially in Britain, as cat 'flu, or feline influenza, is *similar* to human influenza both in some of the signs which occur and in being initiated by viral infection. But the viruses responsible in the cat and in man are quite different. Humans do not get cat 'flu, and vice versa.

In North America cat 'flu is generally known as feline respiratory disease (FRD) or upper respiratory tract infection.

A number of organisms have been incriminated in causing this feline disease and the clinical signs do vary depending on which is responsible. Only rarely is more than one organism involved in a particular animal. At least 80% of cases are due to one of two viruses which appear to be equally important: feline viral rhinotracheitis (FVR) virus and feline calicivirus (FCV). These two viruses are spread from cat to cat mainly by direct and indirect contact, and, perhaps surprisingly, to a much lesser extent by 'aerosol' infection (i.e. the inhalation of droplets, resulting from coughing and sneezing, which contain the virus particles). Therefore, spread mainly takes place wherever large numbers of cats are gathered together, for example in boarding catteries, breeding colonies and cat shows. FRD may be seen in kittens as early as three to four weeks of age where infection is derived from a carrier queen.

FCV survives no longer than ten days away from the cat and FVR virus probably only one day. Therefore, residual environmental contamination is less important than with FIE (FPL). FVR virus is readily killed by most disinfectants; FCV resists certain of them but is destroyed by aldehydes, alcohol and hypochlorite bleaches. The last named are strongly recommended for routine use with cats e.g. diluted Chlorox or Domestos.

Feline reoviruses cause only mild signs such as conjunctivitis (inflammation of the front of the eyeball causing runny eyes) and are thought not to be very important. Also, the bacterial organisms *Chlamydia* (the cause of feline pneumonitis in North America) and the mycoplasms are believed to play only minor roles in feline respiratory disease.

As with most other diseases, bacteria already present in the body may take advantage of a cat's weakened immunity to multiply and invade, and this secondary bacterial infection can lead to pneumonia (inflammation of the lungs) developing.

Q *How can I tell if my cat has cat 'flu (feline respiratory disease)?*

A In general, FVR is a more serious condition than FCV disease. In both, signs appear within ten days of being infected.

Feline Viral Rhinotracheitis FVR virus attacks the nasal chambers and the conjunctiva, producing profuse discharges and sneezing, as well as the trachea, sometimes resulting in a harsh cough. Increased salivation is also seen and there is a rise in temperature accompanied by depression and a loss of appetite.

The discharges from the eyes and nose are at first very liquid; later they become thicker and purulent as secondary bacterial infection develops. This may cause the eyelids to become gummed together and the nostrils blocked, causing difficulty in breathing. Inflammation and ulceration of the cornea in the eye (ulcerative keratitis) and of the tongue (ulcerative glossitis) can occur.

Pregnant queens may abort and therefore (as with FIE) they should not be vaccinated with live vaccines.

Some improvement usually appears after a week and most signs disappear after three to four weeks, though during this period the combination of pain in the mouth and throat, the loss of the senses of taste and smell and the overwhelming feeling of wretchedness make it difficult to persuade cats to eat or drink. Deaths are usually due to dehydration or the development of pneumonia, particularly in kittens or elderly cats, though, fortunately, overall the mortality is low.

In some recovered cats, known as 'snufflers', the infection and inflammation of the nasal chambers persists or recurs, and they show sneezing and snuffling and occasionally a runny nose. In a few, the bacterial infection spreads to the sinuses (cavities within the skull bones), blocking them with thick, sticky discharges and causing pain and swelling between the eyes.

Feline Calicivirus Disease Whereas there is only one strain of FVR virus, there are many different strains of FCV, which vary in their virulence. Some of them produce a disease as severe as FVR while others cause signs so mild as to be undetectable. A characteristic feature is ulceration of the tongue and sometimes also of the palate and nostrils. At times, the paws are eroded. Oculo-nasal discharges (i.e. from eyes and nose), if they occur, are less profuse and most cats are much less depressed. Although in some kittens the disease can prove fatal, in general the signs disappear within ten days or so.

Q *How is cat 'flu treated and controlled, and what can I do to help?*

A As in FIE, your vet may advise the intravenous administration of fluid to counteract dehydration, plus the administration of antibiotics, often in the form of syrups (which are easier to swallow) to control secondary bacterial infection. It may be necessary to resort to artificial feeding in hospital, down a tube inserted through the side of the neck (pharyngostomy tube).

Nursing is of paramount importance in treating feline respiratory disease. Cats should be kept warm in well-ventilated surroundings and the discharges and saliva regularly wiped and bathed away, particularly when the eyelids are gummed together or the nostrils blocked. If the eyelids are not bathed until they can be parted and the discharge beneath them removed, the damage done to the eyeball may be irreversible, resulting in blindness. Placing a smear of petroleum jelly around the eyes and beneath the nose helps to avoid the discharges scalding the skin.

Inhalations of water vapour or vaporized inhalents can be given to help unblock the nasal cavities (as described on page 193). Every attempt should be made to persuade the cat to eat (page 73), and regular grooming and attention are also important in increasing the cat's sense of well-being and giving it the will to fight back. Cats who suffer from difficulty in breathing should be carefully handled to avoid any worsening of their condition. Some chronic 'snufflers' improve if they are housed outdoors. Operations are sometimes resorted to, to drain infected sinuses or remove diseased nasal bones, but often with disappointing results.

All feeding bowls, beds and bedding used by an infected cat, as well as its surrounding environment, should be thoroughly disinfected to limit the spread of the virus. Wearing rubber gloves, which are changed before handling each cat in a colony and then disinfected, reduces transmission from cat to cat. An infected cat should be isolated from all others and new arrivals should be isolated for fourteen days (in case they are incubating the disease) to see whether signs of illness appear.

Cats that have poor immunity or are suffering from stress (e.g. poor nutrition, ill-health from other causes, low environmental temperature, abandonment) are more likely to become infected. Protection can be given by vaccination (usually as two shots three to four weeks apart) which can be combined with vaccination for FIE. Also available is a vaccine which is given as *one* dose in the form of drops placed into the nasal cavities. This intra-nasal vaccine stimulates local immunity in the nose very quickly (within forty-eight hours), thereby blocking the entry of virus by this route. It is believed that this local immunity will be produced even if the maternal antibodies are still present in the blood. Later the cat will develop antibodies in the blood, provided maternal antibodies are absent (see page 139).

However, although more complete protection is provided by the intra-nasal vaccine, about half of the cats receiving it show after-effects of conjunctivitis and rhinitis (runny eyes and nose) and in some this lasts for two to three weeks afterwards. The vaccination for cat 'flu should be boosted at least annually.

Approximately 80% of the animals which recover from FVR continue to carry the virus in their bodies (i.e. become carriers) though they will not usually excrete it unless they are exposed to stress, such as other infections or poor feeding, etc. Between 10 and 40% of cats recovering from FCV infection shed the virus for a month or more afterwards, the higher proportion being in colonies of cats. 25% of cats at cat shows have been found to excrete this virus. Some of them remain life-long carriers and excreters of virus. Such carriers are obviously an important source of infection for other cats, particularly since they may look quite normal and healthy, although fortunately tests are now available which can distinguish them. At times even vaccinated cats may, if they are exposed to a really virulent strain of virus, become carriers.

Q *What sort of a disease is feline leukaemia? Is it like leukaemia in humans?*

A The term 'leukaemia' is used (in any species, e.g. cat, dog or man) when some of the white blood cells circulating in the blood-stream show evidence of cancer. These cells show characteristic cancerous changes which can be recognized under the microscope.

In man and in the dog the cause of leukaemia is not yet established but in the cat it is known to be due to a virus, which has therefore been named feline leukaemia virus, or FeLV for short.

In fact the name of the disease is misleading since most cats infected with this virus do not develop leukaemia, and a much more common problem is that the virus causes cancerous growths (malignant tumours) called lymphosarcomas to develop in one or more of the lymphoid tissues of the body. These are the lymph nodes, the thymus (an organ at the front of the chest), the spleen (an organ in the abdomen) or in the wall of the intestines. The signs shown by affected cats vary according to the site of the growth; for instance, growths in the thymus (which are most common in young cats, especially Siamese) produce difficulty in breathing; in the intestine – diarrhoea; in the lymph nodes of the throat – difficulty in swallowing. They may also grow in other organs, such as the kidneys, nose and nervous tissue.

Furthermore, because cells from the lymphoid tissue are responsible for producing the various antibodies which give immunity against different diseases, the damage to lymphoid tissue produced by FeLV can result in the cat's, especially the young cat's, inability to develop or maintain adequate immunity against a variety of disease-producing organisms. This means that affected cats are more likely to develop such diseases as gingivitis (inflammation of the gums), feline infectious anaemia (FIA), feline infectious peritonitis (FIP) and respiratory infections.

In some cats, including half of those with lymphosarcoma, the virus causes anaemia (a lack of red blood cells) in addition to the other problems. This is because the virus either destroys a large number of the circulating red blood cells, or damages the red bone marrow which produces *new* red blood cells.

The virus can also damage developing foetuses inside the mother causing them to die during pregnancy, either early (not detectable and usually attributed to infertility), or late (abortion), or soon after birth ('fading kittens').

If one or more of these conditions occurs in a group of cats kept together (e.g. in a single household), the possibility of infection with FeLV should be considered.

Q *How can I tell if my cat is infected with FeLV?*

A Currently, there are three tests available which can be performed by certain laboratories (possibly even your vet's own practice laboratory) on a small blood sample collected from your cat. These are a virus isolation test, an immunofluorescent test, and an immunosorbent assay ('Leukassay').

The interpretation of results depends on which test is used. Using more than one can provide valuable confirmatory evidence. In general it is advisable to *repeat* the test(s) three months later. This is because some cats which at first give a negative result may be in the incubation stage of the disease and will later show positive, and some cats appearing positive initially may recover (i.e. get rid of the virus) and then give a negative reading.

Furthermore, not every cat with lymphosarcoma gives evidence of FeLV infection, although the majority do, because lymphosarcoma does have other causes.

Q *What should I do if my cat is found to be infected with FeLV?*

A Unfortunately, there is no effective treatment currently available against *any viral disease*. Therefore the animal cannot be cured and around 70% of infected cats will die inside eighteen months. For those that have lymphosarcoma the outlook is hopeless; no drugs or other treatment will produce improvement. Two other important facts must be taken into account. One is that an infected cat represents a great danger to other cats, particularly those who live in close association with it, and the second is that most infected cats detected by testing will be those that are going to be permanently infected. There is, however, a *chance* that an infected older cat, particularly if not one of a colony, will only be temporarily infected. However, this can only be established by re-testing after three months and again after six months.

Infected cats should be removed from contact with others, either by isolation or by euthanasia. The feasibility of effective isolation obviously depends upon individual circumstances – it is a lot easier if the cat is the only one in a household.

After the removal of an infected cat, all utensils, equipment and surroundings with which it has been in contact should be thoroughly cleaned and disinfected with bleach. At least a month should elapse before another susceptible animal is introduced into this environment. In cat colonies, all infected animals should be removed, all new entrants (unless certified FeLV free) isolated for three months and tested at the beginning and end of that period, and breeding animals (stud cats and breeding queens) regularly tested (every six to twelve months).

Q *Can my cat be vaccinated against FeLV?*

A Although vaccines have been developed, they have not been sufficiently tested for them to be licensed for commercial sale. However, it is hoped that in the early-to-mid 1980s a FeLV vaccine will be generally available.

Q *Is FeLV transmittable to humans?*

A Certainly, at one time this was feared, but all available evidence now suggests that FeLV is not transmitted to man and that cases where leukaemia has occurred in both cats and their owners are purely coincidences. Obviously, however, normal hygienic precautions should be taken after handling known infected animals.

Q *What kind of disease is feline infectious peritonitis?*

A Well, feline infectious peritonitis (FIP) is a viral disease of cats which has been recognized only since the middle 1960s and is apparently becoming increasingly common.

How the disease is transmitted is still unclear, though it is more common in colonies rather than in single-household cats and in younger animals, particularly those under three years old. It seems likely that, unlike FIE (FPL) virus, the virus of FIP does not survive for long in the environment.

In some ways the name of the disease is misleading because it occurs in two main forms. Both have an insidious onset starting with a high temperature, loss of appetite, increasing dehydration and weight loss. One form is the so-called 'wet' form, of which an important feature is peritonitis (inflammation of the peritoneum – the membrane which lines the abdominal cavity and covers the abdominal organs). Inflammatory exudate slowly collects in the abdomen, making it appear greatly swollen, and often also in the chest, producing increasing difficulty in breathing.

The second form of the disease is called the 'dry' form, where there is no fluid accumulation and in which the kidneys, eyes, and nervous tissue may be damaged. Often the colour of the cat's eyes appears to change.

In both forms there can be an incubation period of several weeks or months before signs appear. In some cases, concurrent FeLV infection may trigger the onset of signs of FIP by lowering the cat's immunity.

As well as its increasing occurrence, the importance of the disease lies in the fact that, with or without treatment, the disease is almost invariably fatal, usually within two to five weeks, and that as yet there is no vaccine against it. However, many cats seem to develop a good natural immunity to FIP and clinical disease only appears in about 20% of the infected cat population. To limit the spread of FIP in a colony, the affected cats should be isolated or destroyed and the cattery thoroughly disinfected.

Q *How could my cat get rabies?*

A Rabies is generally transmitted through the bite of an infected animal, by virus particles in the saliva of that animal being implanted in the bite wound. Other routes of infection are possible but much less common; for example infective saliva can enter through a scratch or an existing skin wound, or droplets of saliva may be inhaled. An animal may even eat the carcase of a rabies victim. In countries where rabies is established (enzootic) in the wildlife, cats almost always become infected by bites from rabid animals such as foxes, skunks, or bats. The incubation period in the cat is variable and may be very long (four months or more), though on average clinical signs of rabies appear about three weeks after the infective bite. The signs are due to the virus damaging the nervous system, for example, producing encephalitis.

Q *How would I know if my cat had rabies?*

A The disease characteristically has three phases. First, there is a pro-dromal stage, lasting less than forty-eight hours, in which the cat shows a personality change; sometimes it becomes more affectionate, though more often appears apprehensive and timid and hides away from light and noise. This is followed in turn by a stage of excitability and irritability, and then by a stage of paralysis. An animal is said to have 'furious' rabies or 'dumb' rabies depending on which of these two stages is encountered.

In the cat the stage of excitement generally lasts longer (up to four days) so that cats are more commonly encountered with 'furious' rabies, probably in about three-quarters of cases. Many cats probably die whilst still in hiding, but if accidentally disturbed during the excitement phase (e.g. in a garage) a cat will attack viciously and without provocation. It will scratch and bite, usually not letting go, both at animals and inanimate objects. Characteristically the cat's voice becomes hoarse. During the 'dumb' phase the attacks of rage disappear and paralysis gradually spreads progressively from the hind quarters forwards, terminating in death. Hydrophobia, the fear of swallowing water (because of laryngeal paralysis) or even of seeing water, which triggers off violent muscular contractions and which is seen in about 50% of human cases of rabies, is *not* a feature.

From the onset of clinical signs cats rarely survive longer than eight to ten days, and most die within four or five. During the time when signs are present, and for at least twenty-four hours beforehand, the cat's saliva is infective and bites from cats are an important source of human infection, often second numerically only to dog bites.

Q *Why should a cat showing signs of rabies be destroyed?*

A Regrettably, once clinical signs of rabies are present in a cat, or in man, no treatment is effective and the disease is always fatal. (There is one recorded case of a child recovering but in this instance there was some doubt about the diagnosis.)

Because rabid cats cannot be cured and represent such a source of danger to the human population, *their destruction is necessary as soon as possible.* Furthermore, if a cat exhibiting typical signs has bitten someone, it is important that its brain be examined as soon as can be arranged to enable the diagnosis to be confirmed, and thereby establish whether or not the bitten individual should undergo a course of rabies vaccination. Any suspected rabies case should *not* be handled but confined to an enclosed area from which it cannot escape and the public health authorities or police informed.

Because of the inherent dangers, those engaged in jobs where they are likely to encounter rabid animals, e.g. in quarantine kennels, are routinely vaccinated.

In some countries, such as the United States, what happens to a cat that has recently been bitten by an animal known to be rabid depends largely on whether the cat has previously been vaccinated or not. In both instances, treatment with anti-serum or vaccine *can* be given but the World Health Organization strongly recommends that all unvaccinated cats should be put to sleep immediately because of the risk they represent. If a cat's owner is unwilling to allow this, the unvaccinated animal, whether treated or not, must be isolated and observed for the onset of rabies signs for at least six months. Vaccinated cats, however, are usually re-vaccinated and isolated for only ninety days.

Q *If my cat has been vaccinated against rabies abroad, will it have to go into quarantine?*

A This depends upon the countries between which you intend to transfer your cat. As a general rule, countries where rabies is already well-established in the wildlife do not require cats to be quarantined, e.g. the continental U.S.A. and India. On the other hand, countries which are rabies free *may* insist upon a period of quarantine for cats entering the country, e.g. Australia, Great Britain and Hawaii (despite being a state of the U.S.A.). This requirement for compulsory quarantine may be waived if the cat comes directly from another rabies-free country without being offloaded or otherwise coming into contact with other possibly infected animals *en route* (e.g. from Great Britain to Hawaii, or New Zealand to Australia).

However, Great Britain always requires six months' quarantine for cats, regardless of the country of origin. Cats entering Australia have to undergo sixty days' quarantine if they arrive by ship and ninety days' if transported by air, though if the crates used for transport have had their seals broken this period is automatically extended to nine months. (In fact, Australia and New Zealand will in general only import animals from each other and from Great Britain and Ireland. Animals from other countries have to serve six months' quarantine in Britain or Ireland and then a further six months' residence there *before* they can be exported to Australia or New Zealand.) Cats entering Hawaii from the rest of the United States, whether vaccinated or not, have to undergo a minimum 120 days' quarantine.

Quarantine may appear a harsh measure, but those countries which are fortunate enough not to have reservoirs of rabies in their wild animals wish to avoid this happening, and many believe that a period of quarantine is the most effective method of prevention. The vaccination of dogs and cats against rabies will, in general, prevent them from acquiring the disease and thus from being a source of infection for man. However, with a disease that has such a long incubation period as rabies there is always the risk that a vaccinated animal may in fact be incubating rabies at the time of vaccination. Once admitted to a country, such an animal could readily transfer it to the wildlife, such as foxes, which in Europe are believed to be the main reservoir of infection. Certainly in Britain there is evidence of nightly contact between foxes and cats in urban areas. Therefore, although a vaccination policy is the best one for countries infected by rabies, it is regarded as inferior to a quarantine policy for countries where rabies is not established.

Once there is a reservoir of rabies in the wild animals of a country, these constitute an important source of infection for man and for any unvaccinated domestic animals such as feral cats. Undoubtedly this alters many people's attitude towards wildlife conservation, and indeed avoidance of wild animals is recommended in infected countries. The periodic eradication of wildlife from various areas (by trapping, shooting, poisoning and gassing) may be required in an infected country to stop the spread of rabies. Rabies also causes a great deal of pain and suffering among the wild species themselves.

Q *Can I have my cat vaccinated against rabies?*

A In some countries, or parts of some countries where rabies is prevalent, feline vaccination against rabies is required by law. This is the case in north-eastern France and in certain states of the United States (the regulations for the vaccination of dogs and cats in the United States vary from state to state, and within a state between different counties and even towns). In most countries, such as Italy, Switzerland, Germany and Denmark, vaccination is voluntary; i.e. you can have your cat vaccinated if you want to but it is not compulsory. In some countries such as Sweden and Britain, rabies vaccination is prohibited.

In Britain, rabies vaccination is only permitted for animals which are genuinely being exported to countries that require rabies vaccination to have been performed in advance, and for animals in quarantine kennels and catteries, largely to avoid the risk of infection being transferred between quarantined animals.

The reason for not allowing general vaccination in Britain is that the public would probably tend to rely upon vaccination for protection (even though this could never be 100% protection), and therefore would be less likely to comply with the quarantine regulations and would delay in reporting clinical cases. For a voluntary vaccination policy to be effective, a minimum of 70% of the susceptible animals need to be vaccinated. Experience in European countries with a voluntary vaccination policy shows that usually only around 30% of animals are vaccinated. Finally, vaccination may also interfere with the confirmation of a diagnosis of rabies by producing changes in the brain which have a similar appearance to those occurring in cases of natural infection.

Q *Someone told me that if my cat had anaemia, it would be infectious. Is this true?*

A At one time, especially in North America, feline infectious anaemia (haemobartonellosis) was thought to be the most common cause of anaemia in the cat. Now it is known to cause less than 10% of cases. However, it is likely that in fact there is widespread infection within the cat population, although disease only appears when the cat is subjected to stress.

A small bacterial organism (*Haemobartonella felis*) is responsible. Each organism invades a red blood cell in the circulation, multiplies inside it and then causes the cell to rupture (haemolyse). Then the released bacteria spread to other cells and repeat the process. In addition to the typical pallor and weakness of anaemia, diseased cats show high temperatures with accompanying listlessness and disinterest in feeding. A stained smear of their blood will allow the organisms to be seen very clearly through a microscope.

Feline infectious anaemia (FIA) is seen principally in young male cats, especially around two to three years' old, and is more common in the spring and summer. This strongly suggests that it is transmitted by cat bites because these are the seasons when cats are most sexually active and therefore when most inter-male fighting takes place. Probably, it is also spread by flea bites, and available evidence indicates that it can transfer from the blood of a pregnant queen to her kittens still inside the uterus, i.e. by congenital infection.

A long course of treatment with a broad spectrum antibiotic will eliminate the infection in at least 50% of cases. As an emergency measure, seriously ill cats may require a blood transfusion.

Q *Is ringworm really caused by a worm?*

A No, although in the past this was believed to be the case. In fact, this skin condition has nothing to do with worms. It is due to the effect of parasitic fungi (dermatophytes), and the one which is almost always responsible for the disease in the cat is called *Microsporum canis*. It grows on the 'dead' surface layer of the skin, including the hairs and very occasionally the nails, and does not penetrate 'living' tissue. Young animals are more often affected because they have poor immunity and because of the lower fatty acid composition of their skin. Lesions are intensified if the animal is deficient in vitamin A.

The spores of the fungus are transmitted from cat to cat, and often to humans and dogs as well, by direct and indirect contact. Contaminated combs and brushes are important in spreading infection, and in the environment (e.g. on bedding, baskets, leads and scratching posts) spores can persist for over a year.

Ringworm is correctly classed as an infectious disease, although the signs typical of many other infectious diseases, for example a high temperature and loss of appetite, are absent. In most cases there are small patches of baldness (alopecia) where the hairs have broken off, and often these do not have a regular outline. Generally they occur around the head (especially the ears) and the forelegs. The skin appears crusty and brown debris can sometimes be seen at the base of hairs looking like staining. Rarely does the skin show inflammation or secondary bacterial infection producing pus. Gradually the lesions will enlarge and spread, although itching and scratching are not common features. In general, it occurs in very young cats and spontaneous remission can be followed by very strong immunity to re-infection.

In some cats, particularly long-haired animals, the hairs alone are affected and this may not be readily apparent. Cats without obvious clinical signs can, unsuspected, spread infection widely in catteries and in the home.

In the majority of cases, though not always, the affected hairs will glow with a characteristic yellowish-green fluorescence (similar to that seen on luminous watch dials) when placed under ultra-violet light of a particular wavelength produced by a device called a Wood's lamp. Identification can be confirmed by examining affected hairs under the microscope, and by growing the fungus from them on special culture media.

Q *How should ringworm be treated?*

A In dealing with an infection, it is important to have all cats on the premises checked and to isolate infected individuals. All contaminated articles should preferably be burned, and all surfaces should be disinfected. Efficient disinfectants include solutions of iodophors (e.g. Pevidine), or formalin (though this is unpleasant to use). For disinfecting small articles, alcohol may be used.

The diseased hairs on infected cats should be closely clipped away and burned; but always sterilize the clippers afterwards. Fungicidal shampoos or creams may then be applied (but because of their toxicity any containing mercury should be avoided). However, these measures should *always* be combined with four to six weeks of oral dosing with the anti-fungal antibiotic griseofulvin (which strangely has no effect on bacteria). The drug becomes concentrated in the keratin of the new hairs (or the nails and skin) as they grow, rendering them resistant to fungal attack. Feeding oily food at the same time as griseofulvin is given enhances its absorption. However, it should not be given to pregnant cats because it can produce deformities in the developing kittens, i.e. it is teratogenic.

If any other animal, or person, in a household with a known infected cat develops itchy lesions on the skin, appropriate veterinary or medical attention should be sought.

Q *I have read that pregnant women shouldn't handle cats because they might develop a serious illness. Is this true?*

A Yes, this recommendation has certainly been made. The problem is that the minute protozoan parasite responsible for toxoplasmosis, called *Toxoplasma gondii*, can infect not only the cat but a variety of other species. In all of them some multiplication of the parasite occurs (called asexual reproduction) but only in the cat does it undertake sexual reproduction to produce a stage which the cat passes out in its faeces (an oocyst), and which, after about five days' development, is able to infect other animals. Because of this, the cat is known as the final host of the parasite. The other species which become infected, but don't themselves produce infective stages, are called intermediate hosts. These intermediate hosts include many different animals; for example, the dog, cattle, sheep, the pig, rodents, birds and humans.

In addition two other features serve to make *Toxoplasma* even more widespread. The first is that, although the intermediate hosts don't excrete the parasite, it can transfer from one to the other along a food chain. So that a dog eating an infected mouse, or a man eating raw steak or uncooked ham prepared from an infected animal, will in turn become infected. The second point is that in female intermediate hosts (though not in the cat itself) during pregnancy *Toxoplasma* can transfer from the tissues of the mother to those of her offspring whilst they are in the uterus (womb) and may damage them. In some species this congenital transmission of infection may continue for several generations. The cat itself is usually infected by eating infected rodents or birds.

In both the cat and the intermediate hosts, the parasites are generally present in the lungs, brain, eye, heart and skeletal muscles. If the host has very little immunity, multiplication of the parasite occurs rapidly producing an acute phase (acute toxoplasmosis). But after a time the host develops an immunity, with the result that the rate of multiplication slows down and the parasites become localized in cysts in the tissues. These cysts may remain intact throughout the life of the host and cause no harm. With time, however, the immunity will decline, and if the animal should then be exposed to stress the cysts can break down, releasing the parasites and causing another acute phase (i.e. a relapse). Clinical signs of acute toxoplasmosis (e.g. fever, pneumonia, nervous signs) rarely appear, but occasionally a host may die, or suffer severe injury, because the multiplying parasites have destroyed a significant number of cells in one of the vital organs of the body.

By checking for antibodies against *Toxoplasma*, it is estimated that at least one-third of the cats in Britain and the United States have been infected at some time in their lives. Approximately half a billion humans around the world have also been infected, and in certain areas, such as central France, the infection involves 90% of adults. Infected cats only shed oocysts for about two weeks, but during that time several million can be shed.

Q *What can I do to avoid contracting toxoplasmosis?*

A Drug treatment is given to cats showing signs of toxoplasmosis with the intention of controlling the parasite until the animal has acquired an adequate immunity to it. Such animals should be strictly isolated from others. Measures to limit the spread of *Toxoplasma* infection include the following recommendations:

1 All meat for human consumption should be heated to at least 60°C (155°F) throughout before eating.

2 After handling raw meat the hands should be washed, because the parasite in meat is easily destroyed by contact with water.

3 Only prepared (dry or canned) foods, or home-cooked meat, should be fed to cats; never raw meat.

4 Cat motions should be collected and burned each day before any oocysts they may contain become infective. Disposal of the motions by flushing them down the toilet may simply transfer infection elsewhere. Ideally, cats should be kept indoors so that all motions are passed in litter boxes, although this is frequently not practicable. Litter boxes should ideally be sterilized daily by immersing them in boiling water or using a strong (7%) ammonia solution as a chemical disinfectant.

5 Gloves should be worn when gardening, particularly by pregnant women, to avoid possible contact with *Toxoplasma*.

6 Children's sandpits should be covered when not in use to prevent cats from defaecating in them.

7 Pregnant women should avoid handling and caring for cats, particularly if they live on farms where cats have access to many potentially infective natural prey animals.

Q *I want to give my cat the best possible protection. Which diseases should she be vaccinated against?*

A Commercial vaccines are currently available against three important feline viral diseases. These are rabies, feline infectious enteritis (FIE or panleukopenia), and two types of feline respiratory disease (cat 'flu), feline viral rhinotracheitis (FVR) and feline calicivirus disease (FCD). In North America a vaccine is also available against feline pneumonitis though the disease is regarded as relatively unimportant and there are serious doubts about the effectiveness of the vaccine.

It is simply not true that young cats and pedigree cats are the only ones to contract these diseases, although they are usually worse affected; young cats because they have poor immunity, pedigree cats because they are frequently housed in a group. In Britain only about 20% of cats are vaccinated against FIE and 5% against cat 'flu (FRD), although the Cat Fancy requires cats entering all official cat shows to be vaccinated against FIE.

In most countries where rabies is known to be present it is clearly wise to have your cat protected against the disease even though it may not be compulsory. As has been mentioned (page 134), in some countries where rabies does not (at present) occur, routine rabies vaccination is prohibited. Different types of rabies vaccines are available and some countries specify which ones may be used. Live vaccines containing the low egg passage Flury strain of virus are intended only for use in dogs and must not be given to cats because they will actually cause rabies to develop.

Vaccines against FIE (FPL) produce very good ('solid') immunity. Unfortunately, the immunity produced against FRD by vaccination is not as good as that against FIE, and more frequent re-vaccination is advisable.

Q *How old should my kitten be when it is first vaccinated?*

A New-born kittens receive ready-made antibodies from the blood of their mother which are transferred to them in the first milk, or colostrum, which they suckle. These antibodies are not digested, but are absorbed intact from the young kitten's intestine into its blood stream during the first one to two days of life. (In the cat very little antibody is transferred from the blood of the mother to that of the foetus whilst the young are still in the uterus (womb), although this route is the only one used in man. In the cat 95% of maternal antibodies are transferred in the colostrum).

The transferred maternal antibodies provide protection for the young animal whilst its own immunity is developing, and they persist for about eight to twelve weeks depending on how much colostrum a particular kitten has consumed. It is valuable to boost the amount of antibodies in the colostrum by vaccinating females before mating or during pregnancy, though if the latter is done, only *dead* vaccines must be used to avoid the risk of a live virus damaging the developing kittens. In general, maternal antibodies against FIE and rabies (where applicable) persist longer than those against the respiratory diseases. However, the antibody level in any particular individual cannot, as a general rule, be established.

If a kitten is vaccinated whilst these maternal antibodies are still present, the vaccine can react with and neutralize the antibodies, leaving the kitten with no protection. Therefore, it is usually recommended that where there is no particular urgency to have a kitten vaccinated, the first injection should not be given until it is twelve weeks' old, i.e. the longest period for which maternal antibodies normally persist. However, there is the possibility that the maternal antibodies might *not* last that long, and where there is a high risk of the kitten being exposed to infection during its early life, e.g. if exposed to lots of strange cats acting as carriers of infection, vaccination can be given earlier, though usually *not* before eight weeks of age. To overcome the eventuality that there may, nonetheless, be persistent levels of maternal antibody, all kittens vaccinated before, or at, twelve weeks' old should be re-vaccinated again four weeks later.

In breeding colonies where it is possible that a dam is a carrier of FRD, kittens can either be weaned early (at four to five weeks' old) or vaccinated against FRD much earlier. Vaccines should then be given by injection every three weeks from three to six weeks' of age until twelve weeks' old. Alternatively, vaccination can be given intra-nasally at one week old, three weeks' old and at weaning. (Because there is less interference from maternal antibodies, intra-nasal vaccination can start much earlier.)

In general, rabies vaccines should not be given before three months of age. It can be injected on the same occasion as other vaccines, but it should be given independently, i.e. not mixed, and at a different site on the body.

Q *If kittens are orphaned and don't get any natural protection from their mother's milk, can they be vaccinated at birth?*

A If the kittens haven't received any substantial amount of maternal antibodies, because they never suckled after birth (for example in cases where the mother dies giving birth), then it would seem logical to vaccinate them as soon as possible. However, the value of vaccination depends upon the ability of the kittens' immune mechanisms to be able to respond to the vaccine, and in the first two weeks of life the production of antibodies following the adminstration of a vaccine may be poor. Indeed, giving them live vaccine during that time might even be harmful. Since there are hyperimmune sera available against FIE and rabies, it might appear preferable to give a dose of serum followed four weeks later by vaccination. However, present evidence indicates that the use of FIE antiserum provides less effective protection than multiple doses of vaccine.

Current recommendations therefore are that colostrum-deprived kittens should be vaccinated against FIE *regardless of age*, re-vaccinated at eight to ten weeks' old, again two weeks later, and then possibly at sixteen weeks' of age. Where a mother cat has not been vaccinated against rabies, the vaccine can be given to kittens as young as four weeks' old. Protection against FRD (cat 'flu) can be given by intra-nasal vaccination at one week old followed by further doses (by injection or intra-nasally) every three weeks until twelve weeks' old.

Q *Does vaccination always work?*

A No, regrettably it does not. There is no vaccine which is capable of fully protecting 100% of the animals inoculated with it. One important reason is that there is always a small proportion of animals whose immune systems do not respond in the normal manner to vaccines, or for that matter to natural infections. As a result, these individuals will not develop good immunity. This, however, is a fault of the animal's body and not of the vaccine. Unfortunately, unless their antibody levels are measured, which is difficult to arrange, such animals cannot be distinguished.

The vaccine itself must be administered within its stated expiry date and have been stored and administered correctly, i.e. in accordance with the manufacturer's instructions. Vaccines are stored under refrigeration, though not frozen, because they are inactivated more rapidly at higher temperatures. For each vaccine there are one or more recommended routes of administration (i.e. intramuscular, subcutaneous or intra-nasal) which should be adhered to for maximum success. The entire dose must be given and not divided between cats, and a clean syringe and needle must be used, uncontaminated by any disinfectant or antiseptic in which it may have been stored and which will inactivate the vaccine. Veterinary surgeons will invariably pay close attention to these important points; breeders and cattery owners sometimes do not, with disastrous consequences.

Kittens should not be vaccinated whilst they still have maternal antibodies, as discussed already, otherwise antibodies and vaccine tend to neutralize each other. Also vaccination should not take place if there is evidence of a disease already present (high body temperature, etc.). This is because the antibody-producing cells may already be fully occupied reacting to the disease and will not respond effectively to the vaccine. This is the reason for a cat receiving a clinical examination immediately prior to vaccination. However, occasionally, the cat may, at the time of the examination, be incubating the disease against which it is being vaccinated, so that although there are no clinical signs to indicate the fact, infection has already occurred. Clinical signs may then appear shortly afterwards.

Simply giving the vaccine doesn't mean that the animal can't become infected, but that it has an increased protection against the disease. In some cases an infection can be so overwhelming as to swamp the animal's immunity. However, with FRD, where there are other possible causes than those which can be vaccinated against, disease signs may not be related to any vaccine failure.

Certain drugs given internally will suppress a cat's immune responses (immuno-suppressive drugs) and in general vaccines should not be given during or immediately after treatment with them. Such drugs include corticosteroids, used to treat inflammatory conditions, and anti-cancer drugs, such as cyclophosphamide and azothiaprine.

In situations where the immune response is likely to be impaired, because of concurrent disease or drug administration, vaccination should be delayed. If available, temporary protection can be given in the form of an injection of hyperimmune serum.

Q *How long will vaccination protect my cat? Will her immunity ever need to be boosted by re-vaccination?*

A Unless the cat comes into natural contact with the infectious organisms responsible for the various diseases described, the level of antibodies in her blood will gradually decline. Whether or not this has happened, however, cannot readily be ascertained. Therefore, in order to boost the level of antibodies and keep them at an effective level to combat infection, it is advisable for repeat vaccinations to be performed.

The plasma cells which produce antibodies can 'remember' a particular bacterium or virus and if that organism reappears in the body, they then rapidly produce large amounts of the specific antibody against it.

For maximum protection it is recommended that vaccination is repeated annually, though the persistence of immunity does vary with the disease. Immunity against FIE can last *up to* four years with a live vaccine so that after the first annual booster, others may only be needed every two years or so. In contrast, immunity against FRD (cat 'flu) may be so short that cats particularly at risk, such as stud cats, should ideally be re-vaccinated every six months.

Booster vaccinations are always advisable three to four weeks before known periods of stress and exposure to infection, e.g. before going to cat shows or entering a cattery.

Because great advances are currently being made in vaccine production, and the recommendations for the use of different products vary, this is a topic that should always be discussed with your veterinarian.

Q *I have just taken in a stray cat which, of course, I want to have vaccinated against all possible diseases. Will the vet be able to tell if it has already been vaccinated and will it be harmful if the animal is vaccinated again?*

A First of all, a vet would not be able to tell from examining the cat whether or not it has been vaccinated against the usual infectious diseases; unless, of course it is showing obvious signs of one of them which would strongly suggest that it has not recently been vaccinated against it.

It *is* possible to measure the level of antibody in the blood against a particular organism, although this won't tell you whether it is the result of vaccination or natural infection; not that this matters because the immunity would be the same. However, this type of test is not done routinely and would therefore be difficult to arrange and expensive, particularly since it would need to be done separately for each disease.

More importantly, it would be unnecessary to go to this trouble and expense since routine vaccination would be cheaper and would not prove harmful even if it was quite unnecessary. However, care is needed if your stray cat is found to be pregnant because, as mentioned previously, it is inadvisable to use live vaccines at this time.

─────II─────
Other Diseases
and Operations

Q *What are the causes of the signs of ill-health commonly seen in cats?*

A Ten of the most common signs of ill-health in the cat, and some of the commoner causes of these, are presented in the table on page 144. It must be emphasized that none of these signs is a specific illness with a single cause. As can be seen from the table each has a variety of causes which will usually require individual treatment. Obviously, some causes of illness occur more frequently than others, although to some extent the incidence is dependent upon where the cat lives, i.e. whether in the town or country, and whether in a temperate or tropical climate. Other signs of illness, such as apparent anaemia and high temperature, are discussed elsewhere. Some causes, such as cancer, may act in a number of different ways.

One disorder that can produce a variety of signs, including vomiting, diarrhoea and the poor clotting of blood, is liver damage. Two very obvious signs that can occur with this disorder are distension of the abdomen, due to the accumulation of fluid, and, in the terminal stages, jaundice, a yellow discolouration of the skin (especially obvious in white cats) and of the visible membranes, such as the gums and tongue. Abdominal distension can also occur in association with heart disease and glomerulonephritis (a form of kidney disorder), and is frequently seen in the infectious disease, feline infectious peritonitis. Jaundice can also occur in another infectious condition, feline infectious anaemia, and is found in about one third of feline cases of diabetes mellitus (sugar diabetes). Cats with liver disorders need particular attention because many drugs cannot be broken down as efficiently as usual and therefore may accumulate to toxic levels. In particular the effects of injectable general anaesthetics persist much longer than normal.

Q *What diseases do cats not get?*

A Well, virtually all of the infectious diseases of man and of other animals are not transmissible to the cat, so that, for example, it doesn't suffer from

Table II Causes of Common Signs of Illness

LACK OF APPETITE

Fever/Weakness
* Feline infectious enteritis
* Feline respiratory disease
Feline leukaemia
Feline infectious peritonitis
Feline infectious anaemia
Toxoplasmosis
Heat stroke

Toxicity
* Feline urological syndrome
* Renal failure
Food poisoning
Abscess
Pyothorax
Pyometra or endometritis
Diabetes mellitus (terminal)
Poisoning
* Cancer

Pain/shock/ difficult swallowing
* Dental disease
Accident (fracture, etc.)
Burns and scalds
Corrosive poisoning
Snake bite
Rabies
Ulcers (mouth & throat)
Foreign bodies (mouth & throat)

Obstruction
Hairball

Behavioural
Psychological upset (e.g. home removal)
Aversion to food
In heat (calling)
Pregnancy & giving birth

INCREASED SALIVATION

Increased stimulation
* Heatstroke
Poisoning (e.g. organophosphorus)
Feline infectious enteritis
Pseudorabies
Snakebite

Nausea
Food poisoning
Hairball
Travel sickness
Other causes of vomiting

Difficulty in swallowing
* Dental disease
* Feline respiratory disease
Cancer (mouth & throat)
Foreign body (mouth & throat)
Ulcers (mouth & throat)
Rabies

Behavioural
Fear
Excitement
Delight
Aggression

VOMITING

Fear/Weakness
* Feline infectious enteritis
Feline leukaemia
Feline infectious peritonitis
Feline infectious anaemia

Toxicity
* Feline urological syndrome
* Renal failure
* Food poisoning
* Dietary allergies and intolerances
* Poisoning (including some drugs)
Diabetes mellitus (terminal)
Pyometra or endometritis
Haemorrhagic gastro-enteritis
Roundworms (in kittens)
* Cancer

Pain/shock
Accident (fracture, etc.)
Burns and scalds
Corrosive poisoning
Snake bite

Obstruction
* Hairball
Other foreign bodies
Constriction of oesophagus, stomach or intestines
Hernia
Intussusception

Behavioural
Psychological upset
Pregnancy & giving birth

Travel sickness

DIARRHOEA

Toxicity
* Food poisoning
Renal failure
Roundworms (in kittens)
Haemorrhagic gastro-enteritis

Infectious & other damage
* Cancer
Feline infectious enteritis
Feline leukaemia
Feline infectious peritonitis
Feline infectious anaemia
Tuberculosis
Pseudotuberculosis

Toxoplasmosis
Poisoning
Digestive/ absorbative defects
* Dietary allergies and intolerances
Hairball
Pancreatic insufficiency
Malabsorption
Colitis
Hepatitis
Heart disease
Behavioural
Pregnancy
DIFFICULTY IN BREATHING
Obstructed chest movements
* Lymphosarcoma
Ruptured diaphragm
Pneumothorax (air in chest)
Fluid in chest
Pyothorax
Poor oxygen supply
Heart disease
Heartworm infection
Feline infectious anaemia
Poisoning (e.g. carbon monoxide, fumes, smoke)
Pneumonia (feline respiratory disease)
* **Heat stroke**
COUGHING
Irritation of throat
Dental disease
Foreign body in throat
Swallowing hair
Inefficient liquid dosing
Inhaling dust or fumes
Cleft palate
Damage to lungs/ windpipe

* Feline respiratory disease
* Lungworm infection
* Cancer
Tracheal worm infection
Roundworms (in kittens)
Toxoplasmosis
Asthma (allergy)
Poor blood supply
Heart disease
Heartworm infection
LOSS OF HAIR
Parasites
* Fleas (esp. allergy)
* Ear mites
Ringworm
Head mange mite
Self damage due to other parasites
Persistent licking
'Lick granuloma'
Pseudorabies
Dietary causes
Poor nutrition
Dietary allergy
Other causes
Endocrine alopecia
Thallium poisoning
Local damage (e.g. abscess)
STRAINING
Obstructed intestine
Cancer
Hairball
Other foreign bodies
Fractured pelvis
Hernia
Irritation of intestine
* Food poisoning
* Feline infectious enteritis
Roundworms (in kittens)
Poisoning
Haemorrhagic gastro-enteritis

Blockage of urethra
* Feline urological syndrome
Cystitis
Giving birth
* Normal
Difficult (dystocia)
INCREASED THIRST
Increased water loss
* Renal failure, including that due to cancer
All causes of severe diarrhoea and vomiting
Heat stroke
Salty food
Glomerulonephritis
Diabetes mellitus
Overdosage with drugs (corticosteroids & diuretics)
LAMENESS AND PARALYSIS
Pain
* Abscess
* Bruising
* Foreign body in paw/leg
* Cut on paw
Arthritis
Warfarin poisoning
Damage to bone/nerve
* Accident (fracture)
Cancer
Nerve poisons
Snakebite
Rabies
Interference with circulation
Aortic thrombo-embolism
Heart disease
Dietary causes
Excess vitamin A
Calcium deficiency

measles, or chicken pox, or from foot and mouth disease or swine fever. This is an example of the type of natural (innate) immunity called genetic immunity; the genetic constitution of the cat protects it from these viral diseases. However, this is not necessarily the case for all time. Viruses have a disturbing capability to produce mutations which allows them to attack species which were previously able to resist infection. For example, influenza only became common in man a hundred years ago; before that time the virus principally caused disease in animals. And very recently the canine disease 'parvovirus infection' has arisen, apparently caused by a mutant of the virus (a parvovirus) responsible for feline infectious enteritis (feline panleukopenia). However, the actual virus causing FIE (FPL) in the cat is *not* pathogenic to dogs.

The cat doesn't ever suffer from a broken collar bone (clavicle), which humans commonly injure in falls. This bone is poorly developed in the cat and appears merely as a rudimentary slender rod of bone surrounded by muscle near to the shoulder joint. It is attached to the rest of the skeleton only by soft tissue. The clavicle, however, may serve as a trap for unwary veterinary surgeons. On radiographs it presents an appearance very similar to that of a needle, so that where it is suspected that a cat may have swallowed such an object, care has to be taken to distinguish between the two. Also the cat has no appendix (at the end of the intestinal cul-de-sac called the caecum) so cats don't suffer from appendicitis. Nor do cats suffer from haemorrhoids (piles) or varicose veins, disorders which clinicians attribute to the upright stance of humans. Venereal disease is also virtually unknown in the cat.

And, of course, whether because of lack of opportunity or interest, cats avoid the problems associated with drug abuse, smoking and alcoholism! However, our admiration should perhaps be tempered by the knowledge that the cat's response to cat-nip (page 51) strongly resembles a drug-induced state, and that in laboratory tests cats have voluntarily resorted to alcohol when subjected to stress in their social relationships!

Q *Do you ever get diabetic cats?*

A In general, disorders caused by the abnormal production of one or more hormones (endocrine diseases) occur relatively infrequently in cats, compared with people or dogs. But diabetes mellitus (sugar diabetes) is a condition that occurs in about one in every 800, mainly the middle-aged or elderly.

The condition arises from the deficient production of the hormone insulin by the beta cells of the pancreas. As a result, glucose derived from the diet and from metabolism within the body cannot be stored for future use as an energy source and much of it is simply excreted in the urine. Just as in other species, diabetic cats show the classic signs of an increasing loss of weight and weakness, despite a markedly increased appetite, together with an increased thirst and the passage of large volumes of urine. Later, if no treatment is given, body fat is broken down to provide energy and at this stage the cat loses its appetite, becomes dehydrated, vomits and eventually goes into a coma and would die (keto-acidotic coma).

Following veterinary treatment to resolve the immediate problems, long-term control of the disease requires daily subcutaneous injections of a long-acting insulin preparation, frequent urine testing and regular checkups for the remainder of the cat's life. Any owner unwilling, or unable, to embark on such a disciplined course would be well advised to have their cat put to sleep rather than to subject it to half-hearted attempts at treatment, however well-intentioned.

The most frequent complication in the management of a diabetic cat is the inadvertent injection of an overdose of insulin, which causes the cat to show weakness, confused behaviour and staggering (ataxia) and eventually convulsions and coma. Fortunately, the situation is rapidly reversed by dosing the cat *immediately* signs appear with several tea-spoonsful of honey or syrup, or a specially prepared glucose solution stored in the refrigerator against just such an eventuality.

Q *What parasites do cats get?*

A The accompanying table lists the common external parasites (ectoparasites) and internal parasites (endoparasites) of the cat. Those marked with an asterisk are the ones most commonly found. Those marked with a dagger occur in North America and Australia, but not in European countries, except in imported cats. The table is by no means all-embracing because several other parasites are known to occur in the cat, particularly in warmer climates, although they cannot be considered common. Indeed, some of the parasites in the table are not very often encountered, and for that reason are placed within brackets. For example, the cat fur mite (*Lynxacarus radovskyi*) has been omitted from the list of external parasites. This mite, which is found in Australia, attaches itself to the outer half of the hairs, giving a so-called 'salt and pepper' appearance, but it causes no itching or other sign.

Of the internal parasites in the table, the ascarids (roundworms), hookworms and tapeworms inhabit the cat's small intestine. Other internal parasites sometimes met with are the threadworm (*Strongyloides stercoralis*), which can cause diarrhoea and coughing, and the whipworm (*Trichuris campanula*) recorded in parts of the United States (e.g. Florida) and Australia. In North America the stomach worms, *Ollulanus tricuspis* and *Physaloptera* species, are occasionally found in cats, and the latter may provoke vomiting. As well as the lung fluke, which is included in the table, other flukes (flat, leaf-shaped parasites) are sometimes encountered in cats, especially those infecting the liver (for example *Platynosmum fastosum*, reputed to be the most important cat disease in the Bahamas).

Table III Parasites of the Cat

EXTERNAL PARASITES

[Head mange mite, Notoedres cati]
* Ear mite, Otodectes cynotis
  Fur mite, Cheyletiella blakei
  Harvest mite, Trombicula autumnalis, and related species (North American chigger, heel bug, velvet mite, etc.)
* Fleas; Ctenocephalides felis
  Occasionally other species
  Biting louse; Felicola subrostratus
  Ticks; hard(ixodid) ticks
  † soft (argasid) ticks
  Fly larvae; blow-fly maggots
  † Cuterebra larvae

INTERNAL PARASITES

Nematode worms
* Ascarids (roundworms); Toxocara cati
  Toxascaris leonina
  Hookworms; Uncinaria stenocephala
  † Ancylostoma species
* Lungworm, Aelurostrongylus abstrusus
  Tracheal worm, Capillaria aerophila
  Heartworm, Dirofilaria immitis
* † Bladderworm, Capillaria feliscati
† [Eyeworm, Thelazia californiensis]
Tapeworms (Cestode worms)
* Dipylidium caninum
  Taenia taeniaeformis
  [Diphyllobothrium latum]
  [Echinococcus multilocularis]
Flukes
† Lung fluke, Paragonimus kellicotti

---

* Asterisks denote most commonly occurring.
[ ] In square brackets, seldom encountered.
† Found in N. America and/or Australia, but not in European countries.

Parasitic protozoa, e.g. Toxoplasma gondii, have been included in the table of infectious diseases of the cat.

Q *Why is it so important to get rid of fleas on my cat?*

A Cat fleas (*Ctenocephalides felis*) are parasitic and survive by sucking the blood of their host. However, cat fleas will readily transfer to people and dogs as well as cats; in fact, cat fleas are the most common fleas on both cats and dogs. The adult fleas are small, brown, wingless insects with bodies flattened from side to side, and are just large enough to be seen with the naked eye. Occasionally cats are infested with fleas from other species, such as rabbits, birds, and particularly hedgehogs. In North America smaller fleas, stick-tight fleas, are sometimes found firmly attached to the skin of the cat, especially around the face, and are best removed with tweezers. A survey in London showed that almost 60% of cats were infected with fleas.

They are important for five reasons:

1 Their bites cause extreme irritation so that the cat may bite and scratch at itself.

2 Some cats become allergic to the saliva which the flea injects as it bites and will react to even a single flea bite. They will have very inflamed moist areas of skin, or more commonly several small crusty scabs, usually on the back just in front of the tail.

3 A heavy flea infestation, especially in kittens, can result in so much blood being lost that anaemia develops.

4 As the flea bites, some of the blood taken from one cat may be transferred to the next, and if the first cat was in a certain stage of an infectious disease, along with the blood there may also be transferred bacteria, such as *Haemobartonella felis* which causes infectious anaemia, or viruses such as those causing feline infectious enteritis (feline panleukopenia).

5 Fleas can transmit the common tapeworm of the cat (*Dipylidium caninum*). A cat infected with the tapeworm will from time to time shed from its anus segments of the worm containing eggs. If one of these tapeworm eggs happens to be eaten by a flea larva it eventually develops into a cystic form inside the adult flea. Then if this flea should subsequently be swallowed by a cat as it grooms itself, the cystic form develops into a new tapeworm in the cat's intestine. If the infected flea is eaten by a dog, or even a child, then the tapeworm will develop in the dog's or child's intestine.

Q *How can I get rid of fleas on my cat?*

A Adult fleas spend only short periods of time on a cat, just sufficient to obtain a meal of blood, and therefore may not be found when looked for on the coat. If they are present, they are easily seen with the naked eye as small, dark brown insects moving swiftly over the skin, particularly at the base of the tail and behind the ears. It is more common to find evidence of their presence in the form of flea dirts, looking like specks of dark grit, on the skin surface. These consist mainly of dried blood and can be distinguished from grit by the fact that if they are placed on a piece of damp cotton swab a red-brown stain spreads out from them over the dampened surface.

Fleas will be most numerous in the *environment* of the cat, which is where the female flea lays her eggs. This includes not only the cat's basket and bedding (including chairs and beds if the pet sleeps on them), but also between floorboards, tiles and sections of lino, in the pile of fitted carpets and even beneath skirting boards. Therefore, the successful removal of fleas requires a concerted attack: not only treatment of the cat itself, but also of other animals in the household and of the surroundings.

Many proprietary parasiticidal powders or sprays are available for the treatment of your cat, either from your veterinary surgeon or from a pet shop. If a spray is used take care to follow the instructions *carefully*; it is very easy to overdo the treatment and if the animal licks off, or absorbs, an excessive amount of the spray it may be poisoned. Raise the hair by brushing it the 'wrong' way, and spray against the 'lie' of the coat from six to eight inches away for up to three seconds – no longer, and avoid the eyes and mouth. The hissing noise as the aerosol discharges often startles cats. If powders are used it is advisable to thoroughly dust them into the coat, again brushing the hair the 'wrong' way. Leave the powder in place for half an hour, during which time the animal should be watched carefully to prevent it licking its coat, and then brush out as much powder as possible. Putting the cat in a pillowcase with its head sticking out, or wrapping it in a towel for this half-hour may help to stop it licking.

It is possible to apply special insecticidal solutions to the cat's coat, but because these are not washed off afterwards there is always a risk of the cat licking in toxic amounts. Insecticidal shampoos are also available and since they *are* completely rinsed out these are less likely to prove harmful; their use may sometimes be advised prior to treatment with a powder or spray. Tablet treatments are available as well; the drug in the tablets passes into the cat's blood and kills any fleas which suck blood later. Because these drugs in large amounts are toxic to the cat, the tablets must be used with care and not employed at the same time as sprays containing similar drugs. In general, they are not as satisfactory in eliminating fleas as the powders or sprays.

On soft furnishings and carpets the same parasiticidal powders can be applied and vacuumed off after half an hour (burn the contents of the vacuum cleaner afterwards), or an ordinary fly spray or special environmental spray (e.g. Nuvan Staykil) can be used. *These* sprays are particularly useful for penetrating crevices, but they should not be used directly on cats, and animals are best kept off treated areas for several days afterwards. Old bedding and baskets are best burned. In North America flea bombs, or 'foggers', are available which fill the atmosphere with insecticide, but with really severe infestations it is advisable to call in professional exterminators. Most local authorities can offer help or advice.

After the initial treatment, further treatments of the cat and its bedding are advisable, varying from twice a week to once every two weeks (depending on the preparation) to kill any fleas which have hatched out of eggs in the surroundings since the previous treatment.

Q *Are flea collars safe for cats to wear?*

A Cats are liable to acquire fresh flea infestations from other cats which they meet outdoors (and from hedgehogs). If repeated infestation is a problem the cat can be fitted with a flea collar. Flea collars are impregnated with an insecticide (usually either dichlorvos or lindane) which is released slowly as a vapour to kill the fleas. However, outdoors this vapour is easily dissipated by breezes, and, as with other collars, there is a risk of strangulation if the collar gets caught on a projection. There has also been a number of reports of flea collars causing either localized inflammation around the neck (contact dermatitis) or generalized signs of poisoning (depression, vomiting, diarrhoea, and staggering), particularly if used at the same time as other anti-flea treatments.

If a flea collar is used, it is recommended that after being removed from the packaging material the collar should be allowed to 'air out' for twenty-four hours, and then be fitted so that it is still possible to insert two fingers between the collar and the neck. No other treatment for fleas (tablets, sprays, powders, etc.) should be given to the cat for five days before or after wearing the collar, and it should be removed if untoward signs are seen.

An effective alternative is to hang a dichlorvos-impregnated fly strip above the cat's bed, but again this should not be used at the same time as a flea collar or any other de-fleaing treatment.

Q *Can cats get mange?*

A Yes, they can, but not very often. The microscopic round-bodied mite *Notoedres cati* is the cause of notoedric mange (sometimes called feline scabies) which, although very seldom seen nowadays, is a highly contagious disease spread by direct contact.

The mites burrow into the upper horny layer of the skin between the hair follicles, causing intense irritation. Beginning at the tips of the ears and spreading down across the forehead and face, the skin becomes thickened, wrinkled and covered in grey crusts. Later, hairs may be lost and the wrinkled forehead skin gives the cat an old and worried appearance. From the cat's habit of washing its face, the front paws become infected also.

An even rarer type of mange is feline demodectic mange which usually affects the eyelids and the skin around the eyes. Hairs are lost from this region and the skin appears reddened. The cause is the demodectic mite, *Demodex canis*, so-named because it is principally a parasite of the dog, responsible for causing localized or generalized lesions of follicular mange (red mange) especially in puppies. This cigar-shaped mite also lives below the surface of the skin, in this case in the hair follicles, and like *Notoedres* can only be seen when enlarged under the microscope.

These rare conditions are diagnosed by finding the mites responsible in scrapings taken from the surface layers of the skin. Treatment is with the same type of lotions, shampoos and tablets used for controlling flea infestations, although since neither mite survives long away from the host, repeated treatment of the environment is unnecessary. However, with notoedric mange especially, all the cats on the premises should receive treatment.

Q *What other skin parasites attack the cat?*

A As well as fleas and mange mites, dealt with above, suggestions have already been given for eliminating infections caused by the ear mite, *Otodectes cynotis*, which occurs commonly in cats (page 115).

The fur mite, *Cheyletiella blakei*, is a similar size to the ear mite, i.e. just large enough to be seen with the naked eye, and occurs all over the body from head to rump. Often it produces no itching (pruritus) and the most consistent feature of its presence is a very scurfy, slightly greasy coat. The white mites and their eggs give the appearance of extensive dandruff, though close observation with a magnifying glass reveals that it is moving – hence the popular name 'walking dandruff'.

The cat louse, *Felicola subrostratus*, is a flat, wingless insect which feeds on hair and skin debris, and glues its eggs (nits) onto the cat's hairs. The nits will later hatch out into a new crop of lice and can be most easily removed by clipping off the affected hairs. Although it may prove difficult to find them, the lice are intensely irritating to the cat and in young animals may cause anaemia. In Britain infection is rare, except in farmhouse cats.

Both *Cheyletiella* and lice are transmitted by direct and indirect contact (for instance with contaminated grooming utensils) and they are treated with similar preparations to those used for removing fleas. It is always worthwhile seeking veterinary advice about the correct preparation to use because all of them are toxic to some extent and not all are equally suitable for every purpose. Any instructions and precautions should be carefully observed. As a general rule, special care should be taken with very young, very old, pregnant, nursing and ill cats, and those which require repeated treatment. Unless advised otherwise, avoid using a number of preparations simultaneously because of the increased toxic effects.

The cat louse and all mites, except the harvest mite, differ from the flea in that they spend their entire life on the host. The harvest mite (*Trombicula autumnalis*) and the North American chigger (*Eutrombicula alfreddugesi*) are parasitic larvae which attach themselves to thin-skinned regions, usually the ears and between the toes, as the cat walks through vegetation. They need animal protein in order to develop further; after feeding they drop off and ultimately become adult mites which are non-parasitic and live on decaying vegetable matter. The larvae appear as small orange or red spots, and cause considerable irritation. As its name suggests, infestations with the harvest mite are associated primarily with the summer months. Parasiticidal preparations are required for treatment.

Callophorid flies, otherwise called blow-flies (blue-bottles and green-bottles) may lay their eggs in open wounds or in the soiled coat of an ill or elderly animal. The maggots (larvae) which hatch from the eggs feed from the living animal just as they would from a carcase or piece of meat. They secrete enzymes which digest proteins in the skin producing craters on its surface. This condition (fly-strike) requires the area to be clipped thoroughly, cleaned, and treated with insecticide; treatment for shock may also be necessary.

In the southern and western United States, during the third quarter of the year, the fly *Cuterebra maculata* lays its eggs in soil. The larvae which hatch can attach themselves to the skin of cats, usually kittens or debilitated animals, that lie on the ground and eventually they are able to penetrate the skin. Each larva then grows inside a cyst-like cavity to be three-quarters of an inch long. An opening remains in the skin because this grub needs to breathe. Treatment requires removal of the grub with forceps (generally following enlargement of the opening by an incision made under local anaesthesia) and antibiotic treatment to combat secondary bacterial infection.

Q *Is it true that a tick should not be pulled from a cat's body?*

A Ticks are sometimes acquired by cats outdoors, particularly in country districts. They attach themselves firmly by their mouth-parts, usually to the cat's ears, head, neck or paws, and suck blood; consequently, a heavy infestation may produce anaemia. The cat often seems unconcerned and the small dark swelling, fluctuating in size, which is the tick, may be confused with a pigmented skin tumour. In warmer climates than in Britain, some species of hard ticks produce a toxin which progressively paralyzes the cat. Simply pulling the tick off usually causes the deeply embedded mouthparts to remain behind, and this may result in an abscess forming. Preferably the tick should be caused to slacken its grip by applying a pad of alcohol or ether, or by spraying it with an insecticidal aerosol spray, before carefully removing it with forceps. Removed ticks are best burned.

Q *How does my cat get infected with worms and are they harmful?*

A In general the intestinal worms, roundworms, hookworms and tape-worms, cause no harm to adult cats and only large numbers produce signs of infection, usually in kittens. The other parasitic worms may cause more serious problems. Nevertheless regardless of its effect on the cat, most owners find the presence of even a single worm aesthetically distasteful.

Strictly speaking all the nematode worms should be referred to as roundworms because they are all circular in cross-section. However, by popular usage this description is often reserved for the commonest members of the group – the ascarids.

Ascarid worms produce eggs in the intestine of the cat which pass out in the motions. An infective larva develops inside each egg and if this is eaten by a cat the larva develops into an adult worm in its intestine. (In the case of *Toxocara cati* this only happens after a complex 'migration' around the body of the cat, passing in turn through the liver, heart and lungs.) More usually though the egg is eaten by another species, often a rodent, and it is by eating this animal that the cat in turn becomes infected. In a female cat some larvae of *Toxocara cati* (though not *Toxascaris leonina*) do not develop to adults but remain dormant in the body tissues. If the cat should happen to give birth to kittens these larvae then pass to the mammary gland and out in the milk consumed by the newborn offspring. Consequently kittens can be, and usually are, infected very soon after they are born. Because these dormant larvae are not in the intestine they cannot be removed by conventional worming drugs, although drugs are currently being developed which are able to destroy larvae in the tissues.

Large numbers of these worms in kittens can produce persistent diarrhoea, a poor coat and a pot belly. At times, worms may appear in the motions or vomit and can cause coughing.

The common tapeworms are long, flat worms (like white ribbons), attached to the lining of the intestine with hooks and suckers, though again they generally cause no signs. Tapeworms are hermaphrodite, segmented worms which grow continuously; the oldest segments, containing the eggs, are shed one or more at a time from the end of the worm furthest from its head. To complete their life cycle these eggs, after passing out at the anus, must then be eaten by a particular species of animal. In the case of *Dipylidium caninum* (the commonest cat tapeworm) this 'intermediate host' must be the flea or louse; in the case of *Taenia taeniaeformis*, a mouse or rat. An egg will develop into a cyst-like structure in the intermediate host, and if this host is then eaten by a cat the cyst-like structure develops into a new tapeworm in its intestine. But if tapeworm eggs are eaten by a cat they do not develop further.

Q *What other worms might infect my cat?*

A Hookworms have a more direct life cycle. Eggs eliminated in the motions become larvae and after being swallowed (or alternatively, in the case of *Ancylostoma*, penetrating the skin) these pass to the intestine and develop there into adult worms. A large burden of *Ancylostoma* hookworms can cause severe anaemia and weakness, sometimes even death, because the worms feed on the cat's blood. At times, blood may be evident in its motions.

The lungworm *Aelurostrongylus abstrusus* is extremely common, probably affecting about one-fifth of all cats, but over a third in some areas, such as western Scotland. Adult worms, looking like pieces of black thread, inhabit the airways of the lungs where they lay their eggs. These hatch to larvae which are coughed up, swallowed and appear in the cat's motions. To develop further, these larvae must be eaten by slugs or snails, which in turn are usually consumed by rodents. When an infected rodent is eaten by a cat, the larvae are released, pass to the lungs and become adult worms. Heavily infected cats show persistent coughing, made worse by exercise, and loss of condition.

The tracheal worm (*Capillaria aerophila*) is in general responsible for similar, though milder, respiratory signs. It lives in the trachea (windpipe) of the cat and its eggs pass out in the same way as lungworm larvae, that is by being coughed up and swallowed and traversing the intestines. The larvae which develop from the eggs can infect other cats by being eaten directly, i.e. an intermediate host is not essential. In North America and South Africa the lung fluke (*Paragonimus kellicotti*) can infect scavenger cats causing intermittent coughing. It has a life cycle similar to the lungworm, passing through stages in water snails and crayfish before returning to the cat.

The heartworm (*Dirofilaria immitis*) infects cats in the central and eastern parts of the United States, Australia and southern Europe, though not Britain or northern Europe. However, its occurrence is much less common than in dogs. Microscopic larvae are taken from the bloodstream of one animal and later injected into another by the bites of a mosquito, and develop into adult worms in the heart and the pulmonary artery. The damage and blockage caused by these worms can be severe, resulting in difficulty in breathing and even sudden death.

The bladder worm (*Capillaria feliscati*) is of particular importance in Australia, infecting over 30% of cats in Queensland, even though its life cycle is, as yet, unknown.

Finally, in wooded areas of the western states of the United States, the small, slender worm *Thelazia californiensis* occasionally affects cats following transmission by the deer fly. The worm lives beneath the third eyelid (or haw) causing an intensely irritant conjunctivitis, and has to be removed with forceps or a cotton bud after the eye has been de-sensitized with local anaesthetic.

Q *How can I tell if my cat has worms?*

A Ideally, at intervals throughout the cat's life, a sample of motions should be examined by a laboratory for evidence of worm eggs, though usually this is only performed if the cat is showing signs suggestive of worm infection. If an examination is carried out *after* worming, it is a valuable way of assessing the efficacy of treatment, especially as most modern tapeworm treatments cause the worms to break up within the cat's intestine – so intact worms are *not* passed, and are therefore *not* visible in the motions.

As was mentioned earlier, those segments of a tapeworm furthest from the head, which contain the eggs, are continually being shed and passing out of the cat's anus. These segments are large enough to be seen with the naked eye, and they may be discovered in the motions, or sometimes seen around the cat's anus, or in the bedding. For a time the segments retain the ability to contract the muscles in their walls, and though not capable of an independent existence, may be observed moving over the animal's coat or across the floor. They have the size and appearance of rice grains or cucumber seeds. The eggs of other worms are also passed out in the motions, but individually, i.e. not contained within segments, and these are so small that they can only be seen using a microscope. (The segments of the much rarer tapeworm *Echinococcus multilocularis* are too small to be visible without magnification and can only be detected microscopically.)

Q *I have heard that children can get worms from cats. Is this true?*

A In the case of one or two worms, it *is* correct that they can infect humans, usually children because their immunity is less.

The worm which has received most attention is the roundworm, *Toxocara cati*. In its life cycle the infective larva, still inside the egg-shell in which it has developed, may be eaten by another species, often a rodent, which in turn may be consumed by a hunting cat. At times, however, these infective eggs (i.e. containing the larva) may be eaten by children. A number of factors contribute:

1 The outside of the microscopic eggs are sticky, so that they readily adhere to a cat's coat, at least until it grooms itself, and to human fingers.
2 Young children, especially toddlers, have a habit of putting their hands and various objects, even contaminated soil, into their mouths.
3 The infective eggs can survive for two years or longer in the ground and will withstand all disinfectants, long-term freezing and even short periods in boiling water. Only the use of horticultural flame-guns on concrete runs effectively destroys the eggs.
4 The effects of wind, rain and human activity can spread the eggs over a wide area.

In humans the larvae hatch from the eggs, penetrate the wall of the intestine and disperse to the liver, kidneys, brain or eyes. They do not develop further but remain in those organs, and can cause damage leading sometimes to liver enlargement, blindness or convulsions. This disease, caused by the migration or penetration of the larvae, is called visceral larva migrans, and it chiefly affects children between one and a half and three years old. It *cannot* be considered a common disease by any means, although probably more children become infected than ever show signs. Good hygiene and regular de-worming of your cat are important in eliminating the possibility of human infection taking place. At present there is no evidence that *Toxascaris leonina* can infect humans similarly.

It is also possible for a person, again usually a child, who swallows a flea infected with the intermediate stage of the tapeworm *Dipylidium caninum* to become infected with an adult tapeworm in their intestine, although this very rarely happens.

The eggs of the very small ($\frac{1}{2}$ cm long) tapeworm *Echinococcus multilocularis* may at times infect humans. This parasite (see the table on page 148) can occur in cats in North America and some parts of Europe and Asia. Man plays the role of an intermediate host and the egg develops into a tumour-like structure in the liver. It is of course unlikely that this organ will ever be eaten by a cat which would be necessary if the worm were ever to complete its life cycle. Only recently has this worm been distinguished from *Echinococcus granulosus*, which at one time was believed to occur in the cat although not able to produce eggs, so the true situation is not yet clear. *Echinococcus granulosus* certainly does occur in dogs, and its eggs, when eaten by man, can develop into large cystic structures in the liver, lungs or other organs, resulting in the severe, and sometimes fatal illness, hydatidosis.

Q *Is it a good idea to worm my cat, and if so, how often should I do it?*

A First of all, it should be appreciated that most of the worms with which cats may be affected are not treated for unless they are believed to be present. *Routine* worming (or, more accurately, de-worming) is carried out primarily to control infection with the ascarid worms (roundworms), especially since they can be transmitted to man. The drug most commonly used is piperazine, which is relatively safe, cheap and reasonably effective. It is most definitely advisable to give this worming treatment routinely. However, this drug has no appreciable action against other types of worms, for instance, tapeworms. More recently even more effective drugs against ascarids have become available, some of which are also effective against tapeworms; they are, however, considerably more expensive.

It is generally recommended that kittens should be routinely wormed to remove ascarids at intervals of three to four weeks, beginning at three weeks of age, until they are six months' old. A cat should then be wormed every four to six months if it roams free. If your cat is normally confined indoors, repeat worming can be carried out at the time of the annual booster vaccination. This routine worming is advisable because cats can become re-infected at any age, particularly if they hunt, and it is estimated that at any one time 20% (in some areas 35%) of adult cats are infected.

Newly acquired cats should always be wormed, and pregnant queens should be wormed about a month before giving birth. This will not remove any worms dormant in the mother cat's tissues but it will reduce the contamination of the kittens' environment.

In addition to this routine worming for roundworms, some veterinary surgeons also advise worming cats every six to twelve months to eliminate tapeworms. Since tapeworms are less of a problem in kittens than in adults, any routine treatment is usually not started until six months of age. A number of effective drugs are available; currently bunamidine (e.g. Scolaban) is the most commonly used, but this drug is bitter and tablets must not be crushed.

Treatment to remove the tapeworm *Dipylidium caninum*, however, is usually a waste of time unless infestations of fleas (or lice) are removed simultaneously.

When there is *definite evidence* of a worm infection, worming with the appropriate drug should be carried out as soon as possible and then repeated a month or so later to remove any remaining worms.

Q *Is it safe to use worming remedies bought at the pet shop?*

A In countries (for instance Britain and North America) where there are legal restrictions on what drugs can be sold for this purpose other than by a qualified pharmacist or veterinarian, the answer is probably yes. But it is subject to the proviso that these remedies are used strictly in accordance with the manufacturer's instructions.

Unfortunately, owners may misdiagnose their cat's illness as being due to worms and therefore delay getting proper advice and treatment. Or they may overdose their cat, particularly if the first treatment doesn't produce the expected improvement, which can have tragic consequences. Also, because of restrictions upon sale, several types of worming drugs (anthelmintics) are not sold from pet shops and similar retail outlets, and invariably this includes those most recently developed, and most effective.

In countries where there is no restriction on what remedies may be sold over the counter, a number of drastic purgative treatments and potentially toxic drugs may be on sale, so great care must be exercised.

As a general rule, to ensure that you receive the correct drug to treat your cat's condition, whether it is due to a worm infection or not, together with accurate advice about the dose to administer, it is always preferable in the long run to consult your local vet.

Q *Do cats get cancer?*

A Yes, cancer (or neoplasia, or tumour formation) is one of the most common conditions to affect cats, and as in other animals, including man, it occurs increasingly frequently with age.

A tumour, or neoplasm (often popularly referred to as a 'growth') is a multiplying collection of cells whose growth cannot be controlled by the normal body mechanisms. As a rule, these cells lose their normal functions and concentrate solely on growing. Tumours can essentially be classified into two groups. Those termed *benign* grow slowly and are usually easily separated from adjacent tissues, so that complete surgical removal is generally possible. The problems that they cause are usually related to their site. A growing tumour can press on nearby structures interfering with their function, for example with the flow of blood or urine, or with breathing. Tumours on the skin can easily have their surface broken so that they bleed, or become infected by bacteria. Likewise, those in the mouth might be chewed upon, causing pain and bleeding.

Those tumours that are called *malignant* grow much more rapidly, and spread out into adjacent tissues (invasion and/or infiltration). After a period of growth, groups of malignant tumour cells often break off and are carried away in the bloodstream or lymphatic circulation to lodge in other organs of the body, especially the lungs. This process is referred to as metastasis, and each group of cells can give rise to a new tumour (which is also called a metastasis, or secondary tumour) which will grow and spread in the same manner. Because of their invasive growth, complete surgical removal is more difficult and malignant tumours often recur after an operation. It is this malignant type of neoplasia which is generally called cancer (although some experts use the term cancer to refer to *any* type of tumour). Malignant tumours cause problems, not only because of the same type of local pressure effects, but by their rapid, progressive destruction of body tissues which inevitably leads to organs failing to function effectively.

As well as being classed benign or malignant, the names of tumours vary, depending upon the tissues from which they have been derived.

The signs of cancer depend upon its site, the tissues involved, and the way in which normal body functions have been interfered with. The cause of neoplasia is still imperfectly understood, but essentially it seems that at some time during the repeated multiplication of the body cells, a mutation occurs in the genes responsible for controlling the growth and function of cells. All further cells derived from this 'mutant' will perpetuate the same defects of growth and activity. The genetic make-up of the species, of the breed and even of the individual all influence the likelihood of mutations occurring, but the longer the animal lives, the greater becomes the chance of such mutation appearing. Certain chemicals, e.g. tar compounds, and viruses, such as feline leukaemia virus, stimulate the production of mutations and are therefore held responsible for certain types of neoplasia. Such cancer-producing agents are known as carcinogens.

Q *What kinds of tumours do cats most commonly get?*

A The most commonly occurring tumours in the cat are lymphosarcomas (malignant tumours) which account for one-third of the total. They are an important exception to the rule about cancer becoming more common with age; 40% of cats affected are under three years' old. The organs most frequently involved are the thymus, the kidneys and the intestines.

Tumours of the skin and of the mouth are also extremely common in the cat, and as mentioned before, the lungs are often involved in the secondary spread of tumours, causing coughing and difficulty in breathing.

Tumours of the mammary glands account for almost a quarter of all tumours in female cats (especially domestic short-haired and Siamese cats), and almost all of these are malignant, i.e. cancerous. In fact, a much higher proportion of *all* tumours in the cat are malignant than in most other species. It has been estimated that each year neoplasia arises in between two and three cats in every thousand, and that in 80% of these cases it will be of the malignant form.

Q *Is it possible to treat cancer in cats?*

A Treatment of certain types of cancer by surgery, radiation therapy and drugs (chemotherapy), particularly if commenced in the early stages, *may* be successful in eliminating the tumour and preventing its occurrence. However, overall the results are disappointing; the most that can often be achieved is a slight increase in life expectancy, and to prevent prolonged and unnecessary suffering euthanasia should be seriously considered as a humane alternative.

Q *What other cat diseases come with old age?*

A As well as neoplasia (cancer), there are a number of other conditions which become increasingly common as cats grow older. One of the most significant is kidney failure. The kidneys have the important function of eliminating the waste products of metabolism, particularly those resulting from the breakdown of proteins in the body, and of regulating the composition of the blood plasma. With age, the number of functional units which comprise the kidneys gradually diminishes, and this may be accelerated by severe damage (e.g. from a road accident), lymphosarcoma of the kidney or bacterial infection. When around 70% of the kidney tissue has ceased to work, the waste products will accumulate in the blood and cause such toxic effects as a loss of appetite, listlessness, vomiting, increased thirst, dehydration, weight loss and, after a time, ulcers in the mouth. This condition, chronic renal failure, is not reversible, and to enable the cat to live with it the diet needs to contain less protein than usual to reduce the production of these waste materials. However, such a diet is unpopular with cats, and it can prove difficult to persuade them to accept it. When cancer or some other progressive cause (e.g. amyloidosis) is responsible, euthanasia is advisable.

(Similar signs can arise rapidly at any age (acute renal failure), for example following serious injury, severe dehydration, certain types of poisoning or twenty-four hours after the onset of the feline urological syndrome (FUS, see page 64). Fortunately the loss of function is usually only temporary in this case and if treated promptly normal kidney function can be restored.)

The other common kidney disorder of the cat, glomerulonephritis (caused primarily by damage inflicted on the kidneys by the immune system) initially requires treatment with a *high* protein diet, but eventually may also terminate in chronic renal failure.

In elderly cats, constipation is very common and a lack of muscle tone in the bowel can lead to failure to pass any motions at all or even to attempt to strain. The faecal material may have to be regularly removed by a vet.

Acquired heart disease also occurs more frequently as cats get older, though it can occur at any age. But in cats coronary thrombosis (i.e. blockage of the blood vessels supplying the heart tissue itself with blood) and malfunctioning of the heart valves are rare; the common disorder is cardiomyopathy – failure of the heart muscle to pump blood efficiently. In about half of all cases blood clots form in the chambers of the heart and fragments of these are carried away in the blood. The most common site for them to lodge is the point where the main artery, the aorta, divides into two arteries supplying the hind legs. A blockage here, called aortic thrombo-embolism, reduces, or cuts off, the blood supply to the hind legs so that the hind paws feel cold. There is no pulse in the back legs, and the cat experiences pain in the leg muscles and is unable to walk. Treatment of this type of cardiac disease is, regrettably, often unrewarding.

With advancing years, dental disease (periodontal disease) increases in frequency and arthritis, seen as lameness on rising, may appear. With decreasing efficiency of its immune system, the aged cat may be unable to maintain adequate immunity against feline respiratory disease (cat 'flu) for long periods so that more frequent vaccination becomes advisable, e.g. every six months. Also the cat's immunity to parasites can diminish, with the result that heavy worm burdens may sometimes be present.

Q *Under what circumstances is it advisable to have a cat put to sleep?*

A Where it is known that a cat will have to endure continual or recurrent suffering, with little or no prospect of remission, then almost certainly the most humane course of action is to have it painlessly put to sleep. By suffering is meant not only acute or severe pain, but also the consequences of congenital malformations and serious injuries, and those slowly progressive illnesses which inevitably can only terminate in death, such as paralysis, cancer and uncontrollable wasting diseases; in fact any disease where severe irreversible damage has been caused.

When an animal is clearly not able to enjoy life any longer, it is unlikely that many owners would wish to prolong its suffering and would rather let it die with dignity. Although many owners suspect that their cat knows when it is going to be put to sleep, this, of course, really isn't possible. But certainly a cat can detect when its owner is distressed, and may alter its behaviour accordingly.

In law, the cat is the property of the owner and therefore at the end of the day the responsibility for the decision to have the cat humanely destroyed must be the owner's. This is why a veterinary surgeon will often ask the owner to sign a formal request for euthanasia to be carried out. But naturally enough, faced with such a difficult decision, many owners will rely heavily on the advice and judgement of their veterinarian. Sometimes there is a legal requirement for a cat to be put to sleep because it represents a danger to the health of the general public and other animals, as with those suffering from rabies.

Vets themselves can face very difficult decisions regarding euthanasia – for instance, where owners are unwilling or physically unable, to give essential treatment, or perhaps cannot afford it, or where owners wish to have a perfectly healthy animal put to sleep because they can't, or won't, look after it. In many cases, although the veterinary surgeon feels the task distasteful, euthanasia is usually preferable to a lingering death from illness or to the owner devising his own method of destruction, or simply abandoning the cat.

Q *How do vets put cats to sleep?*

A Nowadays the method usually adopted for feline euthanasia is for a veterinary surgeon to inject an overdose of a barbiturate anaesthetic, usually intravenously, but occasionally in very young, elderly, or weak animals by another route. The cat goes to sleep as if being anaesthetized for an operation but does not recover. This method inflicts no pain and with an intravenous injection is extremely quick, since only a matter of seconds elapses before the animal becomes unconscious. With a very aggressive cat handling can present a problem and it may be necessary then to place it into an anaesthetic cabinet and to let it inhale an anaesthetic gas or vapour. In general, it is preferable for euthanasia to be performed on a vet's premises, since all the specialized equipment and trained assistance will be available there.

Animal welfare societies, faced with the unpleasant duty of having to destroy many unwanted animals, but with limited charitable resources, may be obliged to use a less expensive method. Reports suggest that the most suitable is to induce unconsciousness and then death by using nitrogen to flush all the vital oxygen out of a cabinet holding the animal.

Q *If my cat has to be put to sleep, how could I dispose of his body?*

A Some owners wish to have the body of their cat returned to them for burial at home, although most will prefer their vet to dispose of the body for them. (Subject to local laws, any grave should be made at least three feet (1 m) deep.) Usually the vet will have an arrangement with the local authority to collect any bodies either for incineration or burial, whichever method of disposal is available in the area. Also there are various pet cemeteries and crematoriums that can offer their services, and usually your vet will be able to give advice about the facilities which are available locally.

Q *Can my cat pass on any diseases to me?*

A Diseases that can be transmitted from animals to man are known as zoonoses. Comparatively few of these are spread by the cat, although they do include some that can be extremely important. Because of the relatively poor immunity in younger animals, such diseases are usually most serious in children.

External parasites transmissible to man include fleas, the fur mite (*Cheyletiella*) and ringworm fungi. Cat fleas commonly attack man and in some urban situations have even replaced the common human flea (*Pulex irritans*). They generally come from the cat's environment rather than directly from the cat itself, so that the first bites are usually on the ankles. In adult humans an itchy red rash is found, and in children irregularly inflamed weals which subside within forty-eight hours to leave small, red, raised papules which are intensely irritant. Later these lesions can occur anywhere on the body. The role of the cat flea in transmitting tapeworm infection has already been discussed, and in some parts of the world cat fleas may transmit other diseases to man, including the plague organism (*Yersinia pestis*).

The fur mite is easily able to penetrate clothing and frequently produces lesions even when the cat itself is showing no signs. Small, red spots which itch furiously and develop into yellow, crusted lesions occur most frequently over the forearms and trunks as a result of cuddling the cat, and sometimes also on the buttocks.

However, on occasion the cat in a household has been blamed for transmitting fleas or mites to man when the real cause of human skin reactions have been red mites (*Dermanyssus gallinae*) derived from birds nesting under the eaves of the house.

Ringworm fungi, like the fur mite, can cause a marked inflammatory reaction in humans, even when the infected cat shows no obvious signs. There is also circumstantial evidence that cats can carry types of ringworm acquired from rodents (mouse favus and vole ringworm), again without showing signs, and pass them on to human contacts.

Of the internal parasites of the cat, *Toxoplasma* and the roundworms are of greatest significance. *Toxoplasma* is responsible for widespread infection in the human population, sometimes causing the disease toxoplasmosis, and possibly abortion or developmental abnormalities in pregnant women. As well as the direct transmission from cat faeces, it can also be acquired by eating raw meat products. The cat roundworm, *Toxocara cati*, is known to occasionally infect children, producing the disease visceral larva migrans, described earlier in this chapter.

As was also mentioned earlier, the tapeworm *Echinococcus multilocularis* grows to maturity in the cat in the northern parts of North America and some parts of Europe and may at times infect man.

If human skin comes into direct contact with soil containing the larval stage of those hookworms that infect cats, the larvae may penetrate the skin, resulting in a dermatitis called cutaneous larva migrans or creeping eruption. This disorder is rare in temperate climates but in warmer regions, such as Florida, the migrating larvae are a considerable nuisance and may even progress to the lungs, causing a wheezing cough. In mosquito-infected regions the microscopic larvae of the heartworm (*Dirofilaria immitis*) may be transferred by a mosquito bite from the blood of the cat to that of man and become trapped in the lungs, producing the usually symptomless condition of pulmonary dirofilariasis.

In some parts of the world, especially the so-called under-developed countries, cats can act as 'reservoir hosts' for a variety of parasites, which do not transfer directly to man but infect other species first. These species in turn are able to infect humans.

The transmission of rabies virus to the human population by cats is, of course, extremely important, although, in many countries where rabies is established, routine rabies vaccination of cats is not obligatory. A scratch or bite from a cat will at times cause a disease in man seven to ten days later, known as cat scratch fever, which is presumed to be due to the transmission of a virus. This virus causes no signs in the cat but produces fever, skin lesions and swollen lymph nodes in humans.

Bacteria may also be implanted in bite wounds, causing them to go septic and form abscesses. Salmonellosis (characterized by fever and diarrhoea containing blood) and tuberculosis are other bacterial diseases which the cat may, on rare occasions, communicate to man.

Q *How can I minimize the chance of catching a disease from my cat?*

A The basic methods of controlling the spread of zoonoses to man are the same as for controlling the spread of disease between cats though, with the exception of vaccination against rabies, immunization is not available.

Cats which are discovered to be infected should be treated wherever possible, and/or isolated, depending upon the dangers inherent in the transfer of the disease. With rabies, isolation on suspicion of infection and euthanasia if signs appear are advisable, and in many countries mandatory. Where treatments are relatively innocuous, such as worming, these may be carried out routinely as discussed previously.

Hygienic precautions are also of great importance to break the chain of transference at as many points as possible. The hands should be thoroughly washed after handling cats and before putting the hands to the face or in the mouth, for example before eating. This applies particularly to young children. Cats should not be allowed to lick the face, or to sleep with humans or on their beds. Also cats should not be allowed to lick plates and utensils used for human food, and their own feeding bowls should be washed separately from crockery and cutlery used by humans.

Children's sandpits should be covered when not in use to prevent them being used as litter trays. Litter boxes should be changed daily and the cat's faeces ideally burned, although this should not be carried out by a pregnant woman. It is advised that pregnant women should avoid looking after a cat, and should wear gloves for gardening to avoid possible contact with *Toxoplasma*. These recommendations may appear extreme, but they have been suggested as measures to reduce the hazards of *Toxoplasma* infection in pregnancy.

Cats should be fed only dried, canned or cooked meat to avoid infecting the cat with parasites which in turn could be acquired by man. Also, to destroy *Toxoplasma* in its infective form, all meat for human consumption should be adequately cooked, and hands that have been in contact with raw meat should be well washed with soap and water. Finally, although it is difficult to destroy the sticky roundworm eggs of cats, they can be removed from the environment by thorough scrubbing of affected surfaces with hot detergent solution followed by a thorough rinsing down.

Q *What operations are commonly performed on cats?*

A The operations of spaying (ovariohysterectomy) and castration (orchidectomy) are probably the most commonly performed. An alternative operation to produce sterility in males, vasectomy, is much less often performed. (This involves removing a short length of each vas deferens, the tube along which the male reproductive fluid, semen, passes from the testicle to the urethra, which in turn conveys it to the tip of the penis.)

Also commonly performed are the opening and draining of abscesses, often caused by bite wounds but sometimes involving the tooth sockets or mammary glands, cleaning and extracting teeth, suturing wounds and arresting severe haemorrhage, and removing tumours from the skin, mammary glands and mouth. Foreign bodies (see page 229) may have to be surgically removed from the skin, tongue and pharynx and sometimes from internal organs such as the stomach or intestines (e.g. hairballs).

Orthopaedic surgery to repair fractures in bones is often necessary. The two halves of a long limb bone are usually secured by a strong metal pin passing down the centre of each part. Fragments are often wired together. At times screws and plates are used to get secure fixing.

Male cats suffering from feline urological syndrome, causing blockage of the urethra, need to be catheterized to withdraw the urine which cannot be passed, or if this proves difficult, to have urine removed via a needle inserted through the abdominal wall. At times males that repeatedly suffer from this condition may have the penis removed, thereby eliminating the site of the obstruction, and a new opening is created for the cat to pass urine (perineal urethrostomy).

Q *What other operations do you sometimes perform on cats?*

A Well, sometimes it is necessary to carry out a Caesarian operation to remove kittens that cannot be born naturally – because of their size or the way they are presented in the birth canal, or because of some abnormality of the mother, such as a very narrow pelvic canal, possibly the result of a pelvic fracture. The operation involves opening into the abdominal cavity and then into the uterus (womb). The operation is so named because reputedly Julius Caesar was delivered in this way.

Cats with chronic ear disorders often benefit from the improved ventilation provided by exposing more of the ear canal to the air, using the technique of aural resection.

Occasionally, it is necessary to repair an abnormal opening in the wall of the abdominal cavity which allows part of the intestines to pass through, a fault known as a hernia. Quite often in road accidents the diaphragm is ruptured causing a diaphragmatic hernia. The passage of intestines into the chest cavity interferes with breathing and can have serious, even fatal consequences. When some kittens are born, the abdominal muscles fail to close together at the umbilicus (the point where the umbilical cord is attached), with the result that a small bulge of protruding intestine can be seen or felt beneath the skin, an umbilical hernia. Usually this type is much less serious. Very occasionally parts of organs which protrude through normal body openings, known as prolapses, need to be secured back into position. In the cat prolapses of the rectum and the uterus are sometimes encountered.

Occasionally it may be necessary to amputate a badly injured limb, tail or ear, or to remove a severely damaged eye. Operations on the eyes or eyelids are sometimes necessary, including an operation to correct the curling inwards of the eyelid margin (entropion), which causes it to contact and irritate the front of the eyeball. This condition is found not infrequently in Persian cats.

Also required at times are drainage operations to remove accumulated fluids of various kinds (e.g. blood, lymph and the watery fluids known as transudates) from the abdominal or chest cavity, and even to flush out purulent discharge from the frontal sinus of cats with sinusitis via a hole drilled through the skull.

Opening into a hollow organ or body cavity is indicated by a medical term ending in -otomy, whereas the removal of an organ or part is designated by the ending -ectomy. Consequently opening into the chest cavity (thorax) is referred to as thoracotomy, and into the abdomen (strictly speaking the peritoneal cavity) as laparotomy. The performance of an exploratory laparotomy is a fairly common surgical technique when it is necessary to examine the abdominal organs for lesions which cannot readily be detected by radiography or other means. Laparotomy is, of course, necessary for opening into one of the abdominal organs (e.g. stomach – gastrotomy, intestines – enterotomy, or bladder – cystotomy) perhaps to remove a foreign body or a tumour, or removing a diseased abdominal organ (e.g. kidney – nephrectomy, or spleen – splenectomy). As with the spaying operation discussed earlier (page 26) any skin sutures are generally removed seven to ten days later.

This is by no means an exhaustive list and many other specialized operations may be needed in particular circumstances, usually requiring a high degree of technical skill.

Q *Are there any operations you would not perform on cats?*

A Some veterinary surgeons, especially in Britain, are unhappy about performing operations which will not benefit the animal and are simply for the convenience of the owner, and often describe such procedures as mutilations. The two most common examples in the cat are the removal of the claws (onychectomy) and of the vocal chords (ventriculocord-ectomy). Many cat owners feel that these operations are utterly appalling.

Q *Why did my vet tell me not to give my cat any food or water before his operation?*

A Almost all the surgical operations on cats are performed under general anaesthesia. (General anaesthesia implies a generalized loss of sensation accompanied by unconsciousness.) The use of a general anaesthetic is most important for humane reasons; it prevents fear and pain during the operation, and, by avoiding pain, greatly minimizes surgical shock which would otherwise frequently prove fatal. In addition, general anaesthesia relaxes the muscles and avoids the possibility of movement, which is an important pre-requisite for successful surgery, particularly on delicate or complex structures.

Because of the use of general anaesthesia, the normal reflex movements (automatic responses) are temporarily abolished, including the coughing reflex. Normally any material which attempts to enter the larynx at the back of the throat provokes a violent bout of coughing to prevent its passing down any further, i.e. down the trachea (windpipe).

Under general anaesthesia vomiting can occur if there is food or water in the stomach, and this material will pass up to the back of the throat (pharynx), where the digestive and respiratory tracts cross each other. Because of the lack of an effective coughing reflex, there is then a grave risk that some of the material may pass through the larynx and down the windpipe to the lungs. Such vomited material, containing acid from the stomach, is very irritant and would provoke a severe pneumonia (inhalation pneumonia), which is invariably fatal.

Furthermore the pressure of a stomach distended with food on the abdominal side of the diaphragm can interfere with normal breathing whilst the cat is anaesthetized.

It is to *avoid* these potentially serious consequences that food and water must be restricted prior to general anaesthesia. Because food can be retained in the stomach for several hours, an overnight fast is usually advised, which means that an animal is not fed after its normal evening meal on the day before it is to be anaesthetized.

Water is removed from the stomach much more rapidly and it is therefore usually sufficient to prevent drinking on the actual day of anaesthesia. In all cases follow your veterinary surgeon's advice. Longer periods of deprivation are undesirable because they weaken the cat and reduce his chances of successfully withstanding the stress of surgery.

There are two other important points:

1 Don't feel sorry for the cat and give it a drink against your veterinary surgeon's instructions, because you may literally kill it with kindness.

2 Tell the vet, or his nurse or receptionist, when food and drink was last consumed. If you know, or suspect, that the animal has in fact eaten or drunk after it was supposed to do, say so, don't conceal the fact. It is usually better to postpone the operation than to expose the animal to an unnecessary risk.

Q *Is general anaesthesia safe?*

A In the vast majority of cases, yes. Modern anaesthetic drugs are less toxic and have a greater margin of safety than previously, and in the hands of trained, experienced veterinary staff death from anaesthesia seldom occurs. However, it should be appreciated that, just as in human medicine, there are individuals who may, quite unpredictably, react unfavourably to a particular drug. Fortunately, such idiosyncratic reactions are few and far between.

Certain groups of animals are more at risk from the undesirable effects of anaesthetics – principally the very old, the very young, and severely ill, debilitated or weak animals, especially those suffering from shock. Whenever possible, it is better to delay anaesthesia and surgery until the animal is in a stronger condition to withstand it. But clearly in an emergency situation this is not possible.

Two general rules emerge therefore:

1 Postpone non-essential anaesthesia and operations (e.g. cat spays) on sick animals until they are improved.

2 Perform any really essential anaesthesia and surgery *immediately*, before a cat's condition deteriorates further.

Q *Is a surgical operation the only reason for giving a general anaesthetic?*

A Although not undertaken lightly, general anaesthesia may be applied in other situations:

1 Where the cat's temperament makes it extremely difficult to handle – for example, with some animals it may be necessary in order to be able to clip matted hair from the coat, or to bath the cat.

2 Where a long painful procedure has to be performed which may unduly distress the cat, such as passing a catheter into the bladder of a male cat with a urinary blockage.

3 Where it is necessary for the cat to remain absolutely still – for example for radiographs to be taken. This is particularly necessary if such radiographs involve complex techniques e.g. the injection of contrast media to show up certain structures more clearly.

As with any type of 'photograph', movement produces blurring of the image so that it can be difficult to distinguish important details. For certain radiographic procedures it may be sufficient to keep the animal still by holding it, but this is usually unsatisfactory for complex procedures, as well as exposing the handlers to non-essential radiation.

Q *Couldn't the vet give my cat a local anaesthetic instead of a general one?*

A In most cases local anaesthesia is used to remove sensation from a relatively restricted and superficial part of the body. The local anaesthetic (otherwise known as a local analgesic) in the form of a drug solution, is injected *either* around the sensory nerve endings of an area, *or* around the nerves which receive sensation from that area (the latter is referred to as nerve blocking). As a result, the transmission of sensations, including pain, from that area to the brain is temporarily prevented, and the animal is unaware of interferences to that region of its body.

Spinal (e.g. epidural) anaesthesia is seldom practised on cats, but this technique produces complete blockage of the lower spinal nerves to produce a total lack of sensation, and paralysis in the posterior part of the body.

In all types of local anaesthesia, however, the animal still remains conscious and therefore subject to fear when it observes what is going on around it. It is also able to move. For these reasons, it is unsuitable for any surgical procedures which involve the deeper structures of the body, or where sudden movement could produce severe damage (e.g. near the eye). It is also not appropriate for lengthy procedures, or if the animal resents being restrained.

As a consequence local anaesthesia in the cat is usually employed only for desensitization of the skin prior to the removal of small growths, or for injection into deeper structures to facilitate certain procedures. For example it is useful for desensitization of the skin before emergency drainage of the bladder, using a needle inserted through the abdominal wall, in cases of urethral obstruction.

12

Mating
and Kitten Care

Q *How often do female cats come into heat, and how can I detect this?*

A All female animals undergo cycles of sexual activity called oestrous cycles. The overall regulation of these is performed by part of the brain, the hypothalamus, which responds both to changes taking place in the body, such as hormone levels, and to environmental changes, particularly the number of hours of daylight. The hypothalamus has the role of preparing the animal both physically and psychologically for mating, pregnancy and birth and ensuring their successful completion. It does this through its control of the hormonal output of the pituitary gland (at the base of the brain) which in turn affects the release of the sex hormones, oestrogen and progesterone, from the ovaries.

In the female cat (the queen) oestrous cycles recur throughout the breeding season which extends from late winter to autumn, (approximately January to September in Britain, Northern Europe and North America; October to June in Australia and New Zealand). During the late autumn and early winter there is a period of sexual inactivity called anoestrus, lasting on average four months, which is associated mainly with the decreased amount of daylight (less than twelve to fourteen hours per day), and much less with the fall in temperature. Consequently cats kept indoors with artificial lighting may have no such period, or only a very short one, so that their oestrous cycles then occur practically all the year round.

There are generally two or three peaks of sexual receptivity during the year when the cycles are most noticeable; in the northern hemisphere these are early spring and early summer, and sometimes in late summer/autumn. At other times sexual receptivity wanes and the cycles are less obvious.

An oestrous cycle begins with a preparatory stage (known as pro-oestrus) during which the cat is often more affectionate, though restless and unwilling to mate; she paces up and down, often rubbing against the furniture, and she may roll on the floor. Often she urinates more frequently. Unlike in the bitch, there is little obvious swelling of the vulva and usually no vaginal discharge at this time. Then after one to three days she enters the stage of oestrus, or sexual receptivity, during which she will be prepared to mate.

The previous signs are intensified; the cat rolls on the floor emitting a characteristic howling cry known as the 'call', which is particularly raucous in the Siamese. For this reason oestrus is often popularly referred to as 'calling', or 'being on call'. Other euphemisms describe the queen as being 'on heat' or 'in season'. This behaviour is often so dramatic that owners who have not witnessed it before believe that the cat must be in great pain and seek veterinary attention as a matter of urgency. When stroked the cat adopts the mating posture normally adopted in the presence of a tom, with her forelimbs lowered and her hind quarters raised giving a concave curve (lordosis) to the spine. The tail is drawn to one side, and in this crouching posture she makes treading movements with her hind feet. The cat often goes off her food and may spay urine in the house. If confined she will make determined efforts to escape outside. Even if these signs are not sufficiently distinctive for you to notice them, and this may indeed be the case with a cat pregnant for the first time (the maiden queen), the neighbourhood toms will almost certainly know and congregate outside your home.

Unlike most other mammals, the cat does not release an egg or eggs from the ovaries (the process of ovulation) *unless* she has been mated. (In this respect the cat is similar to the rabbit, ferret and mink.) Ovulation takes place twenty-four to thirty-six hours after mating and this ensures that the egg(s) will not be discharged until there are sperms already present, so that fertilization is much more likely to take place.

If mating occurs, the signs of oestrus decline within one to two days; if not, they will persist for ten to twelve days. If the female becomes pregnant as a result of mating, no further oestrous cycles will normally occur (but see page 171), but if mating doesn't take place oestrus will be followed by a quiescent period (dioestrus) lasting seven to twelve days before signs of pro-oestrus appear again, indicating the start of a new cycle. Consequently, oestrous cycles recur at intervals of approximately twenty-one days. Older queens tend to have shorter oestrous cycles.

In about 12% of queens, and those of the Siamese breed in particular, dioestrus (the 'interval' between successive calls) appears not to occur, and calling can continue non-stop for six to ten weeks or more (referred to as nymphomania) which can be very wearing for the owner.

There are no breeding seasons for male cats and they are able to mate all the year round, although in fact they are more active sexually in the spring and much less so during the winter. Undoubtedly this is related to the presence of calling females at those times.

Q *At what age are cats capable of breeding?*

A The age at which a cat becomes sexually mature and is able to reproduce is known as puberty. In the female this is evident by the cat coming into heat ('calling') for the first time. The age at which a female cat first calls is very variable, depending on the breed and the time of year, as well as individual characteristics.

Most queens come on heat first at between seven and ten months of age, although Siamese and the Oriental Short-hairs often come into heat at five months' old (even as early as 3½ months' old). Burmese and other short-hairs usually call first at about seven to eight months' old, whereas Himalayans and Persians, as well as free-ranging (feral) cats, delay their first oestrus until ten months of age and sometimes until they are eighteen months' old. However, if it is winter (the usual time of sexual inactivity) when the cat reaches the age at which it could be expected to start calling, then calling will generally be delayed until the early spring. In fact the spring is the time when many young females come into heat for the first time. Signs of oestrus will also be delayed if queens are kept in dark surroundings, particularly if they are isolated from other cats. Conversely, exposure to light, and the presence of tom cats and/or other queens in oestrus, usually hastens the onset of puberty.

Those cats which reach puberty early, i.e. at five months' old or earlier, certainly shouldn't be deliberately mated at that age. As a general rule it is not advisable to mate cats until they are a year old, or ten months at the earliest, i.e. until they are fully grown. Otherwise a cat which is still growing itself will find it very difficult to cope with the additional demands of developing kittens for adequate nutrition, and there might easily be difficulties in the actual birth because of the small size of the pelvic canal.

Generally in the United States, breeding queens are mated at the first heat if this occurs after ten months' old, whereas in Europe mating is more usual at the second heat, provided again that the animal is fully grown and well developed. After that, it is good policy to let most cats have only one litter a year so that they do not become weakened by frequent pregnancies, although the Siamese and similar breeds can often cope satisfactorily with two litters a year.

Male cats usually reach puberty at nine to twelve months' old, but again there is a great degree of individual variation and some may mature at seven months of age. Although stud toms are ideally aged between one and six years, males can go on siring kittens until they are thirteen years or more.

Q *Can I prevent my female cat from calling?*

A Unless you wish to breed from your cat, the long-term solution would be to have her spayed (page 24). However, this operation should not be done whilst the cat is actually calling because the inevitable bleeding is more difficult to control and the operation carries more risk. This appears to be due to the effect of oestrogen on blood clotting.

To stop calling that is currently taking place, particularly if it has been going on for some time with no sign of abating (as it may in a Siamese especially), ovulation can be induced artificially. This is achieved by carefully inserting a sterile, smooth glass rod (lubricated with a little petroleum jelly) or a moistened cotton bud into the vagina for about three-eighths of an inch (1 cm). The cat should be restrained on a table by a helper who is holding its scruff. Then the inserted rod or cotton bud should be gently rotated, and moved backwards and forwards a little. It is quite normal for the female to cry out and afterwards roll, rub and lick herself. If ovulation is successfully stimulated, the cat will go off heat in one to two days (as is usual) and then will follow a period of pseudo-pregnancy lasting for approximately forty days. Very rarely this period terminates in mammary gland enlargement and maternal behaviour.

The same effect is sometimes achieved by breeders using a vasectomized tom cat. Such a male cat retains all his normal sexual behaviour but will not implant any sperms, so that matings again will result in a pseudo-pregnancy. Nevertheless, for at least forty-eight hours after ovulation has been induced in these ways (in fact until all signs of oestrus have dis-appeared), care must be taken to avoid a normal mating or the cat may become pregnant.

Q *Could I give my female cat a contraceptive?*

A In many countries it is possible to obtain from veterinary surgeons contraceptive drugs for cats which can be used either to postpone the onset of oestrus or to stop it (i.e. suppress or interrupt it) soon after it has started. These are used chiefly where it is intended to breed from the queen at a later date but not at present, for example in the case of an immature animal, or where it is necessary to allow her condition to improve after illness or the birth of a previous litter. The most widely used drugs for this purpose are progestagens, progesterone-like substances (such as megoestrol acetate and medroxyprogesterone acetate) given orally or by injection.

(Because of their steroid effects, these drugs are also used to control the itching of flea allergy dermatitis (miliary eczema) and to promote healing of the ulcerated upper lip lesion known as an eosinophilic granuloma (rodent ulcer). The action of progestagens in these conditions is quite separate from their control of oestrous cycles.)

After prolonged oestrus suppression with these drugs, usually two or three months will elapse before the queen calls again if oral treatment has been used, or six months following the use of injections. It is recommended that queens should be mated at the second call after suppression, because residual amounts of the drug may prevent conception if she is mated at the first call. Extensive use of progestagens has shown that they will not harm developing kittens, either of future litters or even where the drug has inadvertently been administered *during* pregnancy.

However, progestagens tend to cause cats to increase their appetite and to retain fluid, producing an increase in weight. They can also cause behavioural changes (sometimes a cat is more relaxed or depressed, sometimes more irritable) and an increased tendency towards bacterial infection of the uterus (including pyometra). More recently weaker progestagens (e.g. proligesterone) have been developed which have the same oestrus-suppressant action but appear less likely to give rise to these unwanted effects.

Q *If my cat has been spayed, does it mean that she can never come into heat and have kittens?*

A Certainly the surgical removal of the uterus (womb) means that it is impossible for a spayed cat to have any kittens. The vast majority of spayed cats will not come into heat either. However, on rare occasions, it is possible for a spayed cat to come into heat and show all the usual signs, i.e. calling, etc. This can arise either because a remnant of tissue from the ovary has been inadvertently left behind after the operation, or because in that particular animal there is also a small collection of sex hormone-secreting cells at some *abnormal* site within the abdomen. In such cases the remaining tissue cells produce sufficient sex hormone (oestrogen) to affect the cat's behaviour and to produce signs of heat, although such signs may not appear for up to four months after the operation. In this situation, the only solution is to perform a second operation to search for, and if identified, to remove the minute piece of tissue which is responsible.

Q *Do cats always mate with the same partner?*

A No, under natural conditions a queen will often mate with several different toms during one period of oestrus (over three to four days), sometimes with more than one in a day. This makes it possible for at least two different tom cats to fertilize different eggs, so that kittens in the same litter can have different fathers, a phenomenon known as superfecundation. Consequently, if you wish to obtain kittens from the breeding of two particular cats it is important not to allow the queen access to other males, even after the planned mating has taken place.

The male cat needs to be familiar with the area in which mating is to take place, and increases his feeling of security by spraying and rubbing against the surroundings. For this reason matings arranged by cat breeders generally involve taking the queen to the premises of the stud tom and not the other way around.

Q *Is a female cat ever too old to have kittens?*

A Ideally, cats that are over eight years of age should not be mated, because with advancing age pregnancies often do not last full term and there is a high rate of foetal mortality.

Q *Will it be harmful to my female cat if she isn't mated after calling?*

A Well, female cats that go on calling without being mated can develop fluid-filled cysts on their ovaries which produce sufficient female hormone to interfere with normal oestrous cycles and ovulation, and with the implantation of the fertilized egg in the uterus. Therefore these changes can be the cause of infertility. At present it isn't clear whether inducing pseudo-pregnancy will serve as effectively as pregnancy in preventing this occurring. It is, of course, psychologically distressing for the cat to be continually calling if you don't intend to let her have kittens.

Q *I've heard that if my pedigree cat is mated by a 'mongrel' tom, this will affect all her future litters. Is this true?*

A No, this is really a terrible old wives' tale. It may be disappointing to find out that this has happened, especially if you were intending to mate her with a pedigree tom to obtain a litter of pedigree kittens, but it will in no way taint the kittens of future litters. Each kitten is formed from the union of a mother's egg and a father's sperm. Egg and sperm both carry half of the total number of chromosomes, and therefore genes, that will be found in the cells of the kitten and which will determine its characteristics, such as appearance, temperament, etc. The sperms do not survive any longer than a day at the outside, so there is no possibility of any of a previous father's genes still being present two to three months later to influence the characteristics of subsequent kittens.

Q *My cat has just got out and been mated. Can I stop her having kittens?*

A If a female is in oestrus and has been in the presence of tom cats, it is virtually certain that she has been mated. An injection of the hormone oestrogen, given by your vet as soon as possible, but certainly within forty hours of mating, will stop the development of the fertilized egg(s).

Q *Do you ever get homosexual cats?*

A When there is not another entire (i.e. unspayed or uncastrated) cat of the opposite sex available, male cats and female cats that are on heat *may* mount a member of the same sex and show the typical mating behaviour, including neck grasping and pelvic thrusting. However, this is not true homosexuality since the activity is soon abandoned when an entire member of the opposite sex is present; in the case of tom cats this means a female on heat.

This sort of behaviour is also seen between kittens of the same sex before puberty, occasionally as early as four months' old, and sometimes between males when one wishes to show his dominance, such as his 'ownership' of territory.

Q *How can I tell if my cat is pregnant?*

A The average length of pregnancy (gestation) in the cat is around nine weeks, in fact nearer to sixty-five days. There is, however, a good deal of variation; four days either side is quite normal and even a week either side is not unusual (58 to 72 days). Kittens born more than one week premature rarely survive. Although it has been suggested that Siamese and Abyssinians may have longer pregnancies, results of a survey showed no appreciable difference between breeds. In general, cats with larger litters have shorter pregnancies, and those subjected to stress (e.g. change in the environment) towards the end of pregnancy tend to delay giving birth. However, unless mating is closely supervised, the actual date of conception may be uncertain.

During pregnancy the fertilized eggs (zygotes) pass down the oviducts to the uterus (womb). The human uterus is pear-shaped consisting mainly of a large body and two very small horns (right and left), each of which connects with the corresponding oviduct. This is because usually only one baby is developing at a time. However, in the cat the body of the uterus is very short and each of the horns comparatively long because there are usually a number of kittens. The fertilized eggs distribute themselves evenly along the horns and attach themselves to the uterine wall. Later an encircling placenta is formed which allows oxygen and nutrients to pass from the blood of the mother into that of the developing kittens, and for waste products to pass the other way. However, there is no mixing of the blood of the mother and the foetus; the blood of the foetus, like all its other tissues, is formed during the foetus's development.

Occasionally in the first three weeks of pregnancy a cat will appear less active, and may eat less and even vomit. Usually, however, the first sign of pregnancy is that roughly three weeks after a successful mating the nipples take on a distinctly pink colour (known as 'pinking up'), which is particularly obvious in a cat pregnant for the first time. After four to five weeks of pregnancy, the developing foetuses should be large enough (roughly 1 inch (2½ cm) long) to be detectable by gentle palpation (feeling of the mother's abdomen). However, great care should be exercised because if this is done clumsily the foetuses can be damaged with the result that abortion occurs. It is usually not possible to estimate the *number* of foetuses present.

At about the sixth week of pregnancy, if there are more than one or two kittens being formed, the cat's abdomen usually appears visibly larger than usual, although because of the foetuses' rapid growth at this stage, they are less detectable on palpation as separate entities. After the seventh week, it *may* be possible to detect movement of the kittens and to feel their heads. At this time the queen often becomes restless, searching the home for a good place to make a nest.

During the last week the mammary glands become enlarged, and the nipples are prominent. The cat becomes more withdrawn and less active, and occasionally there may be a little white, mucoid discharge seen at the vulva.

After five to six weeks there may be clear radiographic evidence of the foetuses, although because of increasing skeletal calcification they are much more obvious at seven weeks. However, radiography is seldom required, unless it is to establish whether there might be some abnormality of the kittens or of the birth canal. Unnecessary exposure to radiation is undesirable, especially during the first three weeks of pregnancy when it may cause abnormal development of the kittens.

Some pregnant cats (approximately 10%) show signs of oestrus (calling) during the third and the sixth weeks of pregnancy, i.e. the cat continues to have oestrous cycles every three weeks. This is because insufficient of the pregnancy hormone, progesterone, is produced by the ovary during the pregnancy to stop the development of further follicles from which the eggs are released. If allowed to, these queens will often mate and ovulate, so that these eggs may also become fertilized. The result is that foetuses of different ages are present in the uterus simultaneously (superfoetation). If this happens, all of the kittens may be born together, with the second set premature and seldom surviving, or, less often, the second litter may be born normally at a later date.

Q *Our family cat is pregnant. Should we give her any special treatment?*

A For most of the pregnancy she should be treated just as she is normally and not fussed over, though care should be taken when she is picked up not to put undue pressure on her abdomen (page 76). It's important not to restrict her exercise or jumping until the end of pregnancy because this has the beneficial effect of maintaining muscle tone. Unnecessary medication (including flea powders and sprays) and radiography should be avoided, especially during the first three weeks when the development of the foetuses is at a critical stage.

A good, balanced, high-protein diet should continue to be fed throughout pregnancy, but during the last month the amount should be gradually increased until she is receiving between about a quarter and a half *more* food than usual, depending upon her appetite. This extra quantity is best fed as a separate meal. Care should be taken to ensure that adequate calcium and vitamin A are supplied (particularly in the last two weeks), if necessary by giving calcium tablets and cod liver oil. It's advisable to give routine treatment for roundworms (ascarids) a month before you believe she is due to give birth to reduce contamination of the kittens' environment later, though this is a matter you can discuss with your vet.

Constipation may occur in the last few days of pregnancy and can be countered by giving more milk or oily fish, or a teaspoonful (5 ml) of liquid paraffin. To increase the amount of maternal antibodies which will be passed on to the kittens, a booster vaccination can be given to the queen before mating or during pregnancy, although in the latter case only *dead* vaccines should be used to avoid foetal damage. When the cat's abdomen becomes so large that she has difficulty in cleaning her hind quarters, it is desirable to wash the region beneath the tail with lukewarm water each day, carefully drying it off afterwards.

Q *How will I know when my cat is about to give birth and what should I do?*

A When, about two weeks before the birth is due, the queen begins to wander around looking for somewhere to have the kittens, provide her with a 'nesting' or 'kittening' box. This need only be a large cardboard box approximately 2 square feet (60 cm²) with plenty of newspaper in it as bedding, and preferably a lid or cover so as to provide some privacy. This lid can be removed when kittening actually begins. Blankets may appear to give greater comfort but it is possible for a kitten to crawl into a fold and then be unable to feed until found some hours later.

The box should be placed somewhere warm, about 72°F (22°C) and quiet, and other pets and children should be kept well away from it. To simplify the queen's entry and exit, it helps to cut a hole about 7 to 8 inches (20 cm) in diameter in one side, 5 or 6 inches (15 cm) above the floor. She should be persuaded to use the box by being regularly placed in it, and will usually soon tear up the paper to make a comfortable nest. However, many cats have a natural instinct to establish more than one nest for the security of the litter, so that it is prudent to exclude her from rooms in which you wouldn't relish her nest-making, and if necessary to provide her with more than one box at different sites. It may set your mind at rest if at this stage you take the cat to your local vet for a check-up.

During the last week of pregnancy the queen is generally less active, though often appearing uncomfortable while resting. Check that her motions during this time are not hard because they can provide an obstruction in the pelvic canal; if this appears to be the case, give a teaspoonful of liquid paraffin. Also at this time it is a good idea, especially with long-haired cats, to carefully clip away the hair from around the mammary glands and the vulva (the opening of the birth canal). Make sure that the cat is confined (give her a litter tray) and doesn't go outside to have her kittens, particularly in the winter because it is possible that cold weather may kill them.

Usually anything from twelve to twenty-four hours before giving birth (parturition) the queen enters the first stage of labour and is very restless, spending more time in the nest re-arranging it. She pays frequent visits to the litter tray, straining but without effect. Some females may show signs of a clear discharge at this time. In this stage some (though not all) cats go off their food and/or show a fall in body temperature of 2°F (1°C), i.e. down to 99.5°F (37.5°C). The presence of milk in the teats shows that birth is imminent.

Q *Should my vet be present when the kittens are born? I don't want to bother him if it is unnecessary.*

A You won't necessarily have to call your vet at all; most cats can cope with birth perfectly adequately on their own, or with just a little help from their owners. Nevertheless, it is a good idea to inform your vet beforehand so that he can make arrangements to receive and deal with your cat if an emergency arises.

Q *I have never seen kittens being born. What are the stages of labour in a cat?*

A Towards the end of the first stage of labour the queen may breathe more rapidly (panting), often purring at the same time and sometimes crying out. The rate at which events occur is very variable, and you shouldn't panic if nothing more happens for some time.

The onset of the second stage is shown by marked abdominal contractions, causing the queen to strain, which gradually increase in frequency up to one every thirty seconds. The queen may groan and may appear very agitated, repeatedly licking her vulva. Many cats are reassured by the presence of their owner at this time, stroking and talking to them.

Eventually, after strong contractions, the first kitten, enclosed in the bag of fluid (the amniotic sac) in which it has developed, passes down the birth canal and appears at the vulva. Frequently the sac will burst on its way down and the kitten's appearance is preceded by a flood of clear fluid. Otherwise, the sac appears intact, as a balloon-like arrangement covering the kitten, and is then often burst by the mother's frequent licking whilst it is at the vulva. To do this she will put her head between her hind legs.

Cats will usually lie on their sides whilst expelling each kitten, although they may stand, adopting the same posture as for passing motions if any particularly hard straining is required.

In most cases the first kitten is completely expelled within half an hour, often sooner, although additional time may be needed if the kitten is presented rear end first with its hind legs still tucked inside (a so-called breech birth); fortunately, this isn't common. Roughly two-thirds of kittens are presented head first.

When a kitten has been expelled, it is usual for the mother to lick it, and in so doing to break the membrane over it if this is still present. Her licking stimulates the kitten to start breathing and wriggling. The mother would then normally bite through the umbilical cord (the kitten's life-line attachment to the placenta when it was inside the womb) about two inches away from the kitten's body. If she doesn't show any interest in doing this, you should sever the cord at this point, ideally tearing it with clean fingers because this will simultaneously seal the ends. Be careful not to pull on the cord because this might cause an umbilical hernia. If scissors are used to cut the cord they should preferably be sterile, and before making the cut it is advisable to tie a thread around the cord between the kitten and the cut to prevent any seepage of blood.

If the mother doesn't tear open the membrane, as might happen with a queen having her first litter, you should do this quickly, and then tear or cut the cord and dry the kitten with a rough towel. Try to make sure its air passages are clear by wiping the fluid from them; if necessary, the kitten can be held in the palm of your hand with its head nearest your fingers, and gently swung a few times to remove any remaining liquid. Brisk rubbing will normally stimulate breathing but if this doesn't work, *gently* blowing into its nostrils may start respiration.

In most cases after a few more contractions (generally within five to fifteen minutes), the brownish placenta will be passed, looking like a piece of liver. This is called the third stage labour. The appearance of some brown fluid at this time is quite normal. A primitive instinct to hide the presence of new-born kittens from possible predators usually causes the mother to eat the placenta; if not, it should be removed and destroyed. Unless there are twins, the number of placentas passed should equal the number of kittens. Because a retained placenta can result in uterine infection, it is advisable to count how many have been expelled and if there is any discrepancy present her for veterinary examination.

The remaining kittens may all follow within an hour, although three hours is more usual, and at times it can take up to six. Furthermore, in some queens there is a perfectly normal interruption to parturition after the first one or two kittens have been delivered. This period, during which contractions cease as if parturition had been completed, can last twelve to twenty-four (even occasionally forty-eight) hours before labour recommences and the remaining kittens are born in a quite normal state. The total number of kittens in a litter can range from one to nine but is usually between three and five (in fact, the average number is 4.5). In Persians the average litter size is smaller, just two or three.

Q *During the birth of kittens are there ever any emergencies when I should call on my vet for help?*

A Very occasionally it is necessary to tranquillize a queen that becomes almost hysterical in the first stage of labour, crying incessantly and following the owner around. This is most likely to occur in the Siamese breed.

Veterinary attention should also be obtained if at any stage (before, during or after parturition) the queen produces a foul-smelling discharge or if profuse haemorrhage occurs.

In general, however, the three main indications for obtaining veterinary assistance are as follows:

1 Where the queen has shown strong, forcible contractions for two hours without a kitten appearing.

2 Where the queen appears tired and the contractions get progressively weaker; referred to as uterine inertia.

3 Where the kitten is partially delivered and cannot be dislodged. In this case no more than five minutes should elapse before attempts are made to get help.

A common cause of all three is some obstruction to the passage of the kitten(s) producing difficulty in giving birth (dystocia). The fault may be maternal, in which case it is usually due to a deformed pelvis, caused either by a previous fracture or by deformity resulting from a lack of calcium when a kitten. Rarely, there may be some other cause of obstruction, such as a tumour in the pelvic canal. Alternatively, the obstruction may be caused by the foetus being oversized or abnormally presented. Foetal enlargement may be a normal feature (e.g. Persian kittens have comparatively large heads) or abnormal, as in the case of deformed kittens (monsters) or those that have become swollen following disease or death in the uterus. One type of abnormal presentation is where two large foetuses become jammed in trying to enter the pelvic canal together, but usually problems of presentation occur when the kitten is partially born (**3** above); for example, cases of breech birth (tail coming first with hind legs still inside) or where a kitten's head becomes turned to one side just before it passes through the vulva.

In cases where the head and front legs, or the hind legs, are already outside but there is difficulty passing the remainder of the kitten, an attempt can be made to help the delivery. Carefully grasp the exposed part through a single thickness of clean towelling, push it back in about a centimetre (just over half an inch) and then rotate the kitten a little to one side and then gently pull outwards. It helps if this pull is first slightly to the right, and then to the left, and so on, rather than a straight pull backwards. If this approach fails, or if the presentation is more complicated, veterinary help must be obtained.

If it proves impossible for the vet to overcome the obstruction, it will be necessary to perform a Caesarian operation to remove the kittens, i.e. through incisions in the abdominal wall and the uterus.

After the birth of the kittens has taken place, the following conditions make it advisable to consult your vet:

1 You believe a placenta or a foetus is retained, e.g. if a persistent brown vaginal discharge is present.
2 There was any problem with delivery.
3 You had to tie off the umbilical cord of one of the kittens.
4 Any kitten looks or behaves abnormally, e.g. won't suckle or cries continuously.
5 The queen doesn't eat within twenty-four hours of birth, or is obviously ill, or if these signs develop later.
6 The queen has had problems during and after having previous litters (e.g. the development of uterine infection).
7 There is an unpleasant discharge or marked bleeding. However, a little reddish vaginal discharge is quite normal for three weeks after kittening.

Q *What should I do if the kittens appear abnormal or are unwanted?*

A In the case of grossly deformed kittens, it is much the kindest thing to have them put to sleep immediately; indeed, they may very well not survive long in any case. The deformities include such things as spina bifida (where the spinal cord is exposed), gross umbilical hernia (where most of the intestines are outside the body, covered only by a pouch of skin), and the most common, a severe cleft palate (an opening between the mouth and the overlying nasal cavities, so that in suckling milk passes into the nasal chambers and drips from the nose). Other abnormalities such as extra toes or shortened tails, however, will not present any danger to health. If there is any doubt it is always worth discussing with your vet the chances of successfully treating and rearing a particular kitten.

Unwanted kittens, i.e. those for which no homes can be found, are best put to sleep humanely as soon as possible. This often means having to harden your heart, but it is preferable to increasing the stray cat population. Where possible, two kittens should be left to suckle the mother, not only because of its beneficial psychological effect, but also because it may prevent her developing mastitis subsequently. Where it is necessary, unwanted kittens should always be put to sleep by your veterinarian and not disposed of by other methods such as drowning which is extremely unpleasant and inhumane.

Q *How long will it be after my cat has had kittens before she is calling again?*

A It is believed that this is *most* likely to occur three to four weeks after the kittens have been weaned or removed (this includes those kittens who die or who are removed at birth). Certainly, it is usually related to the length of the weaning period, so that the longer the time before weaning, the longer before calling begins again. Where weaning occurs at the start of the winter period (anoestrus), calling may not be seen again for twenty weeks or more after the previous birth.

However, in a number of cats calling occurs, and mating is possible, soon after the kittens have been born (from two to ten days afterwards), so that it is wise to keep queens segregated from toms even though they are still nursing their kittens.

Q *Is it true that a queen will always kill the runt of a litter?*

A I am afraid this is another old wives' tail, although queens do display instinctive cannibalism towards dead and partially decomposed foetuses or a severely congenitally deformed kitten. At times, such a kitten may simply be rejected, i.e. not fed or groomed. Of course a runt kitten, the most poorly developed of the litter, starts under a handicap and may have difficulty in competing with larger and stronger kittens so that, due to malnutrition, it may not survive.

Sometimes a queen may overdo the licking and biting of the umbilical cord with the result that she damages the kitten's abdominal wall and so-called 'inadvertent cannibalism' may occur, although this is rare. (This licking behaviour of the mother seems to be a response not to the kittens themselves but to the fluids produced at birth.) The very rare rejection of normal newborn kittens, or even aggressive attacks upon them, by the mother is believed to be due to a combination of changing hormone levels and stress.

Q *Is it true that tom cats will kill kittens?*

A It is also a widespread opinion that males will kill and/or cannibalize their offspring. In general, it seems that the killing of kittens arises where the male is attracted to a female coming into heat soon after her kittens have been born. Attempts to mate her, however, are unwelcome and she fights him off. The excited male then attempts to mate with one or more of the kittens but naturally his efforts are unsuccessful, simply because of their relative sizes, and, as his mating grip on the nape of the kitten's neck intensifies, he injures and finally kills the kitten. There is then an instinctive reaction to consume, partially or wholly, the dead offspring. Because of the possibility of this happening, it is always advisable to keep toms segregated from kittens until they are four months' old.

Q *What attention will the mother cat and kittens require after the birth?*

A After kittening the mother will thoroughly wash all the kittens and herself, and can then be given a warm drink and possibly some food before resting; although having consumed the placentas (afterbirth), she may not feel hungry for a few hours. (It may also prove possible for you to remove the soiled newspapers, though don't bother if this disturbs her.) A lactating queen will need about three times as much food as usual, fed in an increased number of meals per day; in fact, it's difficult to overfeed her.

Most newborn kittens suckle within an hour or two of being born, usually soon after being washed. They 'paddle' towards the mother and nuzzle her fur until they find a nipple. Some queens may allow the first kittens in the litter to suckle in between giving birth to the others; others won't permit suckling until the last kitten has been born. If the queen's milk is slow to appear, the sucking of the kittens stimulates its flow.

Most newborn kittens weigh between $2\frac{3}{4}$ and 5 oz (90 to 140 g), with an average of 4 oz (115 g), though Siamese kittens may weigh as little as 2 oz (60 g). They usually feed every two hours, though this soon lengthens to every three then every four hours. If feeding goes well and the kittens are warm and contented, little crying will be heard. However, if a kitten has not fed within twelve hours of being born, it will almost always die from a low blood sugar level and low body temperature.

The most common cause of death in kittens is a lack of milk, so it is wise to check on the flow of milk by gently squeezing the nipples on the day following birth. Any blocked nipples should be carefully bathed with warm water and massaged to stimulate the flow of milk. Blind teats attached to non-functioning glands may sometimes be discovered. At times, mastitis (inflammation) can affect the mammary glands, but usually only one or two. The glands appear hot, hard and painful so that the queen refuses to allow suckling. It can lead to an abscess and a vet should be consulted immediately.

Kittens should gain weight at the rate of $\frac{1}{3}$ to $\frac{1}{2}$ (10 to 15 g) per day; round about 3 to $3\frac{1}{2}$ oz (80 to 100 g) per week. It is particularly important for them to have milk for the first forty-eight hours of life because this is the colostrum (see page 138) containing the maternal antibodies which will provide temporary immunity against infection. Most mother cats remain with their kittens constantly for these first two days.

After two to three days many kittens will return fairly regularly to the same teat and those that have 'established' a right to the rear teats, which are richer in milk, gain a lasting developmental lead.

The queen may pass a little blood-stained discharge for a week or so, but if (as already mentioned) a large amount of blood or foul-smelling discharge is passed, or she has other signs of illness (not eating, vomiting, losing interest in the kittens) then veterinary advice should be sought.

As the kittens grow older, the initially high room temperature can gradually be reduced. For the first three weeks the mother cat licks and grooms the kittens, especially their ano-genital area. At times, as was touched upon earlier (page 178), a mother cat will feel the need to move her kittens to another site in the household; though usually she is perfectly happy if the kittening box is moved there also. The urge to do this seems to be greatest between three and five weeks after parturition.

Q *What is 'milk fever'?*

A Occasionally, a queen will show signs of a lack of calcium, a condition known as eclampsia (puerperal tetany or milk fever). Usually it is seen where there are five or more kittens in the litter and generally it happens two to four weeks after birth, although sometimes earlier, sometimes later. The queen has no interest in the kittens, is restless and staggers, and won't eat. Ultimately she will develop muscle spasms and convulsions, accompanied by a high temperature. Prompt veterinary treatment can rapidly reverse these signs.

Q *How can I tell the sex of a newborn kitten?*

A Sexing kittens will be much easier if there are two sexes in a litter, because then you can compare one with the other. Any problem arises from

How to sex a kitten

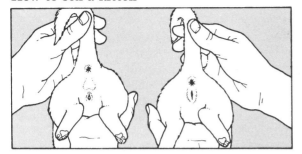

Place the kitten on your hand and lift its tail. In either sex two openings are visible. These will be further apart in a male (left) than in a female (right) and after 4 weeks old, as shown, the testicles may be obvious between them.

the fact that in cats, unlike the larger domestic animals, the urogenital opening in males and females is at a very similar site beneath the tail.

If the kitten is held in the hand with its rear end towards you and its tail raised, two openings will be apparent. The upper one, nearest the tail, is the anus, the opening from the rectum, and the lower one is the urogenital opening. In the female this opening (the vulva) is a vertical slit very close to the anus. In a male two *small* swellings, the testicles, may be evident about half an inch (1 cm) below the anus and just beneath them is the small round opening of the prepuce. However, although at birth the testicles have usually descended to this site (from the abdomen where they have developed), they may not be obvious until four to twelve weeks later. Gentle pressure either side of the opening of the prepuce will cause the small, bright pink penis to protrude.

This is the only way to tell the kitten's sex accurately. The look of its face, the way it urinates and the presence of teats (which occur in both males and females) are not reliable guides. In general, orange (ginger) cats will be males and tortoiseshell cats will be females, but there are even exceptions to these general 'rules'.

Usually sexing is easiest just after birth or at about one month old, though in long-haired breeds it is an advantage to sex kittens early before the growth of the coat obscures the openings.

Q *Is it possible to successfully rear orphan kittens?*

A If for some reason the queen is unable to feed her kittens, it *is* possible to rear them artificially; for instance, if the queen dies whilst, or soon after, giving birth, or if she has a Caesarian operation and is unable to feed the litter for a day or two. It may also be necessary to do this for a time if the queen is ill, e.g. with mastitis or eclampsia, or has no milk, or in those cases where she rejects the kittens. Some people, however, express grave doubts about the long-term effects of maternal deprivation on orphaned kittens and whether hand-rearing them is advisable. Such kittens often do not make good pets; they appear more prone to illness and some turn vicious or suffer from other behavioural problems. (Similarly, if one kitten is rejected by its mother it is invariably destined to become an unhealthy, unsociable individual and it is generally wiser to have it put to sleep.)

Finding a foster mother or mothers for the kittens is always preferable to artificial feeding; for example, a cat whose kittens have died or have had to be destroyed, or one that is still feeding her kittens. Usually one or two kittens can be added to an existing litter without the foster mother caring, provided that this is done when she isn't around. It may be possible to discover suitable foster animals through contacting your vet or local catteries.

Artificial feeding requires the kittens to be fed milk every two hours (though at rather longer intervals during the night) for the first three weeks of life. After that the intervals can be lengthened and the night feeds dispensed with after three weeks. Initially, about a teaspoonful (5 ml) of milk food is required at each feed, rising to two teaspoonsful after a fortnight, although the kitten's appetite is the best guide to its requirements.

Compared with cows' milk, cats' milk contains the same quantity of lactose (milk sugar), slightly more fat, twice as much calcium and phosphorus and three times as much protein. A variety of substitutes can be used. Some of the best and easiest to prepare are the commercial cat milk substitutes (e.g. Lactol and Cimicat) made up according to instructions, or human baby food products prepared at twice the concentration intended for babies, or one tin of evaporated cows' milk or goats' milk plus a third of a tin of water. Alternatively, one can use 1 oz (30 g) of skimmed milk powder in ¼ pint (140 ml) of water with 3 teaspoonsful (15 ml) corn oil whisked in; or again, a ¼ pint (140 ml) of single cream, an egg yolk (plus two to three drops of cod liver oil and a teaspoonful (6 g) of sterilized boneflour) added to a pint (570 ml) of cows' milk. If necessary, additional vitamins and minerals can be added to these formulae as drops (e.g. Abidec).

These milk foods can be made up freshly for each feed, or, in the case of complex formulae, prepared every twenty-four hours and stored between times in the refrigerator. Make sure that all the ingredients are well whisked together so that there are no lumps of powder, etc. This milk should be fed at blood heat (i.e. approximately 100°F (38°C)). Allow the kitten to take it in small amounts so that it can swallow easily, and avoid any going down the windpipe.

Feeding is best done using a special kittens' feeding bottle and teat (e.g. Catac) obtainable from pet stores or sometimes your veterinarian. If this is not available a doll's bottle and teat, or a 5 ml disposable syringe, or an eye dropper, can be used. If the kitten has difficulty taking the milk from the end of a dropper or syringe, a teat, if available, can be fitted. Even a short (i.e. ¾ to 1 inch) length of bicycle valve tubing could be used. These feeding utensils must be thoroughly cleansed after use; e.g. rinsing in cold water, washing in hot detergent water, then rinsing again and immersing in a hypochlorite bleach solution (e.g. Milton) as recommended for babies' bottles. Alternatively, a glass feeding bottle can be boiled for ten minutes immediately prior to use.

After feeding, the kitten's face should be wiped clean with a dampened piece of cotton wool and then the kitten turned over and its abdomen and anal region gently rubbed with this cotton swab to stimulate the passage of urine and motions. It is also important to avoid hypothermia, keeping the kittens under an infra red lamp, or on an electrically heated pad (thermostatically controlled) to produce a temperature of 80 to 86°F (27 to 30°C) in the first week, gradually reducing to 70°F (21°C) over a five to six week period, after which they should be able to generate enough heat to keep themselves warm. Artificially fed kittens can be weaned in the same way as any others.

Q *How should kittens be weaned?*

A Weaning refers to the process whereby kittens make the transition from an all-milk diet to a solid diet, and it is achieved by gradual introduction of an increasing proportion of solids. Where there are large litters, or the mother's health is poor, early weaning will mean that she has to provide less of their total nutrition. Usually, from the end of the first month the mother cat will frequently evade attempts by the kittens to suckle by climbing out of their way, or by lying so that her teats are in contact with the floor.

At about three weeks of age a kitten will often be seen tentatively lapping from its mother's milk dish, and starting at this age it can be given three or four small feeds ($\frac{1}{2}$ to 1 teaspoonful) of a cat's milk substitute, as described in the answer to the preceding question. Then after one or two days small amounts of baby cereal (e.g. Farex) can be gradually incorporated into the milk food, and after a week or so a small quantity of meat-based or fish-based canned baby food, or the meat jelly from a canned pet food, can replace one of these milk feeds.

Regardless of the amount of milk obtained from the mother cat, the number of feeds given per day can remain at around four, although gradually increase their size up to about three to four teaspoonsful or more each time when the kitten is six weeks' old. Also, the proportion of meat and fish-based feeds can increase until at around six to eight weeks' old the kitten can if necessary be removed from the mother altogether, and fed four or five meals a day of a special canned 'kitten diet'. Long-haired cats are rather slower in most stages of development, and may also be weaned a little later.

During weaning the consistency of the supplementary diet should change, becoming more solid as time goes by. Finely minced beef, fish and poultry, which has been lightly cooked, or canned kitten diet can be fed; liquidized to begin with, then fed mashed up so that it is just a little 'sloppier' than usual. Also in the early stages scrambled eggs with butter can be given. Offering a wide variety of foods is valuable because it helps to prevent the cat becoming rigid in its dietary likes and dislikes in later life.

If at any stage of weaning diarrhoea occurs regularly, or the kitten won't feed, consult your vet.

Q *Is it true that tom cats with bad dental decay cannot mate?*

A There is some truth in this apparently bizarre belief. If the male is allowed to mount, he grasps the skin at the back of the female's neck with his teeth before straddling her. Male cats that suffer from severe dental disease may be unable to mate because they cannot grasp the neck properly and thereby get into the correct position.

13
Nursing the Sick Cat

Q *I dread having to give my cat a tablet as he struggles so much and then just spits it out under the table. Is there a proper way to give him a tablet or capsule?*

A Some cats *may* accept the tablet or capsule sealed in a titbit of minced meat or fish, especially if they are hungry. This is unusual, but worth trying first. Simply placing the tablet in a dish of food usually means that the food gets eaten and the tablet left! Crushing a tablet and mixing the powder in with the food is often unsuccessful (especially if the tablet tastes unpleasant) though disguising the flavour with strong-smelling substances, such as fish oils or yeast extract, *may* work. Some people find a tablet crushed in evaporated milk occasionally works. Again, you could try it but always prepare the disguised tablet out of the cat's sight!

If your vet tells you *not* to crush or break a tablet before giving it, *do* follow this advice. Certain tablets (for example, some worming and antibacterial tablets) contain very bitter drugs surrounded by an inert coating. If this bitter material contacts the inside of the mouth, the cat will salivate profusely and breathe rapidly so that its mouth becomes filled with froth, causing great distress. (Some degree of extra salivation normally occurs when dosing with tablets, but not as marked as this.)

In most cases, the tablet has to be placed at the back of the mouth before the cat will swallow it, particularly where repeated dosing is required. If the cat is reasonably good-tempered, you can possibly do this single-handed, although someone else's assistance in holding the cat is often useful. Where the cat is difficult to handle, some assistance is essential. First place the animal on a table or worktop counter about three feet high and where there is a good source of light.

Method 1 This is usually the most effective. If you are right-handed, grasp the cat's scruff (the loose skin at the back of the neck) gently but firmly in your left hand and hold the tablet or capsule between the thumb and index finger of your right hand. If you are left-handed, reverse these instructions. Hold the animal so that it is lying or sitting upright. Your assistant should prevent the animal from scratching by holding its front legs down on the table. Alternatively, the cat can be firmly wrapped in a towel (or placed inside a pillow case or shoe bag) with only its head protruding; then held down on the table. Have a pencil or ballpoint pen within reach.

Rotate the hand which is grasping the scruff so that the animal's nose points upwards (at 45 degrees or more to the horizontal), while at the same time pressing downwards to prevent the cat rising. Usually the mouth will open; if necessary the second finger of the hand holding the tablet can push downwards slightly on the lower front teeth. Now place the tablet as far back into the mouth as possible.

Now take up the pencil or pen immediately, and with its *flat* end quickly, but gently, push the tablet over the back of the tongue, i.e. into the throat. (Using a pencil rather than the index finger avoids the possibility of getting bitten.)

Relax the grip on the scruff, close the cat's mouth quickly and stroke its throat. Wait for it to gulp and lick its nose, which indicates that the tablet has been swallowed. Don't let the cat put its nose down *before* swallowing – he'll simply spit the tablet out again.

There are other ways to place the tablet right at the back of the throat; one which is very simple is to hold the tablet in a pair of artery forceps. This is a specialized instrument, but easily ordered from a pharmacist, and it renders tablet administration as easy as it ever could be. Another is to use a plastic 'pill giver', sold in pet shops, which will both hold and eject the tablet.

Method 2 Some people prefer this method. Again your helper restrains the cat so that it is lying or sitting upright. You can then open the cat's mouth by putting one hand over the cat's head, placing your index finger and thumb well behind the large canine teeth on either side, and then pushing down on the lower teeth with the index finger and thumb. Introduce the tablet into the throat with the other hand, as described in Method 1. Close the jaws quickly afterwards and stroke the throat.

Whichever method is adopted the aim is to be firm, quick and efficient. With successive attempts the animal will become more restless and the job more difficult, so try to get it right first time. Watch the cat afterwards to check that the tablet isn't spat out; if it has been, the procedure will need to be repeated. (Occasionally owners move the furniture to find a dozen antibiotic tablets behind the settee. Before then, they had thought their technique was flawless.)

Giving a tablet is much simpler than giving a capsule. The outer gelatine shell of a capsule becomes sticky on contact with moisture so usually, unless it is put down the throat at the first attempt, the capsule will stick to your fingers or to the inside of the cat's mouth, and successive attempts will become progressively more difficult.

How to give your cat a tablet

1a. *Holding the cat's scruff turn its head so that its nose points upwards. As its mouth opens place the tablet as far back into the throat as possible.*

1b. *Alternatively the cat's mouth can be opened by pushing down on the lower teeth with forefinger and thumb placed on either side. Then pop in the tablet.*

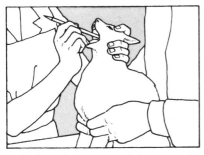

2. *Before the cat can spit it out, push the tablet quickly, but carefully, over the back of the tongue into the throat using the flat end of a pencil or pen.*

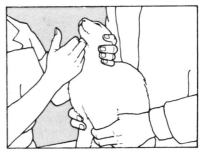

3. *Then close the cat's mouth, and with its head still pointing upwards, stroke its throat until it gulps and licks its nose. Try to get it right first time.*

Occasionally owners attempt to put powdered drugs directly into their cat's mouth. This is almost impossible to do successfully and shouldn't be attempted. Cats usually produce a lot of saliva when being dosed by mouth, and if you do succeed in getting any powder into the mouth, most of it will be washed out again in the flow of saliva.

Q *How can I give my cat liquid medicine?*

A Giving a liquid medicine is usually more difficult than giving a tablet.

Have the cat restrained, lying or sitting on a table top or a worktop, by another family member or a friend. Your helper should stand behind the cat and hold its front legs down to prevent scratching. Or the cat can be rolled up in a towel (or placed in a pillow case or shoe bag) with only the head sticking out; then it can be pressed down onto the table top.

If your cat is reasonably good-tempered, hold its head so that the nose points slightly upwards. If he is more difficult to handle it will be necessary

How to give your cat liquid medicine

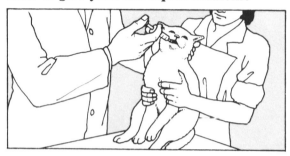

Hold the cat's head so that its nose points slightly upwards. Place the tip of a 5ml syringe (or teaspoon) in between its lips at the side of the mouth and very slowly trickle the liquid out. If the cat coughs and splutters, stop for a while.

to grasp his scruff firmly, and then direct his nose upward. If you are right-handed carry out this restraint with your left hand, and vice versa.

Have the medicine already measured out into a small plastic bottle, or a vial of the type used for dispensing liquids or tablets, or (best) contained in a 5 ml. disposable plastic syringe. A syringe is preferable because it is much easier to handle and avoids any spilling of the medicine; if a spoon is knocked or you cannot pour it easily some of the liquid gets spilled. If a spoon has to be used, remember some useful tips: half-fill two spoons rather than try to manipulate one which is completely full (or else pour a teaspoonful of liquid into a dessertspoon); put a small book, or similar object, under the tip of the handle to keep the top of the bowl horizontal – this will avoid spilling and facilitate picking the spoon up.

Place the end of the vial, syringe or spoon between the lips at the *side* of the mouth and let the liquid trickle out. Do it slowly so that the cat is able to swallow without coughing or spluttering. If there *is* any spluttering allow a pause for the cat to put his head down to recover (though still holding him) before administering any more.

A plastic eye dropper can be substituted for the syringe, but a *glass* eye dropper is best avoided in case it gets chewed on and splinters.

The aim is not *necessarily* to place the dosing implement between the teeth, though this *can* be done with a syringe or eye dropper and will greatly speed up administration. Otherwise let the liquid slowly trickle between the teeth. Certainly do not attempt to open the jaws and place a spoon or bottle between them, either at the side of the mouth or at the front, because this invariably provokes a struggle, resulting in only partially successful dosing and great distress to all parties.

Afterwards it is often valuable to make a fuss of your cat, or to give him some favourite titbit, to reassure him that you are not trying to be unkind.

Q *Does it matter at what time my cat has his medicine?*

A The instructions from your vet (written or verbal) might indicate precisely when a particular medicine should be administered; for example, before or after meals. Many drugs which influence the digestion or absorption of food need to be given just before meals. Of the remaining drugs, most will be absorbed faster and more completely if they are not given at the same time as food.

When the instructions state that the medicine (tablets, capsules or liquid) should be given a certain number of times a day, the intention is for the times of administration to be as equally spaced as possible. In other words, twice a day means every twelve hours, and three times a day every eight hours, insofar as this is feasible. Obviously it is not usually necessary to get up in the middle of the night to give medicine, and times of administration may have to be fitted around working hours, but as far as possible the even spacing of doses should be practised.

Q *The vet has given me an inhalant for my cat. What is it and how can I administer it?*

A Inhalants are volatile substances which are mildly irritant to the respiratory tract – such as oil of eucalyptus, friar's balsam and Vick. In order to work, the inhalant must first be converted to a vapour which can be breathed in. Body heat can do this and so a little inhalant can be applied directly to the cat's chest or chin. However, vaporization is best achieved by adding a little of the inhalant to very hot water. Then both the water vapour and the vaporized inhalant are inhaled. The mild irritant effect of the inhalant on the respiratory membranes causes a runny nose – in other words it increases the volume and decreases the 'thickness' (viscosity) of respiratory secretions. This has the very beneficial effect of washing away the thick sticky mucus which otherwise will block the nasal passages. The water vapour also helps in this and moisturizes the dry membranes. Indeed, because cats tolerate the vapour on its own so much better, some vets prefer not to add an inhalant.

It is unusual for a cat to be co-operative and to hold its head voluntarily over a steaming bowl. Consequently, the best method is to place the cat in a basket the floor of which will allow entry of the vapours – one made of wickerwork or plastic-coated wire mesh, for example. The basket should be firmly supported at either end by a small pile of bricks or books, sufficient to allow a bowl or basin to be placed directly underneath it, and it should be free of bedding.

First apply a smear of petroleum jelly (e.g. Vaseline) to the cat's upper and lower eyelids, and around the nostrils, to avoid undue smarting. Then, with the cat in the basket, place beneath it a small bowl half full of boiling water and containing a *little* of the inhalant, i.e. six drops of liquid or a quarter teaspoonful of solid medicament. Or, as mentioned above, the boiling water *alone* may be used. Now cover the entire basket with a thick blanket, towel or plastic sheet which should reach to the floor all the way around so that the vapour cannot escape. After five minutes, remove the cat and clean away the strings of mucus from around its nose. Then clean the basket as well. Most cats accept this treatment and appear to find relief, but if an animal panics and will not settle down it is best removed straight away. Where the treatment affords some relief, it can be repeated two or three times a day.

Some owners place both cat and bowl of steaming inhalant beneath a table or chair and cover everything with a blanket which reaches to the floor on all sides. Sometimes the cat is shut into a very small room, such as a bathroom or cloakroom, with the bowl of inhalant. However, these methods are best avoided if possible because of the danger of the cat becoming distressed, upsetting the liquid and scalding itself in the process.

Q *Although I don't like the idea, are there any occasions when I should force-feed my cat?*

A As a general rule, of course, it would be unnecessary, but where a cat has lost its appetite, and it has proved impossible to persuade it to eat, so-called 'force-feeding' may be resorted to. There should not be much emphasis on the force; indeed to cram an animal's throat with food or liquid that it cannot, or will not, swallow is likely to lead to some of the food passing down the windpipe (trachea). This usually results in an inhalation pneumonia developing, which is frequently fatal.

The term force-feeding really means using a spoon, an invalid feeding cup or (best) a 5 ml disposable plastic syringe to feed the cat milk, soup, or foods which have the consistency of a paste or cream. Foods of this consistency can be prepared by using a home liquidizer, or by mashing up minced meat, fish or grated cheese with honey or syrup. Alternatively, hydrolized protein products (from your vet or pharmacist) can be fed.

Very liquid foods can be administered using the same technique as mentioned earlier for liquid medicine (page 191): holding the head with the nose pointing *slightly* upwards and slowly trickling the liquid between the parted lips at the side of the mouth. Help will almost certainly be required to hold the cat (as described earlier) and the cat must be given a rest between each mouthful to allow it to breathe properly, especially if its nose is blocked. Don't pour in too much at a time, and, if the cat begins to cough and splutter, stop immediately and allow it to lower its head. It is best not to hold the mouth open and spray the liquid on to the back of the throat because this readily leads to choking.

With more solid food of a paste-like consistency, the mouth can be opened, as described for tablet administration, and the paste either scraped on to the upper or lower front teeth from a finger, or from the *handle* of a spoon, or squeezed on to the tongue from a syringe. If the paste is sufficiently stiff, it can be made into a small ball, placed at the back of the throat and administered in the same way as a tablet (page 189).

Because it is usually not possible to persuade the cat to take very much at a time, it will be necessary to give food frequently, every two hours for example. Force-feeding requires great perseverance to ensure that a cat receives an adequate amount of food. It should *not* be carried out if the cat is not fully conscious. In such animals, the normal cough reflex will be absent and, as mentioned before, inhalation pneumonia may result.

In unconscious animals, or where there is prolonged appetite loss, it may be necessary for your vet to inject drugs to stimulate the appetite, or to feed the cat artificially. This can be done either through a tube which is inserted at the side of the neck and passes down into the stomach, or by using a special solution given intravenously, i.e. into the bloodstream. Unfortunately, even these artificial methods are not practicable for really long term use, and therefore it is important to *try* to get the cat feeding normally as soon as possible.

Q *How should I clean a wound?*

A A wound recently inflicted (especially of the irregular type known as lacerated wounds) may be dirty. An older wound may be infected with bacteria and discharging pus. Both will require cleaning before being dressed or re-dressed.

Cleaning will be made easier, especially in a long-haired cat, if the hair around the wound is first clipped. Before clipping, the wound must be covered or plugged with a piece of moistened, clean cotton wool to stop any hairs straying in.

Then clean the wound using a pad of clean gauze, cotton wool or lint, or even, in an emergency, paper towels. Soak the pad first in tepid water; cleaning will be made easier if it contains a small amount of a detergent antiseptic such as cetrimide (found, for example, in Savlon). This is used primarily because of its detergent effect, not for its limited antibacterial action. Other non-detergent antiseptics should not be used because most of them are poor at killing bacteria and some may cause skin reactions or delay healing. Certainly, do not use any household disinfectants. An alternative is to rub the wet pad on to a tablet of toilet soap, though not carbolic or coal tar soaps because of their toxicity for cats. Washing is much the most effective way of removing bacteria.

Lightly wring out the pad and with it gently dab and wipe away the dirt and/or pus. If you are too vigorous in cleaning you may damage the exposed blood vessels and cause bleeding; if this happens, *immediately stop* further cleaning. The continual oozing of blood can be controlled by holding in place for a few minutes a pad soaked in *cold* water. Dab the wound dry with clean pieces of gauze, lint or paper towels.

To keep the wound clean and to prevent it from being interfered with, apply a pad of gauze or lint (preferably not cotton wool which tends to stick to raw areas), securing it in place either with a crêpe bandage or adhesive tape. If adhesive tape is used, cut a piece long enough to overlap itself when in place.

Q *Most cats seem to hate bandages. Is it always better to let a wound heal on its own rather than to cover it up?*

A Whether a wound is produced accidentally or following surgery, there are a number of reasons for dressing or bandaging it:

1 To stop any bleeding by applying pressure (pressure bandage), though this is usually only a temporary measure.

2 To prevent the wound becoming contaminated by bacteria and other micro-organisms, inert materials such as grit, dirt, loose hair, and even, in hot weather, by blowflies laying their eggs in the wound. These eggs will later hatch into maggots which will feed on the cat's flesh; this is particularly likely to occur in old and debilitated animals.

3 To prevent the cat interfering with the wound. Repeated licking will delay healing, may introduce infection and may give rise to a thick mass of shiny tissue, a lick granuloma. Cats may even remove stitches placed in the skin by biting through the suture material (today usually nylon, or some similar synthetic material) and pulling with their teeth. This can cause the edges of the wound to pull apart before healing is complete (wound breakdown).

4 To provide support, for instance, where there is also a sprain or strain (i.e. tearing of a ligament or a muscle, respectively), or where there may be undue tension on surgical stitches. In cats with fractures the bandages may hold a supporting splint in place.

5 To immobilize a part of the body (a limb or the tail for example). This will prevent further damage which could be caused by the cat putting weight on to a wounded limb, dragging a paralysed limb or banging a damaged tail.

In general, wounds do seem to heal faster if they can be kept open to the air rather than covered. However this presupposes that some other way can be found to deal with the problems described above. Unfortunately, in many cases some form of dressing is essential; the extensive wounds caused by burns, for example, are almost certain to become infected if they are exposed.

The disadvantage of wound dressings is that they may stick to the wound surface. They can also become wet and then rub and chafe the wound. Both of these occurrences will delay healing. Dressings can be wetted by the serum which inevitably exudes from wounds, by exposure to rain, dew on the ground, or puddles, and even by excessive licking or sweating. Serum, or discharge from a wound, can be absorbed by surrounding it with a lot of cotton wool or similar material, but this can make the wound very hot and irritating. If it is possible for the wound to be left open, the liquid will evaporate leaving the wound dry.

Some types of wound are best *never* bandaged, mainly infected wounds with small openings. These include the frequently-encountered punctured wounds caused by other cats' bites (i.e. entry of the top and bottom canine teeth), or discharging channels from abscesses. Such wounds should be left open for drainage and regular treatment. Other small wounds, for example those of the spaying operation, are not usually dressed.

It may sometimes be necessary to fit an 'Elizabethan' collar (see page 201) to prevent the cat from interfering with an exposed wound.

Q *The vet has bandaged my cat's leg. How can I try to keep the dressing dry?*

A If you find your cat spends an excessive amount of time licking the bandage, do your best to prevent it, if necessary by the methods described later (see page 200).

As far as possible the cat should be kept indoors to keep the dressing dry. A bandage which is already wet will have to be replaced with a dry one to prevent chafing of the wound.

It is possible to cover the bandage completely with waterproof adhesive tape. A number of separate short strips, passing in different directions, should be applied to cover the paw, and then the tape wound in a spiral up the leg with each turn overlapping the previous one. However this arrangement can be very difficult to remove again and a simpler method is to place the bandaged limb inside an appropriately-sized polythene bag or sponge bag (the sturdier the better). Any spare width of the bag should be wrapped around the leg and the whole thing secured in place at a number of points with pieces of adhesive tape which pass completely around the limb to overlap themselves. Have one of these pieces of tape right at the top so that half of its width sticks to the bag and half to the cat's hair and skin; this stops the bag working loose and dropping off.

Dry the bag when the cat returns from outdoors and if it becomes punctured remove it and replace it. If the bandage has become wet, it also will need renewing.

One long-term treatment popular in North America was to apply pine pitch (resin) liberally over the bandage and allow it to dry. However pine pitch may be difficult to obtain, and in any case the bandage cannot easily be unravelled afterwards and has usually to be cut away.

Q *How should I apply a bandage to my cat?*

A Fortunately, there are few occasions on which it will ever be necessary to bandage a cat. As a general rule bandaging by an owner is most likely to be a first aid procedure used to stop severe haemorrhage, seal a penetrating chest wound or to provide support, and limit movement, in the case of a fractured limb or tail.

Most of the familiar rolled bandages (called roller bandages) employed by doctors and vets are made from rigid open-weave cotton, which is cut to the required length and discarded after being used once. However, for those unused to bandaging, a crêpe bandage (elastic bandage) is much easier to apply and has a better chance of staying in place. Crêpe bandages

How to bandage your cat
A Limbs and tail

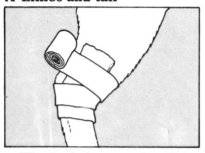

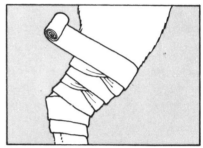

1. *When bandaging a wound on a limb or the tail, start a few inches away from the dressing and gradually work towards the body. Unroll the bandage as you go.*

2. *Each turn of a crêpe bandage should overlap two-thirds of the previous turn. Twist the bandage every 2 or 3 turns to keep it tight. Fasten with a safety pin.*

B Chest and abdomen

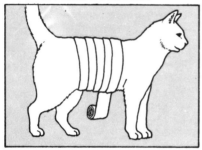

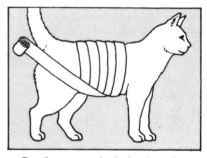

1. *When bandaging the chest or abdomen each turn passes right around the body.*

2. *Bandage towards the head, and after covering the wound go back to the tail.*

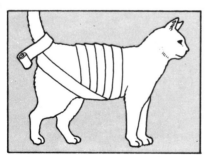

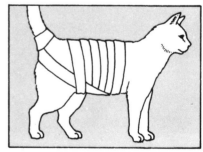

3. *Passing the bandage around the base of the tail helps to anchor it securely.*

4. *Bring the bandage forwards again and, after one last turn, pin it in position.*

are made from a stretch cotton which is much less likely to work loose. They are fastened with a safety pin and, because of their cost, are usually not cut and are re-used after washing and drying. Those of 2 inches' (5 cm) width are most suitable for use on the cat. (Of course, in an emergency any material, e.g. handkerchief, dress belt, scarf, tie, strips of rag, etc., may have to be used instead of a proper bandage.)

Unless the cat is unconscious, it will need to be restrained on a table by a helper holding its scruff, whilst you apply the bandage. If a limb is to be bandaged, the job is simpler if the cat lies on its side with that limb uppermost. And unless the bandage is being applied solely to prevent the cat interfering with a wound, a pad of lint or cotton wool ½ inch (1 cm) thick should first be placed on the surface of the body.

Unroll only a few inches of bandage before you start; have the rest tightly rolled up. Starting a few inches to one side of the area to be covered, gradually wind the bandage round and round the affected part of the body, unrolling it as you go. In the case of a limb or the tail, begin to bandage furthest away from the rest of the body and gradually work towards it. The second turn of the bandage should completely overlap the first; after that each turn should overlap two-thirds of the previous one. If the bandage has to go around the chest or abdomen it will need to be pushed under the body on each turn.

Generally a moderate degree of tension should be retained in the bandage to prevent it becoming slack, though if a pressure bandage is being applied to stop haemorrhage this may need to be slightly tighter in order to be effective. Take care though not to have the bandage *too* tight or it might act as a tourniquet and stop the circulation of blood; around the neck, it might also interfere with the cat's breathing.

It helps to secure the bandage more firmly if, after every two or three turns, the bandage, whilst it is still under tension, is twisted, so that the inside surface now becomes the outside and vice versa; this is called a spiral bandage with reverses. Whether you bandage in a clockwise or an anti-clockwise direction is immaterial and is largely a matter of convenience, depending on whether you are right or left-handed.

After covering the affected area, and going a few inches beyond it, the bandage can be cut and pinned in place. But often to preserve the entire bandage intact, it is preferable to work back over the first set of bandaging until the bandage runs out, and then to pin it securely with the safety pin provided. Take care not to accidentally pin the skin as well.

Check the end of a bandaged limb, or tail, from time to time for any sign of swelling, which would indicate that the bandage is too tight. Then it must be removed immediately and re-applied with less tension. If it works loose, or is interfered with, it should also be removed straight away and re-applied a little more tightly. But bandaging will usually be required only in an emergency; if you are to change dressings on a regular basis your veterinary surgeon will tell you how often to do this.

Using a many-tailed bandage

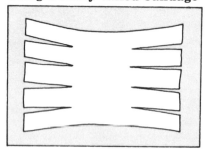

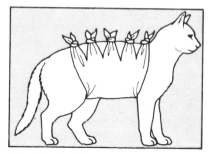

A many-tailed bandage is made from a piece of linen 8 to 9 inches by 2 feet. Deep cuts, about 1½ inches apart, are made along each of the shorter sides.

The 'bandage' is used to cover wounds on the lower chest or abdomen. After the wound has been dressed, each pair of tails is tied together above the back.

Q *What is a many-tailed bandage, and is it suitable for a cat?*

A A many-tailed bandage is a rectangular binder which covers the lower part of the chest and abdomen and is used to protect wounds in those areas. It is not a type of bandage that is often used on a cat, probably because suitable sizes are not made commercially. But it can prove useful, for example in protecting spay wounds where cats have a tendency to interfere with them. It can be made of linen or muslin, or any reasonably strong, closely woven material.

For an adult cat, the rectangle needs to measure approximately 8 to 9 inches (20 to 22 cm) by up to 2 feet (50 to 60 cm), depending on the animal's size. Straight cuts are made about every 1½ inches (4 cm) along each of the short sides. These cuts should run for about one third of the material's width, thus producing a number of 'tails' along each of these sides; the number on each side must be equal.

If necessary, a dressing of cotton wool or lint is first applied to the wound and then (with the cat restrained) the bandage is placed beneath the chest and abdomen with the tails protruding on either side. Each pair of tails (right and left) is in turn brought up the sides of the animal and the tails tied together over the cat's back.

Q *How can I stop my cat from chewing at its bandage?*

A Some cats seem unable to leave a bandage or other dressing alone, and they will repeatedly chew, suck or lick at it. A check should be made that the bandage is not too tight and that the wound beneath it is clean and dry. Having ruled out such causes of irritation, there are really three basic ways to tackle this problem.

The first is to cover the bandage with some very strong, waterproof material. This provides additional protection, and hopefully will prove so difficult to remove that the cat will be unable to penetrate it, and may even give up trying. Very strong adhesive tape (made for sealing cardboard cartons) can be used as a complete covering. Materials like vinyl sheeting or leather have also been employed, either wrapped around a limb and secured with tape, or made up into booties and laced up to fit securely around the limb. However, these coverings are heavy and rigid, often causing the limb to be dragged, and a really determined cat can still chew through them.

The second method is to cover the outside of the bandage in some material that is non-poisonous but tastes so unpleasant that the cat will leave it alone. Again, this is by no means foolproof but can at times be successful. The substances employed are usually those with an acid or bitter taste, or which produce a burning sensation, for example aromatic bitters, white vinegar, lemon juice, Tabasco sauce, or curry paste. Probably the best, though expensive for repeated application, are preparations intended to stop humans from chewing their fingernails.

The third and usually the most successful technique is to enclose the sides of the head so that the cat cannot bring its mouth into contact with the wound. Because of the shape of a cat's head, muzzles are not very effective, but one way of doing this is to make an 'Elizabethan collar' from some stiff material such as vinyl or sturdy cardboard. The idea is to provide the cat with a cone-shaped ruff which fits to its existing collar and encloses its head.

Q *Can you show me how to make an 'Elizabethan collar' for my cat?*

A The pattern for an 'Elizabethan collar' is formed from two half-circles which will finally provide a shape like a thick letter C. The first half-circle should be drawn with a radius equal to the distance from the cat's normal collar to the tip of its nose, *plus* an extra 2 inches (5 cm). The second half-circle should be drawn inside this one from the *same* centre point, but with a radius of only 2 inches (5 cm). Now, by cutting along the lines of the two half-circles, you will be left with the C-shaped pattern.

A series of holes must now be punched along the two straight sides, a little way in from the edge. These holes must be about ½ inch (1 cm) apart and can be made with a stationery punch or sharp tool (even a red hot metal knitting needle). Now fold the material into a cone-like shape around the cat's neck so that it encloses the head. The two straight sides should overlap (by about ¾ inch (1·5 cm)) and the holes line up. If it is much too tight and digs into the neck, trim off a *little* material around the edge of the smaller curve and re-try it until it is just a *little* too tight. Then punch holes at ½ inch (1 cm) intervals all around this lesser curve. Pad the edge of this curve by covering it with a number of narrow strips of sticking plaster, so that it will not damage the cat's neck.

After the final adjustment of the collar's size, place it around the cat's head again and fasten the two sides together by lacing through the holes

Making an 'Elizabethan collar'

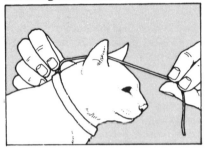

1. *Using a piece of string, measure the distance from the cat's collar to the tip of its nose, passing over the top of its head, and add on 2 extra inches.*

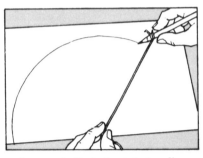

2. *Draw a half-circle of that radius on some stiff material, using a pencil and string. Then, draw a second half-circle, of radius 2 inches, from the same point.*

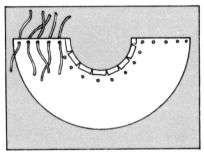

3. *Cut out the 'collar' and punch holes along the straight sides. Try it on the cat; if it is too tight, trim the inner curve. Punch more holes round the curve.*

4. *Using strips of sticking plaster, pad the inside edge. Finally, put it around the cat's neck, lace up the side holes and fasten to the collar with strings.*

with a shoelace or a piece of string – or even fasten the holes together with paper fasteners (with the metal prongs opening out on the *outside*). Then fasten the whole device onto the cat's normal collar with short lengths of string each of which passes through one of the holes nearest the neck.

The Elizabethan collar you have fixed in place must extend a short way in front of the cat's nose, and the acid test of its value is whether the cat can reach the dressing; if it can, there is nothing for it but to make another one a bit longer. You will see that it covers the head but does not (and should not) stop the cat from lying down and sleeping. It *must not* stick out at right-angles to the neck as this makes proper rest impossible.

You may be able to buy from your vet a commercial version of this device, made out of plastic and adjustable for different sizes of cat.

An alternative, simpler and in some ways better method is to use a small plastic flower pot, preferably of the flexible kind used for potting out seedlings. The base must be of the right diameter and the pot sufficiently deep. A child's plastic sand bucket with the handle removed can similarly be used. Cut out the base with a sharp knife, punch holes around the cut edge and, as before, pad the edge with tape to cover any rough projections. Now slip it over the cat's head and again tie it securely in place to the cat's collar.

This Elizabethan collar device is, of course, also valuable in preventing cats from biting or licking at unprotected wounds, from suckling themselves and from scratching at their ears or face.

The cat will not much care for it initially, and may be rather moody and even try to push it off with its hind-legs, but most cats accept it after a short time. It must, of course, be removed for the cat to eat and drink and then replaced; usually it is easiest to undo and refasten the normal collar with the Elizabethan collar attached. However, do keep a careful eye on the cat whenever the Elizabethan collar is not being worn; some cats take advantage of the opportunity for a really good bite at their wound or bandage.

Make sure that the neck is not getting sore; if it is, more padding is called for, and possibly some treatment for the skin. Ensure that the cat doesn't go outside without supervision when it is wearing this device because it can easily get caught up in fences and branches.

Q *If my cat is ill would it be a good idea to give him a hot-water bottle?*

A This is a useful way of supplying heat to an ill or cold animal, but attention should be paid to the following points:
1 The hot-water bottle should never be filled with very hot water, and certainly *not* boiling water. It must always be well wrapped-up in a towel, or else placed in a special hot-water bottle cover which totally encloses it. This is to avoid causing burning of the skin which can be extensive and may result in the loss of skin over a large area of the body.
2 Animals which are seriously ill, or even unconscious, will be unable to move away from a hot-water bottle and this could lead to overheating. Therefore the bottle should be warm, rather than hot.
3 Severely shocked animals (e.g. following a road accident) will suffer if their body temperature is suddenly raised much higher than that of their surroundings. So again, the hot-water bottle should be kept only warm.
4 After filling, check that the bottle is watertight and, at intervals during its use, check that the cover is still in place and that the bottle is not leaking.

An infra-red heater securely fastened at least 3 feet (1 m) *above* the cat's bed could be used instead. It will supply radiant heat continuously and from time to time you should check that the cat is not too warm, especially in summer. Special electric blankets can also be obtained, preferably fitted with a thermostat so that the heat output can be controlled.

There are other alternatives too. If an electricity supply is unavailable, a pet bed warmer can be used. This is a sealed metal box in which a solid fuel stick burns for about eight hours. Again, the warmer should be well wrapped, but not in synthetic fabrics, such as acrylic, which may melt. For

Caring for your cat's eye

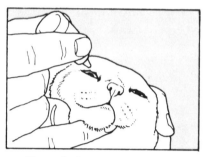

1. *Gently bathe your cat's eye using a pad of cotton wool (cotton) soaked in a warm boric acid solution. Any foreign body or discharge should be wiped away.*

2a. *To apply drops turn the head so the eye faces upwards and, in case the cat moves, hold the squeezee bottle or dropper ½ inch above. Apply 2–3 drops.*

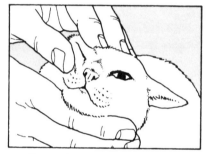

2b. *Eye ointment will flow more easily if previously warmed. Draw the lower lid down and squeeze an eighth of an inch onto its lining, near to the corner.*

3. *Be careful not to touch the surface of the eyeball as you apply ointment or drops. Gently rub the lids together afterwards to distribute the medicament.*

gentle warmth, a temporary bed could be made up for your cat in the airing cupboard.

Q *What is the best method of bathing a cat's eye?*

A Bathing a cat's eye is useful as a first aid measure to help flush pieces of grit or a grass seed, etc., out of the eye, or where the eyelids have become gummed together by discharges.

Either a patent human eye lotion can be prepared as directed by the manufacturer, *or* a warm (*not hot*) boric (boracic) acid lotion can be made by dissolving two level teaspoonsful of boric acid crystals in half a tumbler of lukewarm water. In an emergency, or if nothing else is available, just use warm water. Don't add salt to it; if too much is added the resultant brine will be very irritant and damaging.

With someone else to restrain the cat, soak a small pad of cotton wool or lint in the water or eye lotion, and squeeze the liquid out onto the lids (if stuck together), or onto the surface of the eyeball.

Wet cotton wool, twisted into a spiral, can be used to gently brush away any foreign body from the surface of the eyeball, provided that this isn't repeated too often. With eyelids which are stuck together, the wet pad should be gently wiped over the outer surface, mainly using an outward movement, i.e. from the nose towards the side of the face, until the lids gradually become free. Then the surface of the eyeball should be bathed. Repeated re-soaking of the pad may be necessary. Finally, the surrounding skin area should be dried.

If there is obvious infection beneath the lids, or a foreign body cannot be removed, veterinary help must be obtained. If pain persists in the eye and the animal tries to rub it, place one to three drops of warm (not hot) olive oil into the eye with an eye dropper or, in an emergency, drop the oil from the *blunt* end of a pencil. Try to prevent the cat from undue rubbing of the eye until the vet can attend to it.

Eye baths, as used by humans, are the wrong size and shape for use with cats' eyes, so don't bother trying to find one. Finally, a word of warning: *never* let any dry material (cotton wool, lint, etc.) contact the surface of the eye; it will stick to the moist surface and, when pulled off, will remove the outer layer of cells.

Q *When should I treat my cat's eyes with drops or eye ointment?*

A Don't use drops or ointment unless your veterinary surgeon has advised it. Certain preparations can be quite unsuitable for a particular purpose. For instance, many preparations contain corticosteroids which, if applied to an eye ulcer, will prevent it from healing. Remember too that some proprietary preparations sold for human use are unsuitable for conditions affecting the cat's eye. It is far preferable to seek early advice from your vet about any eye problem.

Q *My vet has suggested that I use hot fomentations to treat an abscess on my cat's leg. What does this mean?*

A A hot fomentation is the application of heat from a pad of lint, gauze, linen or cotton wool soaked in hot water or a hot lotion. It may seem a rather old-fashioned treatment, but it is in fact extremely effective and widely employed. In treating an abscess, the intention is primarily to increase the blood supply to the area by enlarging (dilating) the blood vessels. Consequently, the skin in the heated area looks redder because of the increased amount of blood. Immediately after infection has been implanted in the tissues, after a cat bite for example, hot fomentations *may* prevent an abscess developing. The increase in the supply of white blood cells will destroy the bacteria in the area. If the infection is not discovered until the bacteria are making the area hot and painful, hot fomentation speeds up the formation of the abscess so that it can be drained and healing can begin. Hot fomentations *after* an abscess has been opened surgically, or has burst naturally, promote healing of the wound and ensure that the site is inspected and cleaned regularly.

In other species, though not often in the cat, hot fomentations may be applied to strains and sprains (i.e. torn muscles, tendons and ligaments). In these cases the heat relieves pain and helps to speed up healing.

Hot water alone may be used, or a level teaspoonful of table salt (sodium chloride) may be added to a tumbler of hot water to produce what is called a 'normal' saline solution, a solution exerting the same tonicity as the body fluids. Even better, if you are wanting a developing abscess to 'ripen' (or 'point') or are bathing a discharging abscess, is to use a tumbler of hot water containing a level dessertspoonful of Epsom salts (magnesium sulphate). This exerts considerable osmotic pressure and produces a 'drawing' effect which is valuable in removing toxic products.

How hot should the hot water be? Well, obviously not so hot as to scald the skin or produce discomfort, but tepid water is not hot enough. If it is just bearable to your fingers, that is about right.

Put the liquid into a small bowl and soak the pad of material (at least three inches square) in it. Partially wring out the pad and apply it immediately to the affected part, holding it in contact with the skin. If the abscess has already been opened, gentle squeezing will help remove any infected discharges. It will certainly help if someone else assists in restraining the cat whilst you do this. As soon as the pad has cooled appreciably, remove it, re-soak, squeeze and re-apply. Continue in this way for at least five minutes. The more often you can perform a hot fomentation, the better, but three to four times a day, spaced as evenly as possible, is the minimum.

If the abscess site is on the lower leg, it is usually simpler to make up a double quantity of lotion in a small bowl and place the animal's leg alternately into the lotion and out again, at short intervals for a total of about five minutes.

Poultices are used for a similar effect but these are more difficult to apply and are not routinely used for cats.

14
First Aid for Cats

Q *Is it useful for owners to have some knowledge of first aid for cats? Wouldn't it be better to wait until the vet sees the animal?*

A First aid is the term for the care and treatment given to an individual in an emergency *before* professional help is available – following a serious injury (accidental or otherwise) or the sudden onset of illness. Just as in man and other animals, the principle aim of first aid in the cat is to preserve the life of the animal. The other objectives of first aid are to reduce pain and discomfort, and to lessen the likelihood of the injury resulting in some permanent disability or disfigurement by preventing further damage to already injured tissues.

To be successful in these aims usually requires treatment to be given promptly after the incident. There are signs (described here in order of priority) which necessitate *immediate* treatment to save the cat's life: the absence of breathing (or severe difficulty in breathing) severe bleeding and signs of severe shock (weakness to the point of collapse, panting, pale lips and gums, coldness and trembling). Signs which *may* have equally serious consequences are unconsciousness with or without convulsions and signs indicating poisoning (see page 220).

It is imperative that the treatment of these life-threatening signs receives priority; always leave the cleaning of wounds and other non-essential procedures until later and concentrate on saving the animal's life.

As we have seen in the section on handling, a vital preliminary to the first aid treatment of a cat is the approach to, and restraint of, the injured animal (see page 77), although animals which are very seriously injured are usually those least likely, or able, to offer any serious resistance.

In virtually all emergency situations the help and advice of a veterinarian is *essential*, and his assistance should be obtained *as soon as possible*. Make the initial contact with your vet by telephone to avoid any possible confusion about the reception of the injured animal (see page 14).

The first aid measures described on the following pages are therefore designed to precede, not to replace, proper veterinary attention. Even though a vet might later advise that euthanasia (putting to sleep) of an injured cat would be the most humane course of action, it is not for the first aider to make this decision, and all effort should be directed towards keeping the animal alive until a professional opinion can be obtained.

Q *What is the most common emergency for which a cat would require first aid?*

A There is no doubt that road accidents are the most common emergencies in which cats are involved, especially in urban areas. Many different types of injuries can be caused and multiple injuries are common. At times, these are so severe as to cause the death of the animal immediately, or within twenty-four hours. This is an inevitable consequence of allowing a cat the freedom to wander at will, and other than keeping your cat confined at all times, or only allowing him to exercise when on a lead, there is very little that you can do to prevent such incidents.

The animal may be struck a direct or glancing blow, not only from the front bumper or a wheel, but also from a low slung part of the chassis, transmission or exhaust system as the vehicle passes above the cat. It may suffer crush injuries as a wheel passes over part of its body, and it may at times be dragged behind the vehicle for a distance. In addition to shock, a road accident can produce a variety of external and internal wounds with varying degrees of haemorrhage, fractures, dislocations, concussion or paralysis. Head and pelvic injuries are very common, and sometimes there is a diaphragmatic hernia (passage of the abdominal organs into the chest cavity through a ruptured diaphragm) which causes great difficulty in breathing. At times, the only external evidence of a cat's involvement in a road accident may be frayed or splintered claws (resulting from its attempt to grip the road surface), possibly some loss of hair, and oil and dirt on the coat. Despite the minimal external signs there is often serious internal bleeding.

The animal might remain at the scene of the accident, often dazed or unconscious, or it may run away in a blind panic, only to return home, if at all, several hours or even days later.

First aid treatment for road accidents consists primarily of treatment for shock, plus attention for whatever other serious sign(s) might be present (e.g. severe haemorrhage, difficulty in breathing, fracture, paralysis, etc.) before obtaining veterinary attention. It is of course imperative that if the animal is still in a dangerous position in the roadway it should first be removed to a safer, and preferably sheltered, position.

Q *On what other occasions might my cat require first aid?*

A Cuts and wounds, with a variety of causes, are also common. The majority are 'clean' cuts (incised wounds), resulting for instance from stepping on broken glass or sharp metal concealed in long grass, or falling through a garden frame, or even from licking out cans with a sharp edge.

They can be deep and usually bleed profusely. Cutting wounds can also be produced by wire nooses in animal traps (snares) and by rubber bands placed around the neck, limbs or tail, usually by children. Because of its continual tension, a rubber band gradually cuts through the skin and deep into the underlying tissues, sometimes even down to the bone or through the trachea (windpipe).

Irregular, torn wounds (lacerated wounds) can arise from a dog bite or from a cat being caught on barbed wire or in a mowing machine while hiding in long grass; they bleed less but are more likely to become contaminated. Penetrating wounds, i.e. penetrating the chest or abdomen, are fortunately rare. They may result from the protrusion of a fractured rib after a road accident, from being impaled on a spike (e.g. on a railing after a fall) or from a malicious act such as stabbing or shooting. Typical firearm wounds have a small entry wound and a large, ragged exit wound for the projectile, though sometimes, as with air gun pellets, the projectile remains in the tissues. The explosive release of stored up energy can cause extensive internal damage.

As well as being caused by road accidents, fractures and dislocations can result from being trodden on or kicked, having a tail or a limb slammed in a door, or from an over-ambitious jump or a fall. Many cats discover that they are not as sure-footed as they thought and may fall a number of storeys from a window-ledge or parapet on to concrete or paving slabs, which sometimes results in unconsciousness, fractures (often of the forelimbs, chest and jaws) and internal injuries. However, this does not mean that all cats high up in trees or on rooftops need to be rescued; most will find their own way down safely, especially if tempted by food.

Burns and scalds are also not uncommon in cats and most of these arise in the kitchen. Usually the animal is splashed with boiling water or hot fat, although often this is not recognized at the time. Sometimes a cat investigating an appetizing smell attempts to walk on the cooker hot plate. Quite apart from reasons of hygiene, this reinforces the need to keep cats off kitchen working surfaces, and it is probably best to banish them entirely from the kitchen during cooking. Burns on the feet can also arise from stepping onto the embers of bonfires or the hot charcoal discarded from a barbecue.

So-called chemical burns are due to the effect of corrosive liquids on the skin; this is often diesel oil on account of a cat's habit of hiding beneath motor vehicles. At other times they may walk through such substances as warm tar, creosote, or battery acid. Electrical burns and electrocution usually result from a kitten chewing through a live electrical flex or cable.

Q *Is it true that cats are rarely poisoned?*

A Although cats are more fastidious about what they eat than many species, there are some factors which render them *more* susceptible to

How to give artificial respiration

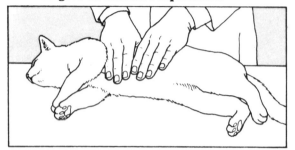

Remove any collar, stretch the head and neck forwards and, with the cat lying on its side, place both hands over the ribs. Every five seconds press down firmly, and immediately release the pressure. At intervals check the heartbeat.

poisoning. Being predators, cats run the risk of consuming prey animals which have themselves already been poisoned. They also have the habit of washing materials off their coats, ingesting them in the process. This problem is aggravated by the fact that the cat's detoxication mechanisms which break down poisons into harmless substances are not very efficient, so that their effects are much greater than in other animals.

Q *How can I administer artificial respiration to a cat?*

A Artificial respiration is required in all circumstances where a cat has stopped breathing, or is breathing irregularly or with difficulty. When breathing ceases, all the body organs, including the brain and the heart, are deprived of the normal continuous flow of oxygen. After a few minutes they will be unable to function and then the animal will become unconscious and die. In an emergency therefore artificial respiration should take precedence over every other procedure. Once it is being performed successfully, attention can then be directed towards other problems.

The cessation or impairment of breathing may in fact be caused by an existing lack of oxygen to the brain (asphyxia), as occurs if the animal is enclosed in an unventilated space (e.g. inside an abandoned refrigerator) or is obliged to breathe smoke or carbon monoxide. An oxygen lack can also result from obstruction of the air passage by a foreign body in the throat or by water in the lungs (as in drowning), or by compression of the airway (as occurs when a cat slowly strangles after its collar has become caught on a projection). The respiratory muscles might be paralyzed following electrocution or the lungs may have collapsed after a penetrating chest wound. In all of these situations the prompt administration of artificial respiration can be vitally important in ensuring that the animal survives.

If there is any foreign material in the air passage or in the lungs, it must first be removed. If the cat has drowned (usually because steep walls prevent it escaping from the water, e.g. in a swimming pool, canal lock, or even a rainwater butt) it is important to first wipe away any oil or mud from the mouth and nostrils, and then to allow as much water as possible to drain from the lungs by holding the cat upside down by its thighs. Obstructions in the throat usually produce choking, coughing or gulping. Foreign bodies, such as bones or needles, should if possible be quickly removed with fingers or a pair of pliers, and any vomit or blood at the back of the throat should be carefully wiped away. After opening the jaws and pulling the tongue forwards the mouth and throat can be checked with a torch.

Artificial respiration will *not* be effective if there is a penetrating chest wound; air can usually be heard passing through the opening and blood coming from the wound appears frothy. Blood-stained froth is also coughed up and appears at the mouth and nostrils. Such a wound must be quickly sealed by plugging the opening with a clean (preferably sterile) piece of gauze, lint or cotton wool, or in an emergency any other clean piece of material. Ideally, this plug should be covered by a further thick pad which is then bandaged in place. However, the immediate problem is to obtain an air-tight seal.

Now with the cat lying flat on its side (with the head preferably lower than the rest of the body in the case of a drowned animal) and any wound uppermost, remove any collar, make sure that the head and neck are stretched well forward and place your two hands on the chest wall over the ribs. Now press down firmly to expel the air from the lungs, but *don't exert too much weight* because you can easily produce crush injuries. Immediately release the pressure allowing the chest wall to expand again and to fill the lungs with air. This procedure should be repeated at approximately five second intervals. Pressing too rapidly will not allow the oxygen to remain in the lungs for a sufficient time to diffuse into the blood.

Once artificial respiration is under way, attention can be paid to other problems; provided that the heart continues to beat, artificial respiration can keep the animal alive almost indefinitely, certainly long enough for veterinary attention to be obtained. If the animal is being transported to the vet's premises and it has not yet begun to breathe on its own, it will be necessary to continue this procedure during the journey. At intervals a check should be made that the air passage is still clear and that there is still a heart beat. The heart beat can be checked by placing a hand around the lower part of the chest between, or just behind, the forelegs. If the fingers and thumb are on opposite sides of the chest, the heart beat can be felt between them. (Try this *now* on a healthy cat so that you will know where to feel in an emergency.)

If the animal begins to breathe regularly and at a steady rate, artificial respiration can be stopped, but regular checks should be made on the cat to ensure that it is continuing to breathe properly.

An alternative method of artificial respiration is to hold the cat by the thighs and to swing it vigorously in a wide arc about ten times. You need space to do this so it is best not attempted indoors. This procedure should be repeated four or five times until breathing starts. If this is unsuccessful, the method described above should be employed.

Q *Can I give my cat the 'kiss of life'?*

A Mouth to mouth resuscitation has been attempted but, because of the shape and size of the cat's mouth, it is usually not very effective. Better is to close the animal's mouth with your hands and to blow firmly and regularly into its nose with your lips closely applied to its nostrils. As described before, it is important to ensure first that the air passage is clear. Blowing should occupy about three seconds, followed by a two second pause, and this should be repeated continuously.

This technique may prove more valuable in providing oxygen than the pressure on the chest method of artificial respiration for those animals with a penetrating wound into the chest cavity.

Q *How is it possible to control severe bleeding in a cat?*

A Minor haemorrhage will stop on its own after a while due to a narrowing of the end of the damaged blood vessel(s) and the formation of a blood clot which effectively blocks the cut end. Consequently, clots which have already formed should not be disturbed because this will allow bleeding to begin again.

However, when a large blood vessel is severed, the flow of blood is so considerable that any clot which begins to form is soon washed away. This is particularly likely to occur when an artery is damaged since it carries blood under higher pressure; indeed, a separate spurt of blood is seen with each beat of the heart.

The best method for controlling severe bleeding is to apply pressure to the damaged blood vessel with a pressure bandage. A thick ($\frac{1}{2}$ to $\frac{3}{4}$ inch) pad of clean and preferably sterile absorbent material such as cotton wool or lint (or in an emergency a handkerchief) is placed over the end of the blood vessel and firmly bandaged in place with a crêpe bandage (or in an emergency a scarf, dress belt, handkerchief, etc.). The rough surface of the material facilitates clot formation.

While such materials for a pressure bandage are being assembled, pressure can be applied to the blood vessel with fingertips preferably covered with a clean handkerchief (or rubber gloves if these are handy). Alternatively, the sides of a large wound can be tightly pressed together. As far as is possible in the circumstances, try to avoid pushing fragments of foreign bodies such as glass further into the wound. Any obvious and easily detached pieces should be quickly removed before bandaging. (With wounds on the neck it may be preferable to hold a pad tightly in position rather than to apply a bandage which can interfere with breathing.) If the pad rapidly becomes soaked with blood, a further pad and bandage

How to control severe bleeding

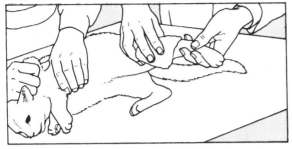

1. *A pressure bandage will control most haemorrhages. With the cat restrained by a helper, place a thick pad of absorbent material, such as cotton wool (cotton) or lint, over the site of the bleeding.*

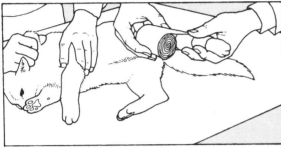

2. *Then firmly bandage the pad in place with a crêpe bandage, or if one is not available, with a scarf or dress belt, etc. If the pad rapidly becomes soaked with blood a further thick pad should be tightly bandaged on top.*

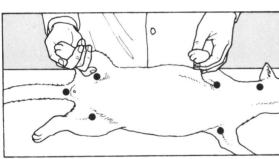

3. *Temporary control of really serious haemorrhage can be obtained by pressing with the fingers at the points illustrated, when there is bleeding from the tail, the hindleg, the foreleg and, though most difficult to control, the head and neck.*

should be applied more tightly on top of the first.

The animal, if still conscious, should be restrained by a helper during this procedure, and if necessary later treated for shock.

The application of pressure to the artery supplying the injured area may be attempted, but only if a pressure bandage is clearly unable to control serious haemorrhaging. Either really hard pressure can be applied with the fingers at places called pressure points (where a superficial artery passes over a bone) or a tourniquet can be applied.

The three major pressure points are located as follows:

1 On the inside of the thigh where the femoral artery crosses the bone (femur) – to control bleeding from the lower half of the hind limb.

2 On the inside of the fore limb just above the elbow joint where the brachial artery crosses the humerus – to control bleeding from the lower half of the fore limb.

3 On the underside of the tail near to the body where the coccygeal artery passes beneath the vertebrae – to control bleeding from the tail.

Pressure can also be applied to the carotid artery in a groove at the lower part of the neck just in front of the fore limb, to control bleeding from the head and neck, although in practice this point is difficult to find and the control of bleeding is often not very satisfactory.

In an emergency a tourniquet can be made from a narrow (1 to 2 inches thick) strip of cloth, a handkerchief, tie, dress belt, supple cat or dog lead or a thick rubber band, firmly tied or clipped into position around the limb or tail. The tourniquet should be nearer to the body than to the wound. Its efficiency can be improved by using the remaining ends of the material to tie a short stick (or even a ballpoint pen) on top of the first knot, and then to twist the stick around several times until the bleeding stops.

Today, however, the use of pressure on an artery (especially with a tourniquet) is *not* recommended for routine use because totally cutting off the blood supply to the tissues can result in their death. Consequently, pressure should never be applied continuously for more than fifteen minutes, and a tourniquet must never be applied around the neck or covered with a bandage, in case it is forgotten. *Pressure bandaging generally produces more reliable control of bleeding as well as being safer and quicker.* If a tourniquet is used in the treatment of snake bite (see page 227) it only need be tight enough to interfere with the lymphatic circulation and not the blood supply.

Bleeding from sites around the head can require special first aid treatment, although in all cases the cat should be effectively but quietly restrained lying down, usually with the site of haemorrhage uppermost.

To control bleeding from the eyeball, hold a pad of lint or cotton wool soaked in clean cold water (*never* dry) over the eyeball. Don't attempt to bandage it in place and prevent the cat from rubbing the eye.

With bleeding from the nostrils, apply a similar pad soaked in cold water over the nose, though don't attempt to cover the nostrils or to poke anything up the nose.

With severe bleeding from the ear flap, first place a pad of cotton wool either side of the flap, like a sandwich. Then fold the ear flap flat across the head with the ear tip pointing towards the top of the skull, and bandage it firmly in that position using a crêpe bandage. Do the same in cases of bleeding from the ear canal but first place a small piece of cotton wool down the canal to assist clotting. Always stop the cat from scratching or rubbing at the ear, and from shaking its head.

With bleeding from the tongue, lips or mouth, keep the cat's head *low* to prevent clots forming at the back of the throat. If the cat is unconscious, blood and clots must be wiped from the mouth and throat to ensure that the airway remains unobstructed.

And, of course, it is essential to arrange for the cat to receive veterinary attention as soon as possible.

Q *What can I do about internal haemorrhage?*

A Internal bleeding refers to bleeding into internal organs or into the chest or abdominal cavities. It usually follows crushing or a severe impact injury such as a fall or kick (e.g. by horses or cattle) or from involvement in a road accident. The fact that haemorrhage is occurring may not be evident until signs of shock appear; this is usually because blood cannot reach the exterior. However, at times blood may be seen. Frothy blood appearing at the mouth or nostrils suggests bleeding from the lungs or air passages (a trickle of blood is usually due to wounds actually *in* the mouth or nose). Vomited blood usually comes from the stomach and appears dark brown because of the action of stomach acid (converting it to acid haematin). Extensive bleeding from deep within the ear canal strongly suggests an injury inside the skull. Sometimes blood may be apparent in the urine or motions after an accident.

Regrettably, it is *not* possible to stop an internal haemorrhage with first aid treatment. The best that can be done is to treat the animal for shock, (see later) wipe any frothy blood from the mouth and nose to keep the airway clear and to obtain the assistance of a veterinarian as soon as possible.

Q *How will I know if my cat is suffering from shock? How should he be treated?*

A Shock is a clinical state in which there is a fall in blood pressure and in the volume of blood in the circulation. The blood flow to the body tissues is poor and the cells, including those of the brain, suffer from a lack of oxygen. Many different types of injury will cause shock but the signs and the treatment are similar in all cases. Shock can result from severe blood loss or a loss of other body fluids (after persistent vomiting or diarrhoea for example), serious pain and tissue damage (from severe wounds and fractures, electrocution and the effects of burns, scalds, and poisons – especially corrosive poisons) and the effect of bee and wasp stings (anaphylactic shock). Internal bleeding can result in 'secondary shock' occurring some time (four to six hours) after an injury.

The tell-tale signs of shock are as follows:
1 The animal is weak and almost always lies down. It is often only semi-conscious and does not respond to stimulation.
2 Breathing is rapid (more than thirty to forty breaths per minute) and shallow, i.e. panting respiration.
3 The lips, gums and tongue appear pale and greyish and feel cold and clammy.
4 The paws feel cold, even though the animal may be in warm surroundings, and it often trembles or shivers. The temperature, if taken, is found to be below normal.
5 The heart beats more rapidly, i.e. more than 120 beats per minute.

6 The pupils are dilated and the eyes appear glazed.

7 The cat *may* vomit.

These signs may already be present when the injured animal is discovered or they may develop later.

Firstly artificial respiration should be given to any animal whose breathing is irregular, and any serious haemorrhage should be controlled. The cat should be kept warm, preferably indoors, by covering it with a blanket. It is important to prevent heat loss, so that if the animal is wet it should be dried, and it should not be allowed to lie directly on a cold or wet surface. Put some insulating material, such as a blanket, coat or newspaper, beneath it. However, because shock is made much worse by raising the animal's temperature above that of its surroundings, the cat should *not* be placed directly in front of a fire or radiator, or given a hot water bottle. The animal should be kept as quiet and undisturbed as possible. If a journey to the vet is required, sudden changes in position (i.e. sudden lifting, turning and jolting) should be avoided because this can cause a rapid deterioration in condition which might prove fatal.

If the animal is sufficiently conscious to drink, and wishes to do so, a small amount of warm milk or water with added glucose can be beneficial. However, withhold liquids if the animal begins to vomit, never force liquids down its throat, and avoid giving any form of alcohol (e.g. brandy). Alcohol can prove beneficial in some types of shock but it is also harmful in others. Because the nature of the shock may not be immediately apparent, the safest rule is to avoid alcohol altogether. Keep the animal lying down, ideally with the hindquarters a little higher than the head, and try to avoid causing pain and fear. Speak calmly to the cat and try to soothe it.

Shock is a serious condition and veterinary attention should be obtained with the minimum of delay. An important part of treatment is the administration of fluid therapy to restore the circulating blood volume and, in some cases, the use of specialized stimulant drugs.

Q *What signs would indicate that my cat had a fracture?*

A A fracture is a break or crack in a bone caused by the application of physical force. The bone most often fractured by the cat is the femur (the thigh bone) in the hind leg. But also common are fractures of the pelvis (often unsuspected), the coccygeal vertebrae (tail bones), usually requiring amputation of the tail, and the lower jaw (mandible).

Fractures are termed open or closed depending on whether or not the skin surface is also disrupted by the injury. Sometimes the broken end of the bone is even pushed out through the skin. Open fractures are, as one would expect, more likely to become infected. Other classifications of fractures are based on the number of breaks, fragments of bone, or on the amount of damage done to the surrounding tissues. However, from the point of view of first aid, such classification is unimportant. The only type which is popularly referred to is a 'greenstick fracture' in which the bone is not completely broken but merely cracked and bent. This type usually occurs in young animals where the bones are still flexible.

There are six main signs of fracture but not all of them are always present:

1 Pain around the fracture site, which makes the animal resent handling and can lead to shock.

2 Swelling around the fracture due to bleeding and bruising.

3 An unnatural degree of movement. The lower part of the limb, or end of the tail, may swing freely or even be dragged along.

4 A loss of function. The cat is not able to move or use the fractured part normally. It may appear lame, because it cannot put weight onto a limb.

5 There may be some deformity such as a lump or sharp edge which can be felt somewhere along the bone. A limb may appear shorter or abnormally twisted, or the skull appear sunken.

6 A grating noise (crepitus) may be heard when the animal moves or the part is handled. This is due to the rough, broken ends of the bones moving against each other (and of course is absent in a greenstick fracture).

If, when you examine the cat, you are doubtful about the shape of a bone, or the degree of movement, it is useful to compare the same part on the other side of the body.

Q *How would I know if my cat had suffered a dislocation?*

A A dislocation (otherwise called a luxation) occurs when one of the bones which form a joint moves out of place. The bones are usually separated by force; dislocation of the hip joint is the most common example following jumping or a road accident. In general, the thigh bone (femur) moves forward making the hind limb appear shorter. The lower jaw is also often dislocated and then the mouth will not close properly. In some cats a congenital defect of the stifle joint allows a small bone, the patella (knee-cap), to dislocate very easily without undue force. This condition is very common in the Devon Rex breed, causing an abnormal gait; in some cases the stifle locks and the cat stretches its hind legs from time to time in an attempt to make the patella slip back into its correct position.

Many signs of dislocation are similar to those of fracture – pain, swelling, deformity and loss of function, but there are useful distinguishing features:

1 Pain and swelling is confined to the region of the joint.

2 Movement is more restricted than usual, not increased.

3 There is usually no grating sound.

4 Bones never penetrate the skin.

It can, however, be difficult to distinguish between a fracture and dislocation, particularly if the fracture is near a joint; occasionally they will occur together.

Q *What first aid treatment should I give a cat with a fracture or dislocation?*

A The general first aid treatment for both fractures and dislocations is very similar. The cat should be carefully approached and restrained, and then carried to a place of safety and warmth with the damaged part carefully supported. A cat basket or large cardboard box is ideal but in an emergency the cat can be carried in your arms. If there is a need for artificial respiration, or treatment for haemorrhage or shock, this must receive priority. Then the cat should be restricted to a confined area to limit its movements – in a cat basket or its own bed (ideally lying down with the affected part or limb uppermost) – until a vet can examine and treat it. This is to minimize pain and, in the case of a fracture, to prevent further damage to surrounding tissues. Make the animal as comfortable as possible and don't handle the area of the fracture or dislocation more than is necessary. Moreover, don't attempt to correct a dislocation; this can be often only achieved after using a general anaesthetic to relax the muscles.

A fractured limb can be well supported and immobilized with a firm bandage. But if there is any possibility that you are dealing with a dislocation and not a fracture, it is best omitted. The procedure is to apply a thick pad of cotton wool 4 to 6 inches long (10–15 cm) over the area of the fracture (usually this will be a limb or tail but occasionally a fractured rib) and then to tightly bandage the pad in place with a crêpe bandage. As a general rule attempts to secure splints to the limbs do more harm than good and are best avoided. If the lower jaw is hanging free it can be supported by applying a crêpe bandage fairly loosely around the head, but check that the animal can breathe satisfactorily, especially if there is bleeding in the mouth.

Spinal fractures and dislocations may result in paralysis of the hind quarters, shown by the cat's inability to move its hind legs and, to avoid further damage, it is important that when such an animal is lifted its spine is kept perfectly straight. Unfortunately, the outlook for such cases is poor and the victims often have to be put to sleep.

Q *What should I do if my cat has convulsions?*

A A convulsion, or fit, is a series of violent, uncontrolled seizures (or spasms) of the muscles, accompanied by partial or complete loss of consciousness. It begins with a series of muscle tremors followed by muscle contractions; the animal falls to the ground and shows 'paddling' movements and champing of the jaws. Often the cat will salivate and pass motions and urine. Upon recovery, the animal may be dazed, confused and unable to see properly. Many cats are extremely frightened and wish to hide away, some may become vicious and others are more affectionate than usual. Most convulsions are over within fifteen minutes, but cats, unlike dogs, may have several convulsions in a day. At times the convulsions become continuous (status epilepticus).

The *most common* causes in the cat are convulsive poisons (e.g. organochlorines, anti-freeze, lead, and metaldehyde) and brain tumours. However, there are a variety of other causes such as head injuries, meningitis and encephalitis (inflammation of the brain and its covering membranes – the result of infection with bacteria, fungi or *Toxoplasma*), diseases of the liver and kidney (due to the accumulation of waste substances in the body) and a low level of calcium in the blood. The last named condition often occurs in the nursing queen and is then called eclampsia (page 184).

It is best to leave the convulsing animal where it has collapsed, unless it is in a dangerous situation (e.g. in a roadway, or near to a coal fire). If it is in danger, try to carefully lift or pull the animal to safety, but avoid getting bitten or scratched in the process (throw a blanket or coat over the cat first). Keep the animal as quiet and undisturbed as possible; at home move nearby furniture and objects quietly away from the animal, draw the curtains, turn off nearby electric or gas fires, turn off the radio, television or hi-fi and, if necessary, arrange cushions or rugs to protect the animal from projections on which it might strike its head. Ask onlookers to leave. Always interfere with the cat as little as possible during the fit; certainly do not attempt to hold it or give it anything by mouth.

Arrange for veterinary treatment as soon as possible. If the fit is continuous, the need for treatment is urgent, but only if there is *no* alternative should an attempt be made to transport an animal that is still having convulsions. It is best done by picking the cat up in a blanket and placing it in a cat basket for the journey.

The fit will usually end spontaneously but still keep the cat confined in the same cool darkened room until it is sufficiently recovered to be transported, or until the veterinary surgeon arrives. Any froth around the mouth and any urine and faeces on the coat can then be gently cleaned up. The cat will usually sleep afterwards.

At times cats indoors show what is believed to be the discharge of a pent-up hunting instinct by suddenly chasing vigorously some non-existent object around the house, before settling down again quite normally. Superficially, this behaviour resembles an attack of hysteria, such as is seen in the dog, but in the cat it appears to be quite normal.

Q *How might my cat be poisoned?*

A Most poisons are taken orally by the cat. Occasionally, a poisonous gas or vapour may be inhaled such as carbon monoxide from a motor vehicle exhaust or a solid fuel burning appliance, though *not* from natural gas. Also toxic are the vapours of organic solvents (e.g. in glues, dry cleaning fluid or fire extinguishers) used in poorly ventilated areas and the smoke and fumes from burning materials, especially plastic foam. Very rarely may a poison be absorbed through the skin.

The evidence for poisoning may be beyond dispute. You might actually see the cat consuming material which you know, or subsequently discover, is poisonous. Or there may be strong circumstantial evidence if the cat develops signs of poisoning and could have had access to a poison – a toxic spray might have been used in the neighbourhood or a rat bait laid. It may be that the cat has been dosed with a drug or its coat treated with an insecticide, or drugs used by members of the household may have been interfered with. Examination of the cat may show signs consistent with poisoning, such as the burning and blistering around the lips caused by a corrosive, a strange smell on the breath, a residue of material around the mouth and, especially, the dribbling of coloured saliva. Many rat and slug baits are coloured and this observation may actually help to identify the poison.

Corrosive poisons are usually ingested by cats as a result of washing these substances from their paws or coat. This type of poison kills by producing shock from the enormous amount of tissue damage and pain created. Corrosive poisons include such substances as acids, alkalis (e.g. ammonia and quicklime), phenolic compounds (creosote, lysol and the Jeyes' Fluid type of disinfectant) and petroleum products (petrol (gasoline), paraffin (kerosene), diesel oil, and white spirit (paint thinners)).

Other types of poison damage the cat's health, and may even cause death, because they interfere with some essential metabolic function. This type generally produces one of four types of signs:

1 Digestive signs such as abdominal pain, vomiting and diarrhoea.

2 Difficulty in breathing.

3 Nervous signs, which can vary in their intensity from staggering, excitement and muscular tremors (twitching) to convulsions (fits), paralysis, coma and apparent blindness.

4 Depression, including a loss of appetite.

This often follows the other signs and precedes death in the case of slow acting poisons. Some rat poisons produce other signs; warfarin, for example, causes internal haemorrhages and anaemia; thallium can produce hair loss, and alphachloralose has an anaesthetic effect and causes the animal to become very cold.

It should be emphasized that *all* these signs can be produced by conditions other than *poisoning*, and there are many instances of cat owners suspecting that their animal is being deliberately poisoned by someone bearing a grudge when in fact the animal is suffering from a disease, often the early stages of some infectious condition. This should be borne in mind before requesting toxicological analyses; testing for any common poison is not cheap, and a blanket test for all possible poisons would almost certainly be prohibitively expensive. Furthermore, the unavoidable delay involved in obtaining analytical test results means that they usually contribute little to treatment, though a positive finding may assist in treating, or preventing, the poisoning of other animals.

Q *If I think my cat has been poisoned, what should I do?*

A The treatment for oral corrosive poisoning is quite different so the first thing to do is to look at the animal's mouth for the tell-tale signs – burning and blistering (with yellow-grey areas on the lips, gums and tongue), pawing at the mouth and often a characteristic odour (e.g. of creosote or disinfectant). If these signs are present, and the cat is not collapsed or unconscious, wash away as much of the chemical as possible from around and inside the mouth. In a conscious animal wipe around the mouth with a pad soaked in water and trickle water into the mouth through a disposable syringe (as for dosing with liquid medicine, page 191). It will be beneficial whether the cat splutters the water out or swallows it. Indeed, rather than attempt to neutralize such poisons, the best policy is usually to dilute them in the stomach with plenty of water. The one real danger is of liquid passing down into the lungs and causing an inhalation pneumonia. If the animal is already unconscious and is perhaps showing difficulty in breathing, treat as for shock and administer artificial respiration. Obtain the help of a veterinary surgeon as soon as you possibly can.

In the case of all other consumed poisons, providing that the animal is still conscious and not having convulsions, the first thing to do is to administer a substance to make the animal vomit. This should ideally be done within half an hour of the poison being taken. And then get the animal to a vet without delay. (Vomiting is not used in cases of corrosive poisoning because further tissue destruction and shock will be caused as the poison passes back from the stomach.) The most reliable method to make a cat vomit at home is to administer a crystal of washing soda (sodium carbonate) the size of a hazel nut. This should be administered in the same way as a tablet (page 189). An alternative is to give a large crystal of rock salt. Giving liquids to cause vomiting is often less successful but the following might be tried if they are available and washing soda is not:

1 Hydrogen peroxide: $2\frac{1}{2}$ ml (half a 5 ml teaspoonful) of the usual 6% (20 vol.) solution; or one 5 ml teaspoonful of a 3% (10 vol.) solution.

2 A strong salt solution: half a level tablespoonful of salt in as little warm water as will dissolve it.

3 English mustard: half a level tablespoonful as a powder mixed in half a teacupful of warm water.

In all cases administration will be simpler using a disposable syringe.

If vomiting is going to occur it usually does so within ten to fifteen minutes. If nothing happens do not give further amounts. If the vet is unable to visit and you have to take the animal to his premises, it could be that vomiting will take place on the journey. If the animal is unconscious you may need to give artificial respiration and/or treatment for shock; and if it is having a fit it should be dealt with as described earlier. Do *not* try to give an unconscious or convulsing animal *anything* by mouth. If you know the name of the poison taken tell the vet, and if you have the packet take that along with you. Otherwise, take a sample of the poison (or suspected poison); possibly it can be identified.

At the vet's the animal might be given an injection of apomorphine to stimulate vomiting if this has not already occurred, and/or have its stomach washed out. It could also be given supportive treatment in the form of fluid therapy and drugs to counteract the particular signs that may have developed. In some cases of poisoning, though by no means all, there may be a specific antidote which can be administered to assist in reversing the effects of the poison. In the case of warfarin, an injection of vitamin K counteracts its anticoagulant effect; with alphachloralose simply keeping the animal warm until its anaesthetic effect wears off is usually all that is required.

If the cat has been poisoned by inhaling toxic fumes or gases, the essential action is to move it immediately into fresh air and if necessary to give artificial respiration whilst waiting for veterinary attention. Do take care, however, that you are not also overcome by the same toxic vapours.

Tar products and petrochemicals are very toxic to cats. Small areas of hair covered with oil-based paints or with tar can be cut off (allow the paint to dry first) but more extensive deposits of tar need to be softened first with vegetable oil, lard or margarine for several hours before being washed out with detergent and lukewarm water. Whilst this softening process is going on, it is advisable to cover the area with a pad of gauze and bandage it in place. Diesel oil, creosote and phenolic disinfectants are corrosive and should be removed quickly. Whilst waiting for veterinary assistance, as much of the material as possible should be wiped away with rags or absorbent paper towels and the area washed with warm water. If the eye or mouth is involved, wash these areas with plenty of water. On no account use liquids such as paint stripper or turpentine on the skin because these are themselves corrosive and will cause further damage.

Q *How can I prevent my cat from being poisoned?*

A The detoxication mechanisms of cats are less effective than those of many other species. This is due to a deficiency of the enzymes needed to bring about the rapid transformation of potentially poisonous substances into harmless compounds. To minimize the risk of your cat being poisoned the following points should be observed.

1 Do not administer any drug which has not been supplied, prescribed, recommended or approved by your veterinary surgeon. Cats react badly to many drugs; in particular aspirin and paracetamol should be avoided. Even a small daily dose of aspirin can prove fatal for a cat within a fortnight. Drugs which, as a side-effect, suppress the production of red blood cells by the bone marrow (such as the antibiotic chloramphenicol and the anti-arthritic drug phenylbutazone) have an especially marked effect in the cat. Mention is often made of the fact that morphine and its derivatives produce maniacal excitement in the cat; in fact this only happens when they are used in high doses. At the recommended dose rate, it does not occur. Consequently, such related drugs as pethidine (meperidine), a valuable pain killer, and apomorphine (used to produce vomiting in cases of poisoning) *can* be used in cats.

2 Keep cats away from poisonous substances. Some of these, for example the rat poison alphachloralose and the slug bait metaldehyde, appear to be particularly attractive to some cats, and animals that get a taste for them may actually seek them out, even though substances are often added to these baits nowadays to give an unattractive taste. Access to such poisons should be prevented by carefully siting or covering the poison. Placing it in the middle of a length of thin drainpipe or under a heavy paving stone raised a couple of inches above the ground is often effective. Remove any dead or dying rodents or pigeons before the cat finds and eats them. Keep the cat off areas of the garden and other land during and after treatment with weed killers, and clean up spilled liquids such as creosote, paraffin (kerosene) and disinfectant which the cat might walk in and subsequently lick off. Again, some cats seem to develop a liking for anti-freeze (containing ethylene glycol) which has been allowed to drain from a car's radiator. Following consumption, the body converts it into oxalic acid and the cat develops signs of oxalate poisoning (depression, staggering and convulsions).

3 Don't apply an excessive amount of any preparation in the form of powders or sprays to kill parasites. Try to avoid the animal licking the coat whilst these are in place; powders should be brushed out after thirty minutes. Never apply DDT or fly sprays to a cat's coat.

4 Don't treat any wooden or wickerwork baskets or beds for cats with wood preservative, or paint them with lead-based paint. Cats are much less likely to chew at the painted surface than a dog, but as the paint flakes off with age the flecks of paint can be licked from the coat.

5 Discourage cats from eating house plants because many are poisonous. Providing a source of grass in the house, e.g. growing a pot of cocksfoot or lawn grass, can help in limiting this behaviour. Ivies and the ivy-like philodendrons, poinsettias and Dieffenbachias are poisonous, as are various outdoor plants – laurels, rhododendrons, azaleas and oleanders. At Christmas time cats may be tempted to eat the mistletoe used for decoration and the shed needles from Christmas trees; both are toxic.

Q *What is the difference between the treatment of burns and scalds on a cat?*

A Strictly speaking, a burn is caused by dry heat (a flame or hot surface) and a scald by moist heat (boiling water, hot fat or steam). But this distinction has no practical value and the first aid treatment for any thermal injury is the same – the immediate application of cold water to the area to remove all residual heat from the tissues. If the animal is actually on fire (occasionally this does happen – sometimes as a result of a malicious act), the flames must be smothered immediately by covering the cat with a blanket, rug or coat. Then water should be applied as soon as possible for five to ten minutes with a spray attachment or hose, or simply poured or sponged on.

Don't try to apply grease to the burn, to prick any blisters, *or* try to pull away any burned material (like a blanket or collar) which is stuck to the skin. If any such adherent material is part of a large mass, the rest can be detached by cutting through it three to four inches away from the skin surface.

All burns and scalds should be examined by a veterinary surgeon unless the total area of skin involved is smaller than the palm of your hand and shows no obvious scorching of the hair, or blistering and swelling of the skin. Even so, if the eye or mouth is involved, or the cat is in a state of shock, veterinary attention is required.

The cat's skin is normally more tolerant of heat than that of humans. Cats appear to feel no discomfort until a temperature of 126°F (52°C) is reached, whereas most people dislike prolonged contact with surfaces hotter than 112°F (46°C).

Classically, burns are described as first, second or third degree. First degree burns produce only redness, slight swelling and pain. Second degree burns result in blistering with considerably more swelling and pain. Third degree burns are those where the complete thickness of the skin is destroyed, even exposing the underlying tissues; with these severe burns, pain is absent, shock is severe and healing takes a considerable length of time. A major burn is a second or third degree burn involving more than 20% of the total body area. Very extensive burning will usually prove fatal and in survivors extreme scarring will produce disfigurement and often difficulty in eating and walking. If a burn involves more than 50% of the body surface, euthanasia is advisable because the chances of survival are slight.

Shock and sepsis are the two major consequences of a burn. First aid treatment for shock is often necessary, otherwise it may lead to other problems such as a failure of kidney function. Burns can go septic because the protective outer layer of the skin has been destroyed, permitting the entry of pus-producing bacteria. For this reason it is essential that burns should be kept clean.

With a mild burn or scald (i.e. involving a small area and showing only slight redness, swelling and pain), it may be sufficient, after bathing in cold water, to clip the hair, wash the area with toilet soap and then to apply an antihistamine cream. Then a pad of sterile gauze should be used as a dressing and kept in place with a crêpe bandage. The area should be redressed (washed, creamed and a fresh pad applied) each day for one to three days, but if a blister or any pus develops a veterinarian should be consulted.

Quite often hot liquids are splashed onto a cat in the kitchen and the resultant scalds are not detected until, in stroking the cat a day or so later, one or more scabs are felt. These may be oozing with serum or pus which is matting the hair. This type of lesion should be referred to your vet, but if some delay is inevitable clean away any pus by washing with mild toilet soap, rinsing and dabbing dry. But don't try to remove the scab.

Skin contact with very cold surfaces produces lesions similar to thermal burns, known as freezer burns, though here cold water treatment is not required. Nor is it needed with electrical burns arising from chewing through a live flex or falling onto an electric railway conductor rail. Here the important points are to separate the animal from the live surface, *after* the current has been switched off, and then to apply treatment for shock and, if necessary, artificial respiration. If it is difficult to cut off the domestic electricity supply, the cat can be pulled away from the live surface after first being covered with a dry coat, blanket or rug for insulation. However, don't attempt this with a high voltage supply that is still functioning, (e.g. a conductor rail or overhead cable), because you may be electrocuted yourself.

Q *Do cats get sunburn?*

A Sunburn is generally rare in cats, though in sunny climates (e.g. Australia and the southern states of the U.S.A.) it can affect the ear tips of cats with white ears, particularly blue-eyed white cats. There is a slow reddening and crusting of the ear margins, without much discomfort but getting worse each year. Eventually a cancer may develop on the ear tip. This is not a first aid condition, but requires affected cats to have the ears protected in summer with sun creams, to be kept indoors during the hours of strongest sunlight (10.00 a.m. to 4.00 p.m.) and, if lesions are well-developed, to have the ear tips amputated.

Q *What is a frictional burn?*

A Frictional burns arise when a cat is dragged behind a moving vehicle or contacts a revolving wheel. They are strictly abrasions (a type of closed wound) and are usually extensive, very painful, ooze blood and are easily contaminated. As a first aid measure they require bathing (see page 195), dressing with gauze and bandaging, otherwise sepsis of the area is a very common sequel.

Q *How should I deal with heatstroke in a cat?*

A Cats can generally tolerate high temperatures better than dogs but, like all animals, they will be affected by heatstroke if kept for long in extremely hot, poorly ventilated surroundings, especially if they are without water. The flat-faced breeds (e.g. Persians) are more likely to be affected because they have more difficulty in increasing the volume of air breathed in and out to cool themselves. Heatstroke most commonly affects animals left in cars parked in the sun during the summer months, but cats in carrying containers left in direct sunlight, or in enclosed rooms or small buildings (sheds and outhouses) in hot weather, will also suffer. It should be borne in mind that areas initially in the shade may later be in the full glare of the sun.

The temperature-regulating mechanism of the body cannot maintain the normal temperature and this gradually rises (hyperthermia). An animal with heatstroke becomes distressed and weak, it pants rapidly, drools saliva and the tongue and lips look very red (later even taking on a bluish tinge). If its temperature continues to climb, the animal will collapse, go into a coma and eventually die.

Immediate treatment is required. The cat must be removed from the hot surroundings and its temperature lowered by applying cold water to the skin. If the animal is unconscious, it can be carefully placed in a bath or bowl of cold water with the head kept above the surface. Usually there is an obvious improvement in the cat's breathing and an increased awareness of its surroundings within five to ten minutes. Care has to be taken not to overdo the lowering of temperature because the disturbance of the brain's usual temperature-regulating mechanism impairs its normal functions. Often the body temperature continues to fall for some time after the application of cold water has ceased. In short, there is a danger of lowering the cat's temperature too much. If you have a rectal thermometer and are able to take the temperature it is wise to stop when the temperature falls to 102.5°F (39.2°C). A cat's normal body temperature is around 101.5°F (38.5°C). It often helps to stimulate the circulation by massaging the animal's legs during this procedure. If necessary, apply artificial respiration.

Dry the cat and let it rest in a cool place with plenty of drinking water. In some cases the temperature begins to rise again although recovery may appear to be complete, and so it is always advisable to seek veterinary attention.

Q *Do cats ever get bitten by snakes?*

A All the available evidence indicates that cats, unlike dogs, rarely suffer from snake bites. In most countries there are one or more poisonous snakes (and the venom which they inject during a bite varies in its virulence). In Great Britain there is only one, the common adder (*Vipera* *berus*); in North America there are several belonging to two sub-families, the pit vipers (including the rattlesnakes and copperhead) and the brightly-coloured coral snakes. It is useful to be able to distinguish between the bites of poisonous and non-poisonous snakes. With poisonous snakes the venom causes a severe swelling in the centre of which are two small punctured wounds where the fangs have penetrated the skin; with non-poisonous snakes the bite appears as a U-shaped or semi-lunar row of tiny punctures with minimal swelling and pain.

Q *If my cat is bitten by a snake what should I do?*

A With a non-poisonous snake bite, cleaning of the wound, and possibly applying some hydrogen peroxide, is all that is required. With a poisonous bite wound, the prime concern should be to obtain veterinary attention quickly so that an injection of anti-venom can be given. In the meantime, the cat should be kept as calm as possible and its movements restricted to limit the amount of venom absorbed from the injection site. Cleaning the wound is useful, though not immediately essential.

If there is likely to be a considerable delay before a vet can examine the animal or if the venom is known to be extremely toxic (as with many American species of snake), the absorption of venom can be further reduced by applying a light tourniquet and an ice pack. However, a tourniquet can be really only applied to bites on the limbs or (improbably) the tail. Most venom is absorbed through the lymphatic system and so the tourniquet doesn't need to be so tight as to stop the circulation of blood. A broad rubber band or piece of elastic placed around the limb (nearer to the body than the bite) and clipped in place with a bulldog clip is very effective. Alternatively, a handkerchief or piece of rag could be tied around the limb. It should still be possible to slip a finger under the tourniquet when it is in place. After each forty-five minute period the tourniquet should be removed for five minutes and then re-applied.

An ice pack can be prepared by placing ice cubes in an old sock, tying up the open end and then crushing the cubes. The pack should then be lightly bandaged in place over the bite. Colder material from a deep freeze should first be wrapped in towels to avoid freezing the body tissues.

(Although the removal of venom by sucking from the wound is valuable, there are practical difficulties about performing this successfully on the cat. It involves incising the tissues between the two fang marks with a razor blade to a depth of about one-fifth of an inch (5 mm) the thickness of two matchsticks, applying your mouth to the incision and sucking. Any fluid thus removed should be spat out and rinsed away. Be careful not to cut into a major blood vessel and not to get scratched or bitten.)

Apply artificial respiration if breathing becomes laboured.

In North America and Australia, though fortunately not Great Britain, bites may also be inflicted by spiders (widow spiders, funnel-web spiders and brown spiders), ticks and fire ants, as well as stings by scorpions. The venom or other injected material can produce severe local swelling and pain, and in many instances nervous signs. Treatment should be along the same lines as for snake bites, with veterinary attention receiving priority.

Q *Do cats ever suffer from hypothermia?*

A Yes; as mentioned previously it occurs in cats poisoned with the rat poison alphachloralose, and also in those suffering from exposure after long periods in very cold, wet or windy conditions, including being shut in the refrigerator. If the animal cannot maintain its normal body temperature, despite shivering, its body activity slows down so that it becomes lethargic and then unconscious. The animal feels cold to the touch, its breathing is slow and shallow, and eventually it would die. Newborn animals and old animals are particularly vulnerable to low temperatures.

The cat should be dried quickly if wet and brought into warm surroundings as soon as possible. However, it should not be subjected to local heat, e.g. by being placed in front of a fire or on a hot water bottle or electric blanket, because the sudden increase in blood flow may cause the animal to collapse. In cases where the animal is comatosed, it should be placed in a bath of water at blood heat for ten to fifteen minutes, dried and wrapped in blankets. If the animal is able to drink, it can be given warm milk, but don't give it alcohol or attempt to force feed it.

Q *Do cats ever get frostbite?*

A Frostbite may affect the ear tips of cats exposed for a long time to sub-zero temperatures. The cat has no sensation in the ear flaps, and they appear pale and very cold to the touch. If frostbite is suspected, gently apply *warm* water with a pad, but *do not* rub vigorously, or apply intense heat suddenly. Later, affected areas may appear red or, in severe cases, black. It is sensible to obtain veterinary advice.

Q *Is it ever necessary to deal with wasp and bee stings in cats?*

A Yes, occasionally it is. Cats who try to catch these insects may get bitten inside or around the mouth. This will result in pawing at the mouth and increased salivation. Attention is usually drawn to stings on the skin by a cry of pain followed by continual licking of the site. Multiple stings can result in severe illness, but the most serious consequences occur if either the tongue is stung (because it can swell so much that it blocks the passage of air through the throat) or if the individual animal is allergic to the sting and goes into a state of severe shock and collapse (anaphylactic shock). Both of these latter conditions demand immediate veterinary attention.

228

If the sting is still present at the site looking like a large black splinter (as is often the case with bee stings but usually not with wasp or hornet stings), it should be carefully removed with a pair of tweezers. Then antihistamine cream should be applied to the stung area. If that is not available, or if the sting is in the mouth, the area should be bathed with a 2% sodium bicarbonate solution (one level teaspoonful bicarbonate of soda in a tumbler of warm water). This solution can be introduced into the mouth in the same way as for a liquid medicine (page 191) and the cat allowed to spit it out.

If there is considerable swelling in the mouth and breathing proves difficult, the cat should be laid on its side and the tongue pulled well forward out of the mouth. Artificial respiration should be applied if necessary and treatment for shock given. Unfortunately, where there is severe obstruction at the back of the throat, artificial respiration will not be sufficient to overcome the blockage and it is imperative to get the cat to a veterinarian as soon as possible.

Q *What is meant by a 'foreign body'?*

A A foreign body is any solid object or fragment which enters part of an animal's body (e.g. a needle, grass seed, piece of bone or glass). Young cats are more likely than older ones to swallow objects. Some foreign bodies penetrate the body tissues, either passing through the skin or through the wall of the digestive tract. Others merely become lodged in a part of the body, usually part of the digestive tract, e.g. mouth, stomach or intestines, but sometimes in the ear or nose, beneath the eyelids or between the pads.

A foreign body usually causes distress, pain and interference with normal body functions, and a penetrating foreign body can spread infection.

Wherever possible, the foreign body should be removed; this is obviously of vital importance where it is interfering with breathing or causing great distress. The cat will need to be well restrained, preferably on a table in a good light for you to do this successfully. If necessary, a torch can be used to examine the mouth, nose or ear. Then supportive measures such as artificial respiration and treatment for shock and/or haemorrhage can be applied.

Q *What signs would indicate that a foreign body is troubling my cat? What should I do?*

A Foreign bodies in the mouth cause profuse salivation, often gulping, frantic rubbing and pawing at the mouth, movements of the tongue and jaws and, if the airway is blocked, choking and gasping. Kittens may attempt to eat balls and toys made of wool or foam rubber, and this can result in obstruction and choking. If, after opening the mouth (as for the administration of a tablet, page 189) the foreign body can be seen, it should be firmly grasped with fine-nosed pliers and removed. If there is a thread attached to a needle, it should *not* be detached because it will serve as a useful guide to the needle's position. Occasionally, a small cooked bone, such as a vertebra, may be speared by a canine tooth, or a piece of bone may become wedged between the teeth. Again it may be possible to remove these with pliers.

Barbed fish hooks which have penetrated the lips or tongue cannot, because of the barbs, be drawn out the same way as they went in. These hooks need to be pushed all the way through, with the animal under a general anaesthetic, and then the barbs cut off with wire cutters so that the shank can be withdrawn.

A foreign body lodged in the larynx (voice box) or trachea (windpipe) may be forced back up by lying the cat on its side on a firm surface and applying a sudden sharp downward push on the abdomen, just behind the last rib, with both hands. If the animal's mouth is open it may prove possible for a helper to grasp the foreign body as it is forced up and to prevent it passing back down the throat again.

Foreign bodies (often grass seeds) up the nose or in the eye or ear should be removed, if protruding, with tweezers. In each instance the affected part will be rubbed by the animal; foreign bodies in the nose also cause sneezing and those in the eye result in increased tear production. If they cannot be removed a vet should be consulted and in the interim a little *warm* olive oil or liquid paraffin can be dropped into the eye or ear. However, do not attempt to place anything up the nose.

Foreign bodies which have been swallowed may cause vomiting, and if they penetrate the wall of the digestive tract the vomit may contain visible blood. If you know that your cat has swallowed some sharp object, veterinary attention should be sought immediately. In the interval before the vet can treat the animal, it may prove helpful to feed small pieces of cotton wool soaked in milk or a solution of yeast extract (e.g. Marmite) to make them palatable, in order to form an inert packing around the object. Foreign bodies such as needles can at times pass right through the digestive tract only to turn just before passing out of the anus, thereby lodging in the rectum. The animal licks at the anus and strains, and there may be bleeding. Sometimes string may be seen protruding from the anus. In these cases do not attempt to remove the foreign body but consult your vet. (Hairballs have been considered previously, page 101.)

Foreign bodies in the paws and skin, such as glass fragments, drawing pins and pieces of tar-covered grit from roads, should be pulled out using fingers, tweezers or pliers wherever possible. If the foreign body has temporarily to remain in a wound, because it is impossible to remove, covering the wound with a thick pad of cotton wool, lightly bandaged in place, can help to limit further trauma.

Q *Is it worthwhile assembling a first aid kit in case an emergency occurs?*

A This is a very wise precaution and it will certainly enable you to deal speedily and effectively with commonly encountered emergencies. The table on page 232 shows what could be usefully included.

Q *I notice that in the first aid kit you recommend having a fine lead. What is the purpose of that?*

A A fine lead is very useful following an accident where a frightened or injured cat will not allow you to approach closely enough to pick it up (as described on page 77). It is used to make a slip 'noose' by passing the end with the clip through the loop by which the lead would normally be held. This slip noose should be dangled in front of the animal's head and gradually, with patience and slow movements, manipulated into a position around the neck. Then a quick pull will tighten it. If a cat basket or other container is available the animal can even be *momentarily* lifted by this noose and lowered into the container, and the lid quickly secured.

Don't worry that the cat will be harmed by lifting it in this way; it will only be suspended momentarily and there is no risk of it strangling or suffering damage to structures in the neck. It is, in fact, an extremely useful method for securing a severely frightened animal which cannot be grasped. In an emergency a similar slip lead can be made by running a narrow trouser belt or dress belt through the buckle, or even by using a piece of thick cord after first tying one end to form a loop through which the other end can be passed.

Table IV Contents of a First Aid Cabinet

ESSENTIALS

A pair of 5-inch flat scissors with rounded (not pointed) ends. These can be proper surgical scissors or an all-purpose pair.

A pair of tweezers with flat (not pointed) ends.

A standard 5 ml teaspoon; (3 teaspoonsful = 1 tablespoonful).

One or two 5 ml size disposable plastic syringes to administer drugs orally.

Two or three 5 cm-wide crepe bandages and a selection of safety pins.

One 100 g box of cotton wool.

One box of sterilized white absorbent gauze.

One 100 g box of absorbent lint.

One role of 2.5 cm-wide adhesive plaster (preferably elasticated).

A small (e.g. 250 ml) bottle of detergent antiseptic such as Savlon, for cleaning wounds.

A small (25 to 50 g) packet of boric acid crystals for bathing eyes.

A tube of antihistamine cream (for application to burns and scalds).

A bottle (100 ml) of 20 vol (6%) or 10 vol (3%) hydrogen peroxide (for producing vomiting and cleaning wounds).

A small clearly-labelled bottle containing large crystals of washing soda (for the treatment of poisoning).

A small (75 to 100 ml) bottle of olive oil or liquid paraffin (for the cleaning of ears).

A packet of flexible cotton buds.

A styptic pencil (to stop minor bleeding).

A small (25 to 50 g) packet of sodium bicarbonate (for bathing stings).

OTHER USEFUL ITEMS

Of course, other items can be added to this list as necessary:

A pair of nail clippers.

A broad rubber band, or length of wide elastic, plus a bulldog clip to act as a tourniquet.

A pair of fine-nosed pliers (for the removal of foreign bodies).

A rectal clinical thermometer.

An Elizabethan collar, which can be made as described on page 201.

A cat basket or some other reliable carrying container, lined with newspaper or a blanket, is invaluable.

Finally, it is useful to be able to lay hands on a fine lead in an emergency to be used as a slip lead (see page 231).

Table V Cat Fact Finder

Length of pregnancy: 58–72 days (average 65 days)

Number of kittens per litter: 1–9, usually 3–5 (average 4.5)

Weight at birth: 2¾–5 oz (average 4 oz)
90–140 g (average 115 g)

Eyes open: 2–12 days old, usually 5–10 days old

First sounds heard: approx. 2 weeks old

First grooms itself: approx. 6 weeks old

Weaning completed: usually 6–8 weeks old

Number of feeds required after weaning: 4–5 per day

Toilet training completed: approx. 8 weeks old

Minimum age for neutering: 5–6 months old

Onset of puberty in females: 5–18 months old, usually 7–10 months old

males: 6–12 months old, usually approx. 9 months old

Growth completed: 10–12 months old

Adult body weight of females: usually 5½–8 lb (2½–3 kg)

males: usually 7½–11 lb (3½–5 kg)

Quantity of 'wet' diet required: usually 6–9 oz per day (adult). Lactating queens need at least 3 times as much

Maximum life span: usually 12–15 years old (neutered cats live longer than entire cats, on average)

Body temperature: 101–102°F (average 101.5°F)
(adult) 38.3–38.9°C (average 38.6°C)
In kittens *add* 0.5°F (0.3°C)

Heart rate (= pulse rate): 110–140 (average 120) beats per minute

Respiratory rate: 20–40 (average 30) breaths per minute

Length of time spent sleeping: approx. 16 hours per day

Rate of hair growth: one hundredth of an inch (0.25–0.3 mm) per day

Number of pet cats: Great Britain: 5 million
(estimated) United States of America: 23 million
Australia: 2 million
France: 7½ million
Italy: 4½ million

Footnote: Parameters such as body weight, onset of puberty and the number of kittens in a litter can be affected by many factors, particularly the breed of cat.

Table VI Environmental Disinfection

Environmental disinfection means the removal or destruction of disease-producing micro-organisms (though not necessarily bacterial spores) from the surroundings and from inanimate objects, such as feeding bowls and litter trays. It is important in limiting the spread of infectious diseases between cats.

EFFECTIVE CHEMICAL DISINFECTANTS*

On the basis of efficiency only 3 groups can be seriously considered:
1. **Phenol compounds** Toxic to cats, therefore unsuitable.
2. **Aldehydes** Formalin (diluted 1 part in 25) is effective but has a very irritant vapour. Glutaraldehyde is expensive. Neither is ideal.
3. **Hypochlorite bleaches** Cheap, non-toxic and effective, especially against FIE (FPL) virus which is resistant to most disinfectants. Therefore strongly recommended for routine use (see page 125).

DILUTION OF HYPOCHLORITE BLEACHES

0.175% sodium hypochlorite is effective against all cat viruses. The concentration in some commercial bleaches when *recently-manufactured* is shown in brackets after their name, together with the degree of dilution required for use.

'Domestos' (8.8%) Dilute 1 part in 50
'Chlorox' (5.6%) Dilute 1 part in 32
'Brobat' (3.5%) Dilute 1 part in 20
'Milton' (1%) Dilute 1 part in 6

All bleaches lose potency with age, and one year after manufacture these dilutions should be *halved*.

HOW TO INCREASE EFFICIENCY

The efficiency of chemical disinfectants can be increased by:
1. **Thorough cleaning** of the area or object *before* applying the disinfectant will remove many micro-organisms, together with protective layers of grease and dirt. It also reduces inactivation of the disinfectant.
2. **Dilution with hot water** instead of cold.
3. **Increased concentration** of disinfectant, e.g. halving the dilution (but see manufacturers' instructions).
4. **Leaving to act longer** before rinsing away. In general leave to act at least 10–15 minutes.

Footnote: *None of these environmental disinfectants is suitable for use on skin, i.e. as an antiseptic.

Index

abdomen, distension of, 143
abscess, 114, 165, 205–6
ageing, 38, 40
aggression, 46–7, 52
alopecia, 135
American Association of Feline
  Practitioners, 9
amputation, 34, 38–9, 166
anaemia, 116–17, 128–9
anaesthetic, agreement to, 11;
  local, 169–70; general, 11, 12,
  167–9
anagen, 112
anxiety, signs of, 46
appetite, healthy, 110; increase
  in, 58; loss of, 57, 73–4, 109,
  124, 130
artificial respiration, 210–11
ascarids, 154
asphyxia, 210–11
aspirin, dangers of, 117, 223
Aujesky's disease, 120

bacteria, 120–22
balance, 34
bandages, 197–201; application,
  197–9; keeping dry, 200–1;
  many-tailed, 200; pressure,
  212–13
bathing, 95–6
bee stings, 228–9
'belling', 45
biopsy, 11
bites, 113–14; snake, 226–8

bladder worm, 155
bleeding, control of, 212–15;
  internal, 215
blood, loss of, 12, 108, 116–17;
  samples, 8, 11; transfusion, 12;
  vessels, 205
blow-flies, 153
boarding, 93–4
bone marrow, 117
bone meal, 55, 66–7
breeds, 17–19; Abyssinian, 18,
  96, 101; American Shorthair,
  101; American Wirehair, 35;
  Balinese, 40; Burmese, 18, 19,
  36, 57, 101, 172; Himalayan,
  19, 40, 101, 172; long-haired,
  17, 18–19, 101–2, 107–8; Manx,
  34; Persian, 18–19, 101, 119,
  172; Rex, 18, 35, 101, 217;
  Russian Blue, 18, 101; short-
  hair, 17–18, 101; Siamese,
  17–18, 23, 32, 36, 40, 57, 63,
  92, 96, 101, 122, 128, 171, 172;
  Sphynx, 101; Turkish, 19, 101;
  white-haired, 36
brushing, 100
burns, 108, 209; frictional, 225;
  treatment of, 224–5; see also
  scalds

Caesarian delivery, 166, 181
calories, 53
cancer, 128, 158–60
candidiasis, 122

feline leprosy, 122
feline leukaemia virus (FeLV), 8, 124–30
feline panleukopenia (FPL), 124, 138
feline pneumonitis, 138
feline respiratory disease (FRD), 125–7, 138–41
feline salmonellosis, 122
feline urological syndrome (FUS), 64–5, 120, 160–61, 165–6
feline viral rhinotracheitis (FVR), 123, 125–6, 138
first-aid, 207–19
fleas, 21, 95, 99–100, 113, 116–17, 149–51, 163
flea collars, 151
flehmen, 48
fomentations, 205–6
foetus, 180–81
force-feeding, 194–5
foreign bodies, removal of, 229–30
foster mothers, 186
fractures, 108, 208–9, 216–18
frostbite, 228
fungi, 122–3, 135
fur mite, 147, 152, 163
furniture, protection of, 17, 91–2

garden, protection of, 90–91
gestation, 176
gingivitis, 103, 122, 128
glands, 35–6; apocrine, 33; caudal, 35; eccrine, 33; lymph, 128; perioral, 35; temporal, 35
glomerulonephritis, 161
glottis, 28
gonads, 25
grass, eating, 71–2
griseofulvin, 136
grooming, 17, 95–107, 110
gums, 116

haemobartonellosis, 134
hair, loss of, 111–12
hairball, 57, 101–2

handling, 75–81; after operation, 79; by children, 19–20; during pregnancy, 76
harnesses, 78, 92–3
head-righting reflex, 33–4
hearing, 50
heart beat, 215; checking, 211
heart worm, 155
'heat', coming into, 25, 27, 58, 109, 170–74
heatstroke, 109, 226
'home range', 89
homosexual cats, 175
hookworms, 154–5, 164
hormones, 25, 38, 42
hospitalization, 12–13
hot-water bottles, 203–4
hunting instinct, 35, 42–4, 67–8
hyperthyroidism, 58
hypothalamus, 170
hypothermia, 38, 109, 228

incubation period, 123
infection, 120–42; carriers, 123
inhalants, 127; administering, 193–4
immunosorbent assay (Leukassay), 129
insecticides, 117, 150
insurance policies, for pets, 14
intensive care, 12
intestines, obstruction of, 52

Jacobson's organ, 48
jaundice, 143
juvenile ataxia, 125

kiss of life, 212
kittens, abnormal, 182–3; at birth, 179–81; body weight, 59; choice of, 21–2; deafness at brith, 36; feeding, 16, 21; grooming, 102; handling, 21, 76; hunting instinct in, 43; living with dogs, 24; living with older cats, 23–4;

kittens (cont.)
newborn, 183–4; purring, 28;
rearing orphans, 185–6; 'runt',
21, 182–3; sexing, 184–5;
shampooing, 99; sleep, 49; toilet
training, 84–5; training, 82;
unwanted, 182; vaccination,
138–40; weaning of, 187–8;
worming, 157–8; worm
infections in, 154

labour, signs of, 179–80
lactating queens, feeding, 56,
183–4
lameness, 109
laporotomy, 11, 167
larynx, 28
leads (leash), walking on, 18, 92–3
lick granuloma, 96
lips, 116, 215
litter trays, 84–7
liver, damage to, 143
lung fluke, 147, 155
lungworm, 68, 155
lymphosarcoma, 128–9, 159–60
Lynxacarus radovskyi (fur mite),
147, 152, 163

maggots, of blow flies, 153
mange, 151–2
mating, 25, 27, 39, 40, 49, 51,
170–75, 182
medicine, administering, 191–3
Microsporum canis (fungus
responsible for ringworm), 135
'milk fever', 184, 219
milk substitutes, 186
minerals, in diet, 65–7
mites, 151–2, 163–4
mouse favus, 163
moving house, 88–9
mycoplasms, 121

needles, swallowing, 36–7, 146,
229

neoplasia, 160
nepetalactone, 51
nephrectomy, 167
'nesting' box, 178
neutering, 20, 24–6, 38, 165,
172–4; age for, 25–6; by drug, 26
nictitating membrane (third
eyelid), 118
nipples, 176
nose, wet or dry, 111
Notoedres cati (mite), 151–2
notoedric mange (feline scabies),
151

obesity, 72–3
oestrus cycles, 170–75, 177
onychectomy (claw removal), 107,
167
operations, 165–8
orchidectomy, 165
orthopaedic surgery, 165
os penis, 39
osteodystraphy, 60
osteogenesis imperfecta (skeletal
disease), 18
otitis externa, 105
Otodectes cynotis (ear mite), 105,
115, 152–3
ovariohysterectomy (spaying – *see
also* neutering), 165
ovulation, 171–5

papillae, 36–7, 39, 101
paralysis, 108, 131, 218
parasites, 67–8, 147–9
pasteurellae, 121
patella luxation, 18
pathogens, 123
paws, 33–4, 108, 215
penis, 39
periodontal disease, 103, 112,
161, 188
pet food, 53–4; dry, 54–6, 62–5,
120
pheromones, 42, 48, 50
pigment, 40

placenta, 179
pneumonia, 125, 168, 221
poisoning, 109, 209–10, 219–20, 223; prevention of, 222–3; treatment for, 221–2
posterior vena cava, 28
pregnancy, 27, 54, 96, 129, 177–8; diet during, 177–8; handling during, 76; signs of, 176–7; vaccinations during, 124–6
pressure points, 213–14
progestagens, 26, 173–4
protein, in diet, 53–4, 56, 59, 70–71
protozoa, 123
pruritus, 113
puberty, 171–2
Pulex irritans (human flea), 163
pulse rate, 111, 136–7
pupils, dilated, 216
purring, 28–9, 46

quarantine, 132–3

rabies, 131–4, 164
radiation, 117
radiography, 11–12
renal disorders, 38, 57, 64, 160–61
respiration, 12, 108, 109, 111, 191–3; panting, 215
'resting area', 89
retina, 30–31
rigor mortis, 117
ringworm, 8, 122–3, 135–6, 163
road accidents, 77–8, 208
rodenticides, 68, 116
roundworm, 68, 153–4, 156, 163–4
Royal College of Veterinary Surgeons, 9
rue, as cat deterrent, 90

saliva, 112–13, 126
scalds, 109, 209, 224–5
scratching, 113
scratching post, 45, 91–2

sedatives, 81
self-sucking, 52
semi-circular canals, 33–4
shampooing, 96–9; dry shampoos, 98–9
shock, 12, 108, 116, 203, 208, 215–16
signs, of good health, 110–12; of illness, 108–10, 144–5; of mood, 46–8; of shock, 215–16
simulated illness, 49–50
sleep, 48–9
slimming, 72–3
smelling (flehmen), 48, 50–51
spaying, *see* neutering
sperm, 175
splenectomy, 167
staphylococci, 121
stereoscopic vision, 31–2
stomach worm, 147
strabismus (crossed eyes), 18
streptococci, 121
stress, 50
'stud tail', 95–6
sunburn, 225
superfecundation, 174
surgery, 11, 165–7, 169

tablets, use of, 12; administering, 189–91
Taenia taeniaformis (tapeworm), 68–9, 149, 154, 157, 164
tails, 18, 34; *see also* 'stud tail'
tapeworm, 68–9, 149, 154, 157, 164
tartar, 37, 102–3
taste, 37
teeth, 37–8, 44; cleaning, 102–4; diseases of, 103, 112, 161
telogen, 112
temperature, increase in, 111, 126; normal, 111; of skin, 40
territory, invasion of, 42, 50; marking, 23, 25, 35–6, 41, 45, 88–9
testosterone, 38, 41
tetanus, 121
thoracotomy, 166